Servants of the State

Servants of the State

The Contested Control of Teaching 1900–1930

Martin Lawn

The Falmer Press

(A member of the Taylor & Francis Group)
London, New York and Philadelphia

UK	The Falmer Press, Falmer House, Barcombe, Lewes, East Sussex, BN8 5DL
USA	The Falmer Press, Taylor & Francis Inc., 242 Cherry Street, Philadelphia, PA 19106-1906

Copyright © Martin Lawn 1987

All rights reserved. No part of this publication may be reproduced, stored in a retrieval system, or transmitted, in any form or by any means, electronic, mechanical, photocopying, recording or otherwise, without the prior permission in writing from the Publisher.

First published in 1987

British Library Cataloguing in Publication Data

Lawn, Martin
   Servants of the state: the contested control of teaching, 1900–1930.
   1. Teachers—England
   I. Title
   311.2'04137311'00942   LB1777

ISBN 1-85000-257-6
ISBN 1-85000-258-4 (Pbk.)

Library of Congress Cataloging-in-Publication Data

Lawn, Martin.
   Servants of the state.
   Bibliography: p.
   Includes index.
   1. Elementary school teachers—Great Britain—Social conditions—History—20th century. 2. Elementary school teachers—Great Britain—Political activity—History—20th century. 3. Education and state—Great Britain—History—20th century. 4. Politics and education—Great Britain—History—20th century.
   I. Title.
   LB2832.G7L39   1988   382.11'00941   87-15603
ISBN 1-85000-257-6
ISBN 1-85000-258-4 (soft)

Jacket design by Caroline Archer

Typeset in 11/13 Bembo by
Alresford Typesetting & Design, New Farm Road, Alresford, Hants.

*Printed and bound in Great Britain by
Redwood Burn Limited, Trowbridge, Wiltshire.*

Contents

Preface	vii
Introduction	ix

I The Serving Teacher

	Introduction	1
1	Masters and Servants	3
2	Teachers in Dispute: the Portsmouth and West Ham Strikes	21
3	Turning the World Upside Down	37
4	The Rhondda and the Teachers	49

II 1919

	Introduction	59
5	A Collegiate Civil Service?	61
6	Working with the Grain: Teachers and Socialism	73

III The Test of Economy, Loyalty and Unity

	Introduction	95
7	Brothers and Sisters in the Struggle	97
8	'A Reasonable Independence'	117
9	Engendered Professionalism	139
	End Note	157
	Index	166

'Teaching, above all things in this world, ought to be absolutely honest and absolutely free. The teacher should never be the servant of the state in this way, that he preaches and teaches what he thinks the Government would like to have him do, whether that Government come from the Right or from the Left or from the Centre.'

Stanley Baldwin, 'Political Education' 1923.

'If the administrative power in education, which was once diffused, is now being concentrated in the Minister, then the power of the teachers, which is at present diffused, should be concentrated too. We should create our own national power centre parallel to that of the Minister.

Ronald Gould, 'Power in the Education Service' 1963.

Preface

This book has been a long time in formation, so long that it began as a personal act of self-defence as a teacher in the world of educational researchers and has ended as a history of teachers acting in self-defence again. Although its pages act as a chronicle of the battles of teachers in the past so many of the issues revealed within those past conflicts are surfacing again today.

There are very many people who need to be thanked for helping me with research for this book. The first would have to be Asher Tropp for writing his history of the schoolteacher: my own research takes a very different position from his, but it began in his footnotes. The second person would have to be Brian Simon, who provided a model of commitment and scholarship in the history of education which always lay before me even if I never attained it. Many conversations with Brighton teachers and other workers helped me, in the mid-seventies, when I was struggling with the organization of the research.

I was assisted by staff at the Marx Memorial Library, the British Museum at Colindale, the University of Sussex, the National Union of Teachers library and the Public Record Office at Kew, as well as by staff in many local libraries and record offices, in person or by correspondence.

I appreciate particularly the advice and help of Bob Bell and Harold Silver who supervised my research, and the Open University for allowing me study leave to work on it, even though I was too immature to fully appreciate the value of that gift.

From the mid-seventies I have been influenced by the analytical scholarship of Jenny Ozga, and I have benefited from sharing research interests with her and from collaborating with her. In many ways this book is also hers.

The book was started as a reaction to the patronizing and discriminatory approach to teachers which I found when I entered the world of the guardians of educational research. So it should be dedicated to many of the teachers I trained with in the late sixties who saw their place in teaching as necessary in the act of social reconstruction, and the teachers in a London comprehensive who impressed me with their militancy in the pursuit of knowledge and state education. Did that generation of teachers realize that they were to become the enemy within?

Introduction

It is a difficult task to reconstruct the world of the elementary schoolteacher. In one way, this study places on record their struggles at work, their ideas for the future of education and their campaigns and alliances to achieve change. It also shows how they were divided among themselves, influenced by major social and political changes and dominated by the varied politics of the local and central state. I have felt it easier to record and understand some teachers rather than others. The nature of the sources used, which were mainly local and national newspapers acting as a conduit for dissenting teachers, leaves some teachers marginalized. So, conservative or religious teachers, who were many, are not clearly seen here nor are those who left few records, like the supplementary teachers. Some teachers are recorded but not understood and the fault here lies with me, for my disagreements with them confused my attempt to understand them. Also, since I have completed the study, the voices of women teachers have been rediscovered and as a consequence their arguments about themselves and their professionalism have made me recognize some of my own gendered assumptions in a way which may not have fully surfaced in this text.

Crises in the state education system have come with some rapidity since I started this research. It is with growing fascination that I found that the debates and correspondence which I thought were about long-lost issues were suddenly having a clear reference to those which were surfacing in the education press of recent years. History may not run in cycles but we have been down this path of centralization before and need to look again at the reasons why it was rejected.

This study is about a time when there was a national curriculum with approved syllabuses for the elementary schools. There were many disputes between teachers and their employers and a debate about local or central control of education. A constant issue was one about the cheapness of the schooling system and the conflict between the economy lobby and the 'human capital' school who wished to modernize its functions. The solutions found to the problems of this period lasted for many years; for instance, the Burnham Panel for teachers' pay, the de-regulation of the curriculum and the promotion of state professionalism. The present proposals for a national curriculum and syllabuses, and the action taken on disbanding Burnham and imposing a teachers' contract, all of which come from the Department of Education and Science, were rejected as courses of action by its predecessor, the Board of Education. In many ways the current right-wing pragmatism which is ensconced at the DES is fundamentally in contradiction with its own past policies.

There are some ironies present in this dismantling, by the Department, of its own past. The proposal to make teachers civil servants, which is echoed today in the new teachers' contract and the reduction of local authority influence, was rejected by the Board in the 1920s for two reasons; firstly, it was argued that this went against the English tradition of checks and balances on central power, something which distinguished us from our main European neighbours, and secondly, that it would allow a radical government, at that time possibly socialist, to quickly change the teacher's work, a possibility which de-regulation would forestall.

The Burnham panel was set up to stop teacher strikes and the possibility of their involvement in 'revolutionary' change. Today it is disbanded in the process of imposing a solution on teachers' strikes. It was initially more-or-less imposed on many local authorities, yet it was to become their major forum in which to bargain with their employees and its dissolution marks their loss of power in the education system. Burnham overcame a major source of problems for teachers, i.e., the way in which local authorities around the country paid teachers what they, the employers, wanted. Its dissolution and the earlier demise of the wage councils will again allow local labour markets to determine teachers' pay.

These points of contact do not allow for a sort of ley-line theory where paradoxes make up the contemporary reading of the past. Decisions were taken in the 1920s by the Conservative Party in its chosen role as the natural governing party, to safeguard the state, to protect itself and to control teachers, which are now being removed. Yet, oddly, they are being reversed in a language of commonsense and national duty with a sleek pragmatism that seems to have little regard for the political dangers and administrative log-jams, never mind the customs and traditions of political power in this society, so often referred to by a Conservative Party which is now forgetting them. The greater irony here is in the disregard for the past which is operating in a party which so often used it to justify its role and which would be expected to pay it some attention in safeguarding its future. 'Eccentric' and 'maverick' are no terms for a politician of this party to use to describe a system so carefully constructed by predecessors of his own political persuasion.

The main purpose of this study, however, lies not in the correction of the policies of the natural governing party or in telling why teachers often turned towards their rivals, the Labour Party, but in the development of a history of teaching for the state. Within this history, the recognition that teaching is work and that teachers have struggled to alter and change the conditions of their work is important. Professionalism is a key concept in this struggle over work but it is not as undivided a concept as it has sometimes been described. The idea of professionalism surfacing in this study was very complex; there were male and female, skilled and unskilled, local and national, radical and conservative versions of it, all bound within this particular context. At its root it involved a struggle over the kind of work teaching should be and the responsibilities of society for its education which were deployed in ideas of a loyal servant, an apolitical policy, a syndicalist self-government and a Labour alliance depending on whether this was a view promoted from within the state or within the teachers. Tensions arose between the teachers as to which path, and its attached rhetoric, to follow.

What is very clear from this study is the way in which teachers began to see themselves as workers. If they were to be treated as servants then they would organize, if their pay was low then they would strike, if they were penalized and wished to renew their fight for a new education then they would vote for or join the Labour Party. Those who rejected this path could be, paradoxically, men teachers, those who are often regarded as militant. They were, of course, but often only to defend their own relatively privileged position vis-à-vis women teachers.

The historical study of teachers' work is to be encouraged. People are diminished by the lack of a collective memory and the struggles of the past can illuminate teachers' work today. Memorials to the classroom teacher need to be built out of the spoken word of their testimonies or autobiographies. This study should help in raising the questions to be asked of them.

I. THE SERVING TEACHER

Introduction

In 1900, teachers who were working in rural voluntary schools were divided by gender and qualification and only a minority organized within the National Union of Teachers; the rest were unorganized. The certificated excluded other teachers from membership of the Union; employers paid male teachers more than female teachers and the cheaper teacher was preferred for employment in many places. Yet although they felt themselves to be patronized and harried at work by local ratepayer representatives and the church, they began to be seen by many social commentators as a growing force in society, involved in politics and campaigning.

For the teachers in the NUT, their professionalism was an expression of their craft unionism and was an appeal to the skilled, certificated teacher, often to men, and was intended to help them control their conditions of work and influence the development of the system. From 1900 to 1919 teachers began to change. They campaigned for better pay and conditions of work and in so doing, turned the rural world of status and servitude upside down, and in the urban areas allied themselves with progressive labour societies and trade unions. Their greatest successes came with active support from these groups and when they opened their own ranks in the NUT to other teachers.

The salaries campaign was growing steadily but then was halted for two years on the outbreak of war. Financial pressure and concern over the destructive educational policies operating in many local authorities led to the campaign re-opening. Many local teacher associations were to be in dispute with their employers but the biggest breakthrough came in the Rhondda valley in a strike which was to electrify and transform the Union.

Chapter 1

Masters and servants

In 1900, teachers were divided from each other by geography, qualifications, pay, sex and educational location. The National Union of Teachers represented only one section whose membership, in this year, was mainly male and certificated. The others were unorganized. The education system, locally organized with powerful managers, and a state agency, the Department of Education, was, in the main, hostile to the teachers. They were seen as servants, with a parallel attitude to pay, conditions of work and duty. The system in which they worked has been characterized as one of:

> — hesitation, confusion and uncertainty. A measure is taken then partially retracted; a step is made forward, then backsliding begins.[1]

In opposition to this attitude and struggling to free the curriculum from restriction, to develop welfare services in schools and to improve work conditions, teachers began to drift naturally into alliance with people who were themselves out to convince the wider labour movement. These were the Socialists of the Social Democratic Federation (SDF), the Independent Labour Party (ILP) and the Fabians. Though of differing political viewpoints, they were, in common with other smaller socialist societies, in a ferment of discussion, contradiction and argument. A craft union approach, more commonly characterized as a professional Trade Union, dominated the NUT but was, in turn, altering under the pressure of new ideas and changing work circumstances, not the least of which were the large numbers of relatively unqualified teachers. Key elements in the craft approach, such as defining and protecting skills, in opposition to employer controls, began to metamorphose under the pressure of socialist ideas in the new unions and the rise of the unskilled worker. In addition, the idea of service became a key element in constructing new alliances with the Labour movement.

However, as noted above, the teaching force was deeply divided and seemingly unable to alter the depressing conditions of employment which it suffered. Men teachers were paid on different scales from women teachers. The certificated were paid more than the uncertificated, and the supplementary teachers and the ex-pupil-teachers were paid very little at all. Teachers were divided by religion, working for secular School Boards, Nonconformist or Church of England Schools, each of which had different conditions of employment from the others. The urban and rural teachers were very different; the former working in large schools and in teachers' associations, the latter teaching all grades by themselves or with another, and geographically separated from other teachers. Teachers' associations had primarily recruited from their religious or School Board faction and the National Union of Teachers took only the certificated. From the 1870 Act to 1900, the small group of certificated teachers, who were mainly male, were overtaken by an influx of various kinds of untrained or partly trained teachers, all of whom were paid less than the certificated teacher and who, in some areas, reduced all teachers' wages to low levels. Nothing strikes the observer so much as the divided state of teaching in 1900, and consequently the teachers' weakness in altering or improving their salaries and conditions of work. Without a strong, united Union and powerful allies, teachers were pushed hither and thither, in accordance with the law of supply and demand, just as Robert Lowe, the Victorian architect of 'payment by results', expected them to be. The laws of a capitalist political economy and a Department of Education concerned mainly with reducing costs by altering the conditions of entry into teaching, created a servile, cheap, labour force for schools. Furthermore, each group of teachers tended to see the others as the cause of this state of affairs. The male teachers blamed the influx of cheap, partly trained women and the certificated teachers blamed the unqualified.

Their position with regard to their employers was generally that of the supplicant, whether it was the local farmers or Church of England vicar, the Voluntary School Managers or the School Board members and officials. These were the people who controlled the social and economic lives of their workforce, and they were aided by the School Inspectors, at one time visiting annually to examine classes and ascertain grants. The exception to this servility of attitude by teachers was in the urban areas where well-developed local associations attempted to impinge on the management consciousness by means of deputations and letter-writing.

In the rural areas, teachers were often paid very poorly indeed and these areas were the base of the supplementary teacher, the untrained female teachers who often acted as school caretakers as well as teachers. They taught in one or two room schools, very often converted from other uses. These schools were often voluntary schools where teachers were responsible to the local vicar in the Parochial, Church of England or National Schools, and to local School Managers in the Wesleyan and British Schools. Pay was low in these schools, regardless of the teacher's qualifications. Writing in 1902, MacNamara showed how the qualifications, school expenditure and salaries were lower in the voluntary (i.e., mainly rural) schools as opposed to the urban Board school.[2] The working conditions in the voluntary schools were much worse than the Board schools — an NUT pamphlet described one school:

> Seated on ten broken desks are sixty children, working as best they may, it is some time before one can see them clearly, so gloomy is the place. There is but one room, that formerly served as a stable ... in winter lamps are lit all day, so few and small are the windows. Maps, blackboards, books and stationery are antiquated, dilapidated or scarce. The playground is swimming in water, so is the approach to the latrines, which are never cleansed.[3]

This was, the NUT said, no worse than many others. The teachers working in the schools were at the financial mercy of the managers, usually local farmers, and were often pressured to release children from the school for the various arable and corn harvests, grouse beating or stone picking. Even when the Agricultural Children's Act (1873) tried to impose restraints and penalties on the use of village children in this way, the teachers were often warned off aiding prosecutions.[4]

The most pressing problem for the rural teachers was insecurity of tenure. Added to this were the extraneous duties that were little more than compulsory. *The Schoolmaster* in the late Victorian and Edwardian period is full of complaints about these duties in rural areas, and a Union Survey in 1891 had shown that one in three teachers in the sample depended for their tenure on the performance of these duties.[5] These included organizing the Church choir, playing the organ or acting as Sunday School superintendent.[6] One teacher, living in the clergyman's house, took her meals in the kitchen, sang in the choir, organized the Sunday School and taught the clergyman's child the piano as well as undertaking her school duties.[7] Insecurity of tenure meant that the Union was the only real help a teacher in this position could rely on. At Fingringhoe, near Colchester in Essex, a teacher was dismissed on December 24, 1895, because he had refused to sublet a house from the Vicar at a high rent. With local and Union support, the teacher was reinstated. Another case was of a headteacher who was asked to resign by a new Vicar because 'a new clergyman always gets on better with a schoolmaster of his own appointing'. These duties served to enslave the rural teacher, already geographically isolated from other teachers, and made teaching in the rural, voluntary school a tied occupation, similar to the conditions of the local farm labourers.

Although Board Schools were very different from rural schools, there was a shared sense of interference and control. In a well documented study of the London Board Schools, it can be seen that teachers bore the brunt of management moves for increased efficiency. Unlike the rural schools or even the smaller Board Schools, the London School Board increased the efficiency of its schools by controlling the school policy and curriculum. Teachers were expected to be in their schools 10 minutes before the school day started; they signed into a book which was read by the School Managers. Quite often, the Managers had special rooms set aside in the school for their own purposes, sometimes with access from their own staircases. During the 1880s and 1890s, the teachers complained about the increase in attendance register marking (including duplicates), schedules and certificates that had to be filled, as well as quarterly attendance cards, Penny Bank supervision and the gradual increase in clerical work associated with pupil health and nutrition. At the same time, the Board felt that teachers were trying to influence its right to manage. It wanted to compel teachers to do things yet felt that their duty did not end with school hours. It created a number of Board Inspectors to examine its schools and resisted any idea that teachers had a place in curriculum matters:

> The decision of what is taught does not rest with the teachers employed. It would be nothing short of a revolution to maintain that the agent is to dictate to the employer what his employment is to be.[9]

The businessmen on the School Board constantly visited the schools and applied their own ideas and standards to their functioning. As the Metropolitan Board Teachers' Association grew in response to this interference and became concerned with problems of promotion and salary, the Board itself talked more of the teachers' duty and interest in their work, replacing pecuniary interest alone. Between 1873 and 1900, the MBTA managed to enrol 90 per cent of the Board teachers in its ranks and pursued interests in tenure, promotion, superannuation, curriculum and staffing ratios.

Although London was exceptional, it illustrates in microcosm the gradual rise of unionism among the certificated teachers. They were better organized in the towns than in rural areas. The Union (founded in 1870) had grown from 6,880 teachers in 149 local associations (1873) to 43,615 teachers in 431 associations (1900) (approximately two thirds of the certificated teachers). Although it had grown rapidly, it was outnumbered by the large number of unqualified or partially certificated teachers which had entered the teaching force since 1870. This problem was to dominate its activities as a Union for many years, in opposing the uncertificated teachers who undermined its progress in salary and tenure problems, and in opposing the Board of Education that created new groups of teachers as and when the need arose.

The teachers in these schools were of various kinds. The supplementary teachers were practically all women, and their only qualification was a personal approval by an Inspector, that they were vaccinated and over 18 years of age.[10] They tended to be local village girls or the wives of the local schoolmasters, and were 16,000 in number in 1899.[11] There were also the pupil-teachers. These were selected from children of the manual working-class, a method created earlier in the century to provide:

> The cheapest means of supplying Elementary Schools with additional staff, and the main source from which to draw future masters and mistresses.[12]

They were often in charge of classes, though normally school apprentices, and could be awarded certificates without examination by an Inspector, between 1870 and 1873, to take charge of small, rural schools.[13]

Indeed, since the 1870 Act, the old teacher's certificate had been greatly devalued as the State intervened in the production of teachers to ensure there was a sufficient supply. Not only was there the large number of supplementary teachers but the pupil-teachers had doubled in number (from fourteen to twenty-nine thousand) between 1870 and 1875, to meet the new requirements.[14] Tropp described this period as one in which the certificated teachers were 'immersed in a growing flood of untrained certificated teachers, assistant teachers, additional women teachers, pupil-teachers and probationers'.[15] The certificated teachers, by 1899, could include people without any proper training, or those who had one or two years' training in a college. Indeed, the Certificate could be gained without attendance at a College or a local pupil-teachers' centre at all, just by correspondence. Uncertificated teachers were teachers who were still in the process of taking the certificate exams or had any other qualifications (including a university degree) but not the Teacher's Certificate.[16]

It was not only the proportion of the untrained or uncertificated which was increasing (approximately in the ratio of 1:3 in 1900), but also the composition of the force. Men teachers were becoming the minority. They had dropped from half to a quarter of the force by 1900, overwhelmed by the influx of the cheaper recruits to pupil-teacher and uncertificated teacher status, one of the few job avenues open to women.[17]

The effect of this cheaper labour in teaching was that wage scales were depressed over all the country. Supplementary teachers were replacing pupil-teachers in some schools, as they were cheaper and had no restriction of their duties. Uncertificated teachers were cheaper than the certificated, and women teachers were cheaper than men teachers at all levels. In each local area post-1900 economics meant that the cheaper teacher was often employed after dismissal of the expensive teacher. For instance, in York, the Education Committee had consistently reduced the quantity and quality of its teaching staff for economic reasons. It did this, not by dismissal, but by a steady process:

> it was decided that steps be taken gradually to remove such teachers as it seemed possible to dispense with, no one to be discharged, but reduction in staff to be made, if possible, when a teacher left or by making transfers of teachers from one school to another e.g. assistant master left and assistant mistress appointed. Uncertificated mistress appointed in place of certificated mistress. Ex-pupil teacher left.[18]

This policy, widespread in the period, was obviously resisted by the National Union of Teachers, but with a tendency towards a craft union approach, despising the female, unqualified diluted labour and trying strategies addressed to the employer to eliminate them. Not until the next decade (1910–1920) did the Union seriously consider altering its approach to these teachers and in turn, reassessing the role of the State in the past creation of these teachers. In 1900, though, teachers were divided against each other as a result of the post 1870 expansion of the workforce and the ways in which the State and local employers divided them in pursuit of a cheap labour policy.

In the period between 1902 and 1914, the education system was characterised by its mixture of *ad hoc* remedies proposed by the Board of Education and the local resistance, tardiness or enthusiasm within the Education Authorities (created in the 1902 Act in replacement of the School Boards). The signs of release from the straitjacket of payment by results and a powerful Inspectorate, in the encouragement of curriculum change and the development of a caring professionalism, aligned to the growth of school welfare facilities were constantly confounded by the penny-pinching resistance of the rural and town Education Authorities. The Board of Education was not and did not wish to be in control of a centralized system of education. It operated through a series of ambiguous clauses attached to Exchequer grants-in-aid. The key word 'efficiency' could be applied to release changes in the working or provision of local authority education services but this was rarely used. Indeed in future decades (disputes in West Ham, Herefordshire and Abertillery), teachers expecting pressure to be applied to their local authorities who had run-down or patched their education services found this power of the Board to be used entirely at whim — related to wider tactical purposes in which the Board needed to goad an

Authority or restrain teachers. This power was, then, a useful way to influence and direct the system without overtly controlling it. At all times except in a crisis it could be expected to work well — in the Board's terms.

The post-1900 growth of new school-based facilities and teacher involvement with them is a sign of a changing policy towards schools. The post-Boer war unease in Government circles at the poor quality of the army recruits and the increasing attempts by local and national ILP and SDF councillors and union leaders (like Will Thorne and Margaret MacMillan) to expand welfare facilities for children, led to legislation on school meals and school medical services. Again, local authorities varied in their adoption of school nursing posts and the creation of school canteens or local baths. There is evidence that teachers become involved with pupil cleanliness and nutrition on a personal level or in an organized policy: the provision of cocoa or soup in the classrooms, helping the school nurse or doctor, or in the creation of toothbrush clubs.[19] Teachers involved themselves with political organizations that fought for these welfare facilities — at this time, this had to mean the ILP or SDF or Trades Council groups opposed to the ratepayer domination of local councils.

The building of new schools, the supply of staff and, from this period, the extension of welfare facilities, along with provision of roads, lighting and other municipal services, caused financial strain in many local authorities. These tended to be in urban areas where population increases due to the establishment of new industry or the emigration from the countryside had occurred in a short space of time. The government grants-in-aid did not grow in proportion to the demands on services in these areas, which lead to an entrenched reaction to further developments on the part of ratepayer groups, represented in the Conservative or Liberal Parties. Expenditure rose but the proportion met by Exchequer grants fell between 1905 and 1912.[20] The ratepayers were having to pay more for services they did not tend to use — the elementary schools. This was a constant source of friction between teachers and local councils.

Interest in curriculum change had been growing among the teachers, especially when the link between curriculum subjects, school grants, and examination results had passed with the end of payment by results. The 'rigidity and calculation'[21] of the 'Reading, Writing and Arithmetic' curriculum, with its rote learning, lack of individuality of approach and fact-grading were going. They had not gone, by any means, as many teachers would have worked throughout their teaching experience within such a system. The new Code of Regulations, issued in 1904, emphasised the needs of the individual child and a widened list of curriculum subjects that could be taught (though this list also eliminated other subjects nearer to secondary subjects, like science which was popular in London). The Code appeared at the same time as the growth of a New Education approach which was affecting the old certainties of the masters of method. Herbartian psychologists, Montessori kindergarteners, Deweyans, moral trainers and heuristic scientists, all debated and argued about the child and the curriculum.[22] The very idea of an elementary education, and, of course, the teacher, was changing and expanding.

On financial and educational grounds, teachers sought allies, who in turn, were sought by those people in the labour movement who wished to see a new kind of elementary school develop. An example of this tentative relationship came with the production of the Board of Education Circular 709. This circular asked Local Authorities to lower class sizes, in particular, to make 60 pupils the maximum.[23] Immediately, several Authorities tried to get the Circular withdrawn and the NUT produced a leaflet (*Smaller Classes and Better Teaching Staff*, 1909) addressed to the 'workers of the country' appealing for support against these Local Authorities. It argued that the Circular would only cost more where the Local Education Authority had already insufficient or unqualified staff. The need to win allies lead the NUT inexorably to the working-class although it coyly adressed their 'various organizations' without name. The appeal was direct — it asked them 'to show their determination to secure for their little ones greater advantages at school than they themselves enjoyed'.[24]

This appeal was made by people who were themselves from working-class backgrounds, a point which had not escaped the Board of Education. The cheap and relatively efficient elementary education system, with its narrow, heavily supervised curriculum and a teaching staff derived mainly from the manual working-class had become insufficient. One of the grounds for this insufficiency was the class background of these teachers.[25] The need for a 'well-equipped body of teachers' meant that the 'disposition to maintain the educational barriers between class and class no longer existed',[26] and that the old pupil-teacher recruitment led to a 'narrowness of intellectual and professional outlook'. The use of the term 'professional' here has further resonances in this study and suggests that working-class teachers teaching working-class children were creating a possible threat to the new needs of the State and its education system. To deal with this, recruitment from the new secondary schools where intending pupil-teachers would not be segregated on class lines but be able to mix freely with other pupils 'destined for different professions' was recommended. The whole Circular was addressed to an issue it saw clearly as a social class-based education system which was creating a narrow, class-based teaching corps, separated from members of the professional classes (it later referred to this class as civil servants, typists, shop assistants and post office workers). It was a plea against a working-class alliance about elementary education which it saw as determined within a 'narrow professionalism' — one that saw a natural link between teachers, workers and workers' children. The flaw in the plan was that the new second school graduates would still be proletarianized by an economic system operating within a *laissez-faire* capitalist system determined to create cheap sources of labour. What it hoped to alter was the *ideological* outlook of the teacher.

Social observers, in the Edwardian era, began to remark upon the social position of the elementary teacher and the fact that large numbers of them existed. Both these facts created a feeling of unease in the observers. W.H.D. Rouse talked of the 'deep discontent' among the teachers, discriminated against financially and by their employers.[27] He didn't, but he could so easily have quoted from John Morley, when making his criticisms of clergymen, describing teachers as their 'creatures' or their relationship as 'master and servant'.[28] C.F.G. Masterman, a Liberal MP writing in 1911, began to see a political importance attached to teachers:

> They appear as the mainstay of the political machine in suburban districts, serving upon the municipal bodies, in work clear-headed and efficient, the leaders in the churches and chapels. They are taking up the position in the urban districts which for many generations was occupied by county clergy in their rural districts.[29]

A more disapproving version of teachers' growing political presence was written in the *Morning Post*, an extreme right-wing daily paper.

> Not only is the NUT probably the best organized Trade Union in the country, but the teacher is a very keen politician and a powerful canvasser. Strong majorities in the County Councils have ere now melted away at their battle cry. Hence it is unwise to ignore what they are thinking and saying . . .[30]

W.R. Lawson, writing in a book for 'Parents, Ratepayers and Men of Business' was concerned by the elementary teachers outnumbering Church of England clergymen, barristers and doctors, and by their continued rapid growth in numbers. But it was not their numbers, rather their ideology that worried him. Among them, there were 'secularists and socialists' produced by the new municipal colleges and reflecting the 'prejudices and limitations' of their class, the working-class. In effect, they were doing the bidding of the 'Socialist leaders' and in a 'discreet way play(ing) the Socialist missionary'. As evidence of this, Lawson cites the rise of trade unionism concurrent with the growth of a State education system. His advice to the 'ratepayers and businessmen' echoes Circular 573 on Pupil Teachers: teachers had to be recruited from a higher social class, free from narrow biases. Lawson was a propagandist for just those people who were opposing the teachers and their allies in the Local Education Authority districts. Although, like the *Morning Post*, he had a tendency to over-estimate the teacher's power, and reflected a fevered conspiracy theory, he commented upon two important features of the elementary teachers identified by the middle-class observers — their growing interest in socialism (following a secular tradition already observed in Board School areas)[32] and their working-class interests. He concluded:

> In these days, when class jealousies are being so unscrupulously fostered and exploited for political purposes the real state of the account as between the working class and those above it should be clearly understood. As regards education it shows a large balance in favour of the working class. Not only is much more done for their schools than for those of any other class but they have a practical monopoly of the teaching in them.[33]

This was just what some councillors wanted to hear; it provided them with an excuse to contrive restrictive policies on schools and a clear link between their political opponents and schoolteachers, a link that teachers appear gradually to make themselves.

At this time, complaints began to arrive at the Board of Education about teachers being involved in political activities. These were usually made by either Conservatives or Liberals (depending which party the teacher belonged to) and concerned election periods when teachers acted as election agents or allegedly gave special holidays or taught party songs to the children. The Board felt obliged, in this new climate of concern for teachers' growing social and political power, to distinguish between political rights and political involvement and they defined a policy which was to continue for several decades. There was to be no general prohibition of political activity even when the teachers were socialists except if it could be proved that the curriculum was affected by teacher bias or that the law was being broken. One reason why they could not prohibit teachers directly was that this would make clear the relations between the teachers and the State. It would be used by them as 'an argument in favour of according to them the status of civil servants'.[34]

However there were inhibitory factors in the creation of a working-class alliance in elementary education. One of the most important was corporal punishment. It is clear that a system of education that was seen by many parents and children as coercive would have difficulty in creating any educational alliance on class lines. Corporal punishment was a vital part of a system which included attendance officers, and which depended on strong controls over very large classes. Although it was often meant to be administered only by headteachers, assistant teachers protested if there were any restriction of their use of the cane. Yet it was the cane that caused open conflict between teachers and parents and children. In many areas, schooling involved a running battle between teachers trying to impose order in the classroom and parents or children defending pupils from the cane.[35] This conflict could place teachers on opposite sides to their erstwhile allies in the ILP or SDF[36] who were opposed to corporal punishment just as much as they were *for* a better, freer education system. School strikes against the cane, which were not uncommon, could often be led by the sons or daughters of local socialists or be influenced by the actions of local trade unions.[37]

Corporal punishment was one wedge between teachers and the working-class, another was the apolitical ideology adopted by the NUT. From its early days, the Union needed to strengthen its unity in the face of strong religious divisions between its members and the way in which religion was bound up with the employer in rural and town schools. As part of this need for unity and not wishing to antagonize its membership who were in political parties, the Union lobbied Parliament and exerted influence on the Department (later Board) of Education by means of sponsored MPs — in 1895, it had two, Grey (a Conservative) and Yoxall (a Liberal). A part of its apolitical ideology was its interest in professionalism. The key to understanding its use of the term 'professional' is its context. The NUT was a mainly male craft union, small in number in 1870, faced with an influx of diluted labour into teaching and needing to reassert its expertise and case for adequate renumeration for trained, certificated teachers. Its chief aims, from the beginning, are a reflection of this craft union approach: it wanted to control entry into teaching by means of a register; to reduce the amount of employer interference; to gain job security, adequate salaries, and pensions; and to be eligible for recruitment into management (the Inspectorate).

The essential feature of craft unionism is its attempt to secure a monopoly over a craft by means of uniting people with similar interests: in this case the preservation of remuneration and promotion related to certification. As the number of uncertificated, supplementary and pupil-teachers increased, the certificated teachers in the Union (and not all were[38]) found that their attempts to restrict entry into teaching were unavailing. A professional register of teachers and control over entry examinations were the very things that could not be given to the teachers. Attempts to place the craft union approach within a professional frame were partially unsuccessful, as professionalism was seen as 'duty'[39] involving deference, and removed from control. The admission of the Union to consultation was only accepted by the Department of Education in the 1890s and this policy was practically reversed by Morant in the next decade. In common with other craft unions, such as the Amalgamated Society of Engineers (founded only twenty years before the NUT), the Union found that the greatest threat came from the semi-skilled, though it was similarly distressed by compulsory overtime (extraneous duties), a flood of apprentices (uncertificated and pupil teachers), 'illegal' women (the supplementaries) and piece-work rates (a version of 'payment by results').[40] The semi-skilled teachers were able to do the same work as the certificated teacher for less money, and if they were women, for even less. The social exclusion practiced by the craft union came to be fundamentally threatened and then revised during the period from 1900 to 1920.[41]

The craft unions organized to maintain or raise their standard of living, and the only way they could effectively do this was by controlling the supply of workers. If the supply were controlled by them, and not by the employers, then they could increase the value returned to them from the sale of their labour power. The greater the oversupply, the more depressed the salary level. As the Union grew and organized, it constantly tried to restrict teacher supply, by means of a professional register, the elimination of the supplementaries, a pension fund and tenure rights. At the same time, the Department of Education strove to create new sources of qualified teachers to reduce costs and to supply demand. What helped the Union was its ability to mobilize its resources (legal department, finance and propaganda) against the relatively weak Local Authority employers, though it always depended upon the strength of the local teachers' organization. Yet for the first thirty years of the Union's existence it mainly occupied itself with securing Parliamentary representation, Education Department deputations and electoral pressure. The early concern for a professional register was confounded by a Bill that actually excluded elementary teachers from membership. The Bill declared that:

> The relation in which such teachers stand to the Education Department forbids the interference of any other authority. Those who act as elementary teachers are trained so to act and are paid for their services by the State. It is not unreasonable to expect that the paymaster, acting on behalf of the public, should insist on imposing his own conditions, and seeking precisely the qualifications which he may deem adequate for the fulfilment of these conditions.[42]

This was the first of a series of humiliations for the Union that the demand for a register of skilled teachers gave rise to.[43] A later register separated the elementary teachers from the secondary school teachers which allowed the Secretary of the Union, Yoxall, to express his further claim, consistent with craft union notions of skill, that the new Register was a symbol of the struggle taking place:

between the existence of teachers and teaching as a profession . . . and the demand of administrators in this country to reduce teaching to a state function and teachers to state functionaries.[44]

The rethinking that took place on this validation of the policy of certificate exclusiveness was profound and became part of the change in approach to unionism and the uncertificated discussed in this period (1900–1920).[45]

It is possible to argue that the NUT was always a Trade Union yet observers saw either ambiguity about its actions or saw no conflict at all. In other words, it was agreed to be Trade Union-like but what confused the contemporary observer was its connection to the idea of professionalism. As we have noted, Beatrice Webb described the NUT as 'like a Trade Union' and in its objects and methods 'a marked approximation to the Trade Union type', yet she felt that its success was mainly due to its Legal Department. Although she added that it had a professional code of conduct (an afterthought in 1911), she pointed out the very crux of the Union's problem: it had failed to control the supply of teachers and their qualifications and so was unable to raise the market value of its labour. Webb explained that this was because of control over entry by the State, and so, logically, the notion of a Professional Register must be a failure (even though it allowed some elementary teachers to meet Eton Masters and University Dons!).[46]

What was described as professionalism was in fact a strategy common to all craft unions but with key words derived from the historical past of educated, service groups. Professionalism was used as a term describing a service to the community and freedom from state control. What it meant was a determination to define and control the skill of teaching in ways that were often oppositional to the definition or control over teaching imposed by employers. When teachers talked of autonomy or a 'free hand'[47] or of 'professional dignity',[48] it has to be seen in a context of imposed and arbitrary control, of a direct and humiliating nature, exercised by managers, clergymen or School Board businessmen and an indifferent Department or Board of Education. It was an attempt to unite the certificated teachers within a definition of skill that they had socially constructed for themselves; not one seen as part of a devalued, cheap teaching service nor just a technical class control nor a dutiful, loyal workforce. That may be how others saw them but *they* saw themselves as a craft union with a skill which was not just a question of knowledge (certification) but attitude. The education service was failing because it did not allow them the relative freedom to give of their 'best' nor did it include the creative aspects of 'skill' nor did it serve the community (the workers' children) adequately. 'Professionalism' was a particular term used by teachers to symbolize their attempts to define and control their work and was part and parcel of their opposition to employer control — over pay, tenure, cheap unskilled teachers and compulsory overtime. It was not a word in wider currency among the manual working-classes but it generated in the teachers the will to take on extra welfare duties, join labour societies or groups, or resist child labour, and yet at the same time, resist an imposed notion of duty, social controls by the local squirearchy or commercial classes, and inferred roles as narrow and ill-educated. Of course, professionalism is contradictory. It has ideological overtones, in this period, of a political nature. The Register is seen as an almost magical solution to all teachers' problems. The teachers in 1900 were at the point of examining their past strategies and evaluating their progress, and this continued apace after the 1907 West Ham strike and the start of the 1913 Salary Campaign.

The question of 'service' is one key element in understanding the term 'professionalism' (not status or class). Each improvement in the teacher's conditions and pay helped the child, each improvement in resources or buildings helped the teacher. Webb pointed this out in 1915. With far more opportunity than was open to the manual worker, when the teachers fought for better salaries or tenure they were rendering an improvement in the quality of the service offered. She illustrates this by estimating the increased teaching load on teachers since they freed themselves from 'payment by results', by the campaign for smaller classes, against child labour and penurious Local Authorities and all attempts to limit the duration, quality or content of the elementary education.[49] It is the element of service which was to become the key to a change in the direction of the teachers. It helped to create the alliance with labour, especially the socialist element within it (in the broadest sense), using a common political discourse, and developing a class consciousness. It is this alliance with labour which has been described as composed of, for professionals:

> an ethic of service, intelligence and expertise in pursuit of humanitarian ends and a civilizing mission . . ..[50]

Other elements of professionalism that changed and altered in different periods, and in 1900 were at the point of shifting, were based upon social status. As the certificate was undermined, strategies to save the related standard of living were unsuccessful and status as a reflection of differentiation from the teacher's own class background lost ground to a reaffirmation of teaching within a wider alliance, constructed on a different union model.[51]

By the time of the West Ham strike in 1907 (a significant victory for the teachers) elements of new approaches to Union organization and a wide alliance on educational progress and against retrenchment and local reaction, came to the fore. The contradictions in the teachers and the labour movement were also exposed. It is to this strike and the contradictions and advances that it illustrated that the next chapter is devoted.

Notes

1 Selleck, R.J.W. (1968), *'The New Education 1870–1914'* Isaac Pitman & Sons, p. 44.
2 MacNamara, T.J. (1902) 'Burning Questions — The Education Bill' Swan Sonnenschein.
   Expenditure per scholar Vol. Sch. £1. 15s. 2d.
   Board Sch. £2. 5s. 2d.
   Number of children per Vol. Sch. 103 [3,043,000 children]
   certified teacher   Board Sch. 76 [2,662, 669 children]
3 Hurt, J.S. (1979), *'Elementary School and the Working Classes 1860–1918'* R.K.P. p. 108.
4 Hurt, J.S. (1979), p. 200, ibid.
5 Horn, Pamela (1978) *'Education in Rural England 1800–1914'* Gill & MacMillan, p. 192.
6 Thompson, Donna (1927) *'Professional Solidarity among the Teachers of England'* Columbia Univ. Press, p. 62.
7 Thompson, D. ibid. p. 63. [also Horn, p. 193].
8 Williams, R.A. (1953) *'The Development of Professional Status among the Elementary School Teachers under the London School Board 1870–1904'* London, unpub. Ph.D.
9 Williams, ibid. p. 122.
10 MacNamara op.cit. They were created in the 1875 Code.
11 Tropp op.cit. p. 118.
12 Board of Education Circular 573 (1907) *Memorandum on the History and Prospects of the Pupil Teacher System.*
13 Tropp op.cit. p. 114.
14 Tropp op.cit. p. 114.
15 Tropp op.cit. p. 117.
16. In 1899. Certificated teachers: 62,085
        Uncertificated/ex-pupil teachers: 30,233   [Tropp, p. 118]
        Supplementaries: 16,171
        Pupil Teachers: 30,783
        Probationers: 2,500

Distribution:	Cert.	Uncert.	Supps.	Pupil T	
Vol. schools	38	23	18	21	
Board schools	51	21	5	23	[MacNamara]
London Board	81	4	0	15	

17. Horn, P. 112. Uncertificated etc. 1875 13%   —
                                       1914 41% teaching force
18. City of York E.C. *1st Triennial Report* 1903–1906
                     Annual Reports 1907–1913
    This policy was reversed after 1907; certificated teachers were appointed to the new, larger classes. It was reversed again in 1915, as it was felt there had not been a sufficient gain in efficiency. [Yorkshire Herald 21 July, 1915].
19 Hurt, J. op.cit.

20 Gosden, P.H.J.H. (1972) *'The Evolution of a Profession'*,
   Blackwell.   1905/6   53.9% of total cost   (p.35)
   1911/12   48.2% of total cost
21 Selleck, op.cit. p. 44.
22 Selleck, op.cit. passim
23 It also recommended the withdrawal of all male supplementaries, restrictions on the use of this class of teacher and their regular inspection.
24 NUT Pamphlet (1909) *Smaller Classes and Better Teaching Staff*.
25 A circular addressed to this problem was 573 Board of Education *'Memorandum on the History and Prospects of the Pupil Teacher System'* 1907.
26 as (25) above.
27 *Contemporary Review*, August 1900, quoted in Gosden. See note 20.
28 John Morley (1873) *'The Struggle for a National Education'* Chapman & Hall.
29 Masterman, C.F.G. (1911) *'The Condition of England'*. Methuen quoted in Partington, G. (1976) *'Women Teachers in the 20th Century'*, NFER.
30 *Morning Post*, 24 November, 1911 in Tropp. A point echoed in Beatrice Webb *New Statesman* Supplement, Sept. 25, 1915.
31 Lawson, W.R. (1908), *'John Bull and his Schools'*, Blackwood.
32 Williams, R.A. op.cit. One third of Metropolitan teachers had refused to teach Scripture in school (1893) and their association fought off attempts to bar these teachers from promotion (p. 167).
33 Lawson, op.cit. p. 220.
34 PRO Ed 24/412 *Miscellaneous Complaints regarding teachers' political activities 1909–1910*.
35 For a litany of examples of this conflict over the case and pupil/parent resistance to it (and to the restricted curriculum) see Humphreys, D. (1981) *'Hooligans or Rebels? An oral History of Working Class Childhood and Youth 1889–1939'*, Blackwell.
36 McCann, W.P. *'The Trade Unionist, Cooperative and Socialist Organisations in relation to Popular Education 1870–1902'* Unpub. Ph.D. Manchester 1960.
   Not until much later did corporal punishment decline — at the time of the breakthrough in child-centred education and the socialist alliance in the '20's. See Musgrave, P.W. 'Corporal Punishment in Some English Elementary Schools 1900–1939' in *Research in Education* No. 17, May 1977.
37 Humphreys, op.cit. p. 62–89. Also Lee, Jenny p. 62/3.
38 Tropp, op.cit. p. 157. 1895. 83% of male certificated in the Union and only 35% of female certificated teachers.
39 Williams, R.A. op.cit. p. 82.
40 The parallel can be explored in Penn, R. 'Skilled Manual Workers in the Labour Process 1936–1964' in Wood, S. (Ed.) (1982) *'The Degradation of Work'*, Hutchinson.
   Webb described payment by results as 'a demoralising type of piecework with a perpetual downward thrust in favour of a purely mechanical product manufactured in the cheapest possible way', *New Statesman* Suppl. Sept. 25, 1915.
   Other aspects to craft unionism were suspicion of state intervention and lack of interest in Labour representation — Schofield, I. 'The Labour Movement and Educational Policy 1900–1931' unpub. M.Ed. Thesis (Manchester) 1964.
41 Even before Union policy changed, to include uncertificated teachers in membership, (1919), local associations of teachers (in Bradford, Rhondda etc.) often included them.
42 The Educational Times January, 1891 quoted in Parry, N. and Parry, J. (1974) 'Teachers and Professionalism: The failure of an occupational strategy' in Flude, M. and Ahier, J. (1974) *'Educability, Schools and Ideology'*, Croom Helm.

43 It is also of interest in the clear way teachers are seen as state (or civil) servants, something which is later to be denied and abhorred in numerous Board of Education memoranda, H.A.L. Fisher and Lord Eustace Percy (both Presidents of the Board of Education).
44 Reported in 'Review of Incorporated Association of Headteachers', March 1909 and quoted in Baron, G. (1953) 'The teacher's registration movement' *Brit. Journal of Educ. Studies*, Vol. 2.
45 This movement was heightened by the lowering of the connection between certification and headships. In 1855, most certificated teachers could become Heads, by 1895 only 60% could be and by 1918, only 30%. Ozga and Lawn (1981) '*Teachers, Professionalism and Class*', Falmer Press, p. 72.
46 *New Statesman* Sept. 25, 1919. Supplement: English Teachers and Their Professional Organization.
47 Webb quotes a NUT Conference Resolution 1903 — 'right to a free hand to conduct their schools according to their own judgement'.
48 Webb, 1880 Presidential Address and in pamphlet (1913) '*The NUT: Its Activities, Achievements and Aspirations*'.
49 For a discussion of the social construction of skill. More, C. (1981) 'Skill and the English Working Class 1870–1914', Croom Helm.
50 Gareth Stedman Jones 'Marching into History'? *New Statesman* Jan./Feb. '82.
51 Service is a concept shared with other municipal employees although they were organized later than teachers. As municipal services grew, so an associated white collar workforce had as its standard 'service to community'. The National Association of Local Government Employees was one such association. It shared with teachers the idea of a natural 'justice' that was gainsaid to them. In other respects, NALGO showed the same difficulties in organizing as did the NUT, reflecting the craft to industrial union shift.
Spoor, A. (1967) '*White Collar Union: Fifty Years of NALGO*', Heinemann.
Klingender, F.D. (1935) '*The Condition of Clerical Labour in Britain*', Lawrence and Wishart in Ozga and Lawn (1981) op.cit.

Chapter 2

Teachers in Dispute: the Portsmouth and West Ham Strikes

In the late Victorian and Edwardian period, town councils mainly consisted of ratepayer representatives, whether Liberal or Conservative, who tended to see their function as the efficient management of local authority services. Efficient management meant, in essence, that rates should be kept as low as possible and while grants-in-aid from the central exchequer may be accepted, outside political control related to the grants should be kept to the minimum. Conservative and Liberal councillors tended to resist any extension of Local Authority services, even with grants-in-aid, if they meant a consequent rise in local rates. Not until the late 1920s was any kind of weighting given by central to local government, on the basis of the rateable value present in the area or the special factors with which they might need assistance, such as a rise in the local population of small children or large scale unemployment. Before then, Local Authorities varied considerably in their capacity to raise local rates and meet the urgent needs in their areas.

Pressures on the local education system occurred where an area of medium rateable value had a prolonged increase in population due to the establishment of new industries or trade. This was the case in two disputes which altered the debates in the NUT about its work as a teachers' organization and its natural allies in that work.

The condition of Portsmouth's schools between 1883 and 1894 was one of gradual deterioration. There was a complete lack of any new building yet the population of the town had grown continually. Even the Education Department had cause to remind the local School Board of its obligations, after 1888, and this suggests conditions were indeed poor as it was uncommon for the Education Department to intervene, although it had the power to do so if the local authority was inefficient or extravagant.[1] At the time of these reminders, in 1890/91, the average number of pupils per teacher was 100, if headteachers and pupil teachers were excluded.

The election of a new School Board in 1892 enabled the local NUT secretary to visit the School Board President to discuss the perturbing conditions of the schools and the teachers' low salaries. Bramsdon, the President, later recalled the visit and the agreement reached between them:

> That the teachers, in view of the existing difficulties, could not persist in their demands, but would wait a reasonable time if a promise were made to give their salaries proper attention. The promise was made and the strike did not take place.[2]

At the annual meeting of the Portsmouth and District Teachers' Association in January 1892 the question of local salaries was emphasized by the President and ex-President. The ex-President's speech is of great interest here:

> .. He did not know of an Association in England where the percentage of members was so great as in Portsmouth. He touched on the question of salaries ... the only way to attract notice was to agitate public opinion by a general strike (hear, hear). They were not prepared for such an event just at present, but there was no doubt that before long there would be a strike against the miserable salaries now received (Applause) ...[3]

The dispute between the teachers and the School Board, although in abeyance for four years, overrode the fact the new School Board was an improvement on the last one. A local headmaster described the Board as 'generous' and 'just' in meeting the teachers' claims, the officials as courteous, and felt they were at the mercy of the financial position they had inherited.[4] Certainly members of the School Board were politically progressive; two of the members had recently addressed a local Trades Council demonstration alongside Tom Mann, the ILP leader. The teachers' concern and anger was concentrated on the conditions of work and their improvement. For a period of several years the teachers waited for an improvement in the local salaries.

There was also the question of compulsory overtime. Teachers at Portsmouth were expected to attend school at 7.55 am for clerical work and to instruct pupil-teachers. As the clerical work took only a few minutes and the greatly-reduced number of pupil-teachers were instructed by the Headteachers, another reason for the Board's steadfastness on the 7.55 rule was necessary. This is suggested by the School Board who mention in their discussions the necessary discipline of their workforce, the fact that they were large employers in Portsmouth, and that adherence to School Board regulations was essential to discipline.[5] In a curiously contemporary aside,

Bramsdon was to blame the teacher unrest on those teachers not brought up in the local schools and the town but on 'imported teachers'.[6]

According to the teachers, though not some headteachers, the 7.55 rule was not only superfluous but had been operated in a casual manner until the School Board had suddenly tightened up its observation. A memorial sent by certificated assistants to the Portsmouth School Board included the suggestions:

> that the aforesaid regulations be so amended as to prevent the necessity for the attendance of all teachers at their respective schools at 7.55 a.m.... That your scale of salaries for certificated assistant teachers be so amended as to provide that the salaries of the assistants in your service shall be equal to those paid by similar Boards in other parts of England.[7]

Within a week of this memorial, four teachers were dismissed from one school for 'disobeying' the rule over a period of a year. Although this step was obviously taken to intimidate the local NUT, the Board did not feel they were likely to cause more trouble. Bramsdon was certain that 'There is nothing like organized opposition amongst our teachers to the rule of the Board'.[8] The *Hampshire Telegraph* was not so certain.

> ... it seems hard that they (the teachers) should be punished vindictively ... Moreover it would be a serious thing for the Board to have to fight so strong and well-organised a body as the National Union of Teachers. The result of such a contest would hardly be in the Board's favour.[9]

Three teachers were transferred to the dismissed teachers' school, but within a few days they returned to their previous schools where they were refused the right to teach, being locked-out. The following day, February 25th, the remaining two teachers at the school, Highland Road School, handed in their month's notice. On Wednesday, the Board received the notices of seven teachers at Penhale Road schools, who particularly referred to the new strict enforcement of the 7.55 rule. The impression given in the *Telegraph* and the *Schoolmaster* is that many more teachers would hand in their notice over the issues raised. Speakers at a meeting of the District Teachers' Association on March 21st described the overtime rule as 'a great evil in Portsmouth for a long time past'. Reprimands had been given by School Board members to staff for arriving a few minutes late in the morning, yet the teachers were often working late in the evenings. A speaker at the meeting mentioned that:

> when a vacancy occurred in a local school, the teacher was told he must work until 5 p.m. . . . (and) . . . two schools worked overtime regularly all the year round[10]

That the Portsmouth conflict was of interest to other teachers in England can be ascertained from the twenty-one telegrams approving the teachers' action from other local Associations, with many personal letters of support, as reported in the *Schoolmaster*. The National Federation of Assistant Teachers published letters of support in the *Schoolmaster* in which they clearly saw the Portsmouth fight, not as a local one but on the principle of unionism and its national defence, viz:

> it is no exaggeration to say that the future comfort and freedom of thousands of teachers will be very largely affected by the outcome of the fight now going on.[11]

The School Board accepted a local deputation of teachers, accompanied by the NUT solicitor, Mr T.A. Organ. Gradually under pressure they promoted some teachers to a higher level of salary — in fact, to new pay scales created in November 1895 but hitherto never put into operation. Although a gradual process, this meant the teachers had forced the Board to adopt the scale they had previously shelved. The Board initially refused to take back the dismissed or resigning teachers. It took another three months of agitation before the Highland Road teachers were reinstated, and the further point, the 7.55 rule, was changed to 8.30 am.

The Portsmouth dispute illustrates a number of factors in the employment and organization of teachers in this period in the towns. Firstly, teachers were employees and their wages and conditions of work were created solely by the local School Board. The Board could alter or ignore any salary agreement it had made and the teachers were often in no position to influence the Board. The Board quite often ignored the existence of the teachers' union, seeing it as in conflict with their right to manage and as alien to the local community, imported from elsewhere; this view generated statements about 'our' teachers as opposed to the union teachers. Secondly, although the Board might have no qualms about seeing the Union as potential troublemakers, the teachers were often very moderate in their attitudes and demands. At Portsmouth, they were in some sympathy, initially, with the financial difficulties of the Board and its attempts to alter its position. The local Associations had some difficulty in fighting a School Board or the later Local Education Authority effectively. A hard and dangerous battle for the teachers might only end in a partial success and it was quite likely that the composition of the Board, their employers, would remain unchanged. A local dispute was well publicized in the *Schoolmaster* and though the lessons of a dispute, such as ways to organize, or the use of tactical resignations, may not be brought out, the detail of the dispute allowed other Associations to draw their own conclusions, in addition to sending solidarity greetings. Portsmouth had an encouraging effect on teachers intimidated by voluntary or Board School managers elsewhere and on those who wanted the NUT to organize itself as a union with a sustentation fund and divisional organizers.

The dispute at West Ham in 1907 occurred in an urban area which, politically and socially, differed significantly from Portsmouth. West Ham was the base of the new Gas Workers' Union, led by Will Thorne, and the large working-class population, working in the gasworks, shipbuilding and engineering works had been politically revolutionized by the effects of the new unionism. Thorne was a member of the Social Democratic Federation, a Marxist organization led by H.M. Hyndman, but he laid greater stress than the SDF on municipal elections rather than on political agitation in the unions.

Thorne was elected to the West Ham Council in 1891 on a programme which included the eight-hour day, provision of municipal baths and washbasins and municipalization of the tram service. He had always been a great supporter of working-class education and rectifying the almost total lack of schools in West Ham was one of his priorities as a Labour councillor. Thorne put together a disciplined coalition of trade unionists, Radicals, Irish Nationalists and Labour groups, and in 1898 they became the first Labour group to win a town council, although only by a narrow margin. Thorne said then that the Labour Party as a whole would be judged by the progress it made in West Ham.

Although the political and social unity present in West Ham was unlike that present in Portsmouth, the two areas shared the same economic tension in council affairs. Again, a small middle-class ratepaying section of the population had to pay for the social and municipal services of a large working class. Every demand for better municipal services, including education, was resisted by the ratepayers. The West Ham council was mainly composed of people determined to resist extension of services and to reduce the cost of operating those they had. In two specific ways Labour group policies affected the education system. Within a short time, they were building new schools and paying 'trade union' rates to their teachers. At the same time they were extending municipal services to include housing, libraries and tramways, and making union membership compulsory for council workers.

By 1900, they were defeated on the charge of 'high rates and extravagant spending'[12] as they had succeeded in uniting every ratepayer interest group against them. It was the ratepayer alliance that in 1907 altered the teachers' pay scales. The previous scales had attracted teachers into West Ham, when male teachers, for instance, were scarce in London. The teachers had been guaranteed by the Council:

> That any modification of the scale of salaries shall not act to the detriment of a teacher already in the service of the Council.[13]

In 1905/6, West Ham had very high unemployment rates, unprecedented in the borough, and this must have decided the ratepayer group on a course of new economies, hence the new teachers' scales. In March, 1907, the Council created four new grades of certificated teachers, with newly diminished increments and lower scale points. The elaborate scheme affected over 300 teachers who lost relatively large sums of money and who would have to wait longer periods for the next incremental stage.

The teachers had been affected by the gains made in the Labour municipalization programme, such as in pay and services, and the economies were seen as the beginning of a dismantling process. The solid NUT membership organized public meetings and deputations, supported by local Labour councillors, the Trades Council and Will Thorne (the newly elected Labour MP for West Ham South). The teachers' fight became one platform on which to resist the de-municipalization process, for the Labour movement, as well as a reflection of the greater political unity created by the new unionism ideas and the wide political alliance organized by Thorne. The Union organized a strike headquarters in a West Ham shop they rented and formed a permanent strike sub-committee of Executive and local members.

It was clear that the West Ham Council needed to weaken union power in the area to reduce rates and recreate a flexible workforce. The *Daily News* said:

> They have commenced the task of smashing the educational machine which has been the pride of the borough. They have attacked the scale of salaries and called upon the teachers to accept reductions of the most substantial character. Naturally the teachers have objected and having one of the best trades unions in existence, they promise to offer a resistance of a very effective kind . . .[14]

The Union Executive felt that the high rates led education to be sacrificed, and that this almost inevitable response could only be solved by a new national system of rating, and Government grants to heavily-rated areas. Teachers were the most readily accessible target for reducing local educational expenditure. The tone of regret that is present in the writings of the Executive of the period was outweighed in the borough by an insistent and vital unionism. This unionism was locally in alliance with labour organizations. Yoxall recognized this in a large public meeting on the 17th April.

He made a clear statement about teachers' natural allies:

> ... There were present that night in addition to so many working-class parents, a number of leaders of labour organisations. The teachers who were appealing for fair play that night ... were not teachers of the favoured, fashionable and costly schools of the country. They were teachers in the schools of the people, and when they stood up for those schools, they stood up for the people and for the children of the people.[15]

He emphasized this by referring to his correspondence with Labour organizations about secondary education for the working classes, and the fact that most teachers were the children of the working class.

By April 27th, sixty teachers were threatened with dismissal for refusing to accept the new grades, and the Union agreed to pay them the higher grade for five years after dismissal. The Executive decided that if the Council was willing to continue the old scales for its present employees, they would be willing to accept the new grades for new teachers. This compromise would have created an impossible situation for the Council, who would have won in principle but in practice would still have had an education service it regarded as too expensive. As the *Tribune* had said, 'what does it matter how good or bad the teacher is, as long as he's cheap'!

The Council itself was split, although unequally, between those who wished for this 'cheaper and more efficient' service and those, educationists and labour supporters, who demanded a decent education service and the fair treatment of its workforce. A local by-election address at the time illustrates this — an Education committee member, Duncan Best, opposed the 'socialist scheme of equal pay for unequal ability' with the return of a grading system, which would, by recognizing 'aptitude for teaching, intelligence, knowledge and diligence ... promote ... efficiency and will gradually effect a real economy'.[16]

In other words, this dispute was about the right to operate unions and the employers' need to operate a cheap, flexible workforce, hiring and firing at will, to provide a cheap education service. Local NUT Associations throughout the country gave messages of support to the strikers, and some agreed to a levy,[17] recognizing by their actions the importance of this general conflict, exemplified at West Ham.

Worsening conditions in the schools, with insufficient staff and overcrowded conditions[18] led the Council to give their School Management Committee chairman the right to transfer the teaching staff from one school to another. The Council also continued their standby tactic of 'divide and rule' by allowing head teachers to remain on the old scale, and increasing uncertificated teachers' salaries. The effect of the former action was to increase the number of teachers handing in their dismissal notices. Young pupil-teachers were given control of large senior classes and infant teachers were taking boys' classes. Married women teachers, who customarily were dismissed on marriage, were invited by the Council to be re-appointed to the service. Although Labour councillors forced the Council to agree that the 5-year-contract was worth as little as the 'detriment' clause, it was stated in the Council meeting[19] that a teacher who had been banned from teaching in any London County Council school had been appointed.

The reported discussions of the Council made it plain that their purpose was 'to break the tyranny of the Union'.[20] That this was the intention is further suggested by a member of the Council visiting young women teachers in the borough, and promising them seven years guaranteed service, with a heavy financial indemnity in the event of failure to carry out the agreement — the only condition being 'that the teacher should withdraw from the National Union of Teachers'.[21]

By early June, fifty-seven teachers had been dismissed, and fifty-eight had resigned. Most of the teachers (including all of the men teachers) had obtained other appointments. The Special (or strike) Committee was endeavouring to keep the remaining teachers at work, but resignations increased when 'blackleg' or emergency teachers were appointed. Support was regularly coming in by way of local and regional Associations motions, and the always favourable local press. The Chicago Teachers' Federation also sent a telegram of support.

A major source of help for the teachers were the labour councillors on the West Ham Council.[22] Although they were constantly defeated, they were publicly reported in the *Stratford Express, Evening Chronicle* and the *Schoolmaster*. They worked closely with the teachers — for instance, on the 'class size' figures in the schools or in particular cases of dismissals, etc. One of this group, Councillor Hayday, made an impassioned speech during the dispute about the council's policy:

> Too much power had been placed in the hands of one man. If 150 applications were received in response to the advertisements, he would have power to immediately discharge 150 known members of the Union . . . There were councillors who cared nothing about education if only they could save salaries. He had heard Councillor C. Mansfield say 'Sack them all'. They wanted to cripple the legitimate aspirations of those teachers who thought it right to join their Union for mutual protection. . . . Councillor Byford had said he was going to destroy the Labour element on the council . . . People talked about olive branches. The Union would find they had to fight reactionary Councils, just as the trade unions had to

fight employers or Trusts. They would have to become more aggressive.[23]

Members of the majority group of councillors were informed by the Clerk to the Council, Dr Hilleary, that it could not offer special five-year contracts with teachers to encourage them to leave the NUT and continue work (that is, 'blackleg'). The contract with the teachers could not be binding on any future Council, and the Labour Group was definitely opposed to it. Yet contracts were still offered by a Council desperate to ease the problem of classroom overcrowding and teacher resignations. An attempt by the Council to advertise for 600 teachers in Scotland met with unexpected failure when the *Educational News*, their journal, refused the advertisement out of solidarity.[24] The government gave no public encouragement to the Council yet, when questioned by the General Secretary of the Union, and a union-sponsored MP, Yoxall, in Parliament, suggested that the over-crowding was due to seasonal problems and generally small schools!

The Education Committee meeting of 10th July contained a heated debate around a resolution from the South West Ham Free Church Council, which seemed to take the NUT position that 'the new financial regulations should not apply to teachers already engaged'.[25]

This position was unacceptable to the majority of the Council, and yet as a Labour councillor pointed out:

> There was hardly one trade union in ten which would settle the question on such a basis as the teachers were prepared to accept. A trade union would want concessions for those who came after as well as for those immediately affected, but the teachers were not urging that.[26]

That point reveals the differences between the NUT and the Labour allies. It must have been a source of discomfort for the Labour movement to support an organization that said it was fighting for a Labour principle, the right to unionize, yet was willing to compromise from the beginning on just that principle, by allowing NUT members to be employed at a lower than standard rate.

Indeed one councillor, Jones, went on to say that he thought 'the teachers were giving half their case away'. Further he suggested:

> So far as they (the Labour members) were concerned, they were not there to advocate merely the case of the teachers, but the teachers belonged to an organisation, and they had a perfect right to belong to it, and therefore had a perfect right to follow any tactics organised by that body. *He had no particular love for teachers as a class* . . . He was fighting for the teachers on principle.[27]

The support the teachers were getting from the Labour movement was based on the principle of unionism, and yet it obviously rankled with some members of that movement that the teachers were insecure in their use of principle, and made difficult allies.

The blithe disregard for the increasingly overcrowded conditions in the schools was bolstered by the Board of Education's lack of concern, to the dismay of the Labour group who constantly expected the Board to fulfil its grant aid conditions, and withdraw the grant on the grounds of the overcrowding or lack of teachers. Though most of the councillors may have been concerned in private, in the publicly-recorded Education Committee they voted steadfastly to continue. Council Hutt stating that:

> ... a good many other public bodies were going to follow West Ham's example, and it was a fight in which West Ham must pull the chestnuts out of the fire for someone else[28]

suggests that it was not only the NUT that was getting countrywide support, and that West Ham was not exceptional in its work conditions, and that any one of a number of local councils could have begun this particular dispute. It happened to be West Ham because of a particular set of conditions — the strength of the Union locally and the recent election of a strong Conservative and Ratepayers group (the Municipal Alliance party) on the issue of the high local rates.

To replace the often long-serving teachers (whose number was increased by 200 after a Union meeting on the 18th of July) the Council was recruiting where it could. Although it was tacitly supported by the Board of Education, who constantly denied in Parliament that the Code was being broken by the overcrowding,[29] the Council came under attack for the kind of teacher recruited. Because these teachers were designated as 'on supply', the Chairman of the Education Committee refused to give details of their background, testimonials and credentials to the opposition councillors. If any enquiries were to be made, they would only do so after the strike had been broken.[30] The zealots on the Committee saw the struggle as 'the right to govern' — consequently, hiring new staff, transferring staff from school to school, overcrowding the classrooms, was their affair, not the teachers'. The notion of unionism, and even arbitration (constantly mentioned in the Committee) was alien to them. Councillor Best, a recent by-election winner on this issue, said:

> They could meet their own teachers if they came to them, and there was no reasonable request they might make that would not be granted, that course had always been taken when a deputation had

been received. If the teachers had come to the Education Committee in the first case, everything might have been settled.[31]

If Councils changed their minds, contradicted previous practice or ignored previously agreed employment classes, that was seen by this group as their prerogative.

A Church of England vicar, a councillor,[32] suggesting a meeting with 'their own teachers'. The very question of national union recognition is absent from even this moderate solution — a fundamental precept of unionism, recognition, was ignored. Arbitration, even, was overwhelmingly rejected by the Council on July 23rd.

By late July, the dispute had been growing for three months, and the number of teachers resigning was increasing weekly. At the suggestion of the Head Teachers' Association, the Education Committee proposed a:

> round-table conference ... between the representatives of the Education Committee and the accredited representatives of the teachers.[33]

This formula, which excluded the term 'National Union of Teachers' yet could include the NUT locally and the national executive members, was acceptable to most of the Committee — to the Labour Councillors because it allowed no collapse of union principle, and to the moderates, because it allowed them to save face, and yet defy the zealots. The Chairman of the Education Committee, who was also the Deputy Mayor, was totally opposed, but seemed in the week July 16th to 23rd to have lost control over the moderates. The latter group would in 'fair weather' support the right to manage but had been defeated by the teachers' united action.

The next Education Committee (29th July) was completely given over to the selection of the representatives to the Conference — the Mayor was controversially appointed Chairman of the Conference, then eventually a ballot provided the remainder of the group. The meeting took so long to decide its representatives because of the continuing tussle between Labour and the hardliners, with the new group of moderates also hoping to be represented. Eventually, after several ballots, it was decided to include elected and appointed members, mainly of moderate and hardline persuasion. There was no obvious Labour representation.

The conference began at 11 am on Wednesday, July 31st and lasted for nearly ten hours. A settlement was achieved on the issue of salaries and scales which for the Union was a victory. The first impression gained from the *Schoolmaster* and West Ham newspapers after the strike, is one of conciliation, and a concern for the re-establishment of a cordial relationship. The *Stratford Express*[34] declared the trouble a mere misunderstanding:

> There need be no bitterness now. There have been honest misunderstandings and a pretty hard fight in consequence. The misunderstandings are cleared up, and in this country we don't bear malice after a fight.

The *Schoolmaster*[35] said that 'A friendly interchange of views — a round-table conference — was all that was required to secure peace'. These naive, if harmless, pleasantries were useful at the time to heal the wounds of the combatants but they do not explain the significance of the dispute. A Local Authority had for the first time since the Portsmouth dispute eleven years before been successfully fought on a point of principle. The strength of the Union was introduced to a new generation of teachers.

In its appraisal of the dispute, the *Schoolmaster* pointed the way to a policy which the NUT, in the actions of its Executive, invariably followed in the future:

> The West Ham struggle marks a new phase in the history of the Union. It was a fight between a great Union on the one hand, and one of the largest and most important Education Authorities . . . on the other . . . We trust that in any future disputes Education Authorities will see the value of calling into conference the Leaders of the Union at the beginning of a struggle. We are confident that if such a course be adopted it will lead to an earlier and more satisfactory settlement.[36]

The creation of a partnership in educational decision-making, myth and reality, must stem from this period even though there is little evidence to sustain it as other than a reassurance to the two battered parties and a Union Executive eager to avoid further trouble.

The Union changed — sometimes in more overt ways than others. Firstly, the Special Committee, a new institution, had successfully organized a strike, acting as a direct link between the Union Executive, the West Ham NUT Executive, and the local teachers. It was constantly at work in the borough, operating from the strike headquarters. It had held:

> no less than 80 meetings . . . including public meetings, conferences and committee meetings. In addition, hundreds of teachers were personally interviewed by members of the Committee, who at the same time dealt with the Executive and Committee work that would have fallen to their share in the ordinary course.[37]

Yet under this great strain and in an almost unprecedented situation for the teachers' organization, it had to:

formulate a policy that would not only fit the West Ham fight, but would be a precedent for future fights. They had to take strong lines, yet act with the greatest care. A false move might have caused confusion and defeat.[38]

The actions of unionism, and not just tentative ideas, are the legacy of this dispute. The Union defended unionism against a strong employer attack. It had centralized discipline and leadership, and the local initiative, morale-building and tactics of an industrial union.

The Union avoided a special levy for the strike but wary of the future, decided to increase the subscription to the Union, mainly for the purpose of strengthening the sustentation fund — the fund from which members are paid in a local dispute.[39]

Like the Portsmouth School Board, the West Ham Education Committee was fighting for the right to manage the local education service without obstruction. Obstruction to them meant the local association of teachers, as only by reducing wages could the books be balanced and the rates kept down. If councillors wavered in their determination to fight the teachers they could be replaced by the local Conservative/Ratepayer alliance. To smash the Union was their only logical course as this was the force that was trying to maintain wage levels and determine council policy. Council policy was not only to reduce general wage levels for teachers but by breaking the recognized scales, to pay teachers according to their own criteria, creating a flexible workforce. As much as possible they used the divisions between the teachers against them, putting headteachers against the class teacher, the certificated against the uncertificated, and the men against the women teachers. This was not very difficult sometimes as the number of teachers in the NUT was, in this period, only about a quarter of all teachers. Large sections of teachers were non-Unionised and used as a source of cheap, supply labour; the use of married women teachers fits this category, constantly excluded or reintroduced to the teacher labour market when a temporary shortage of teachers occurred.

The moderation of the teachers' union faced with management hostility and the concentration of executive powers in one individual is consistent with the Portsmouth dispute. To have forced the Union to open a strike headquarters and to delegate Executive members to oversee the strike operation was a sign of the total intransigence of the employer, not of a natural militancy or strong syndicalist position within the Executive and membership. West Ham was the first of a number of strikes to occur mainly in the next decade where the Union had to fight just like any other Union. The immediate effect of a strike is that the employer saves money on salaries and so new tactics of struggle had to be devised in the Union. A natural source of allies was the parents of the working-class elementary children and during strikes or disputes, after West Ham, a series of appeals and meetings were addressed to them. In West Ham, it was no coincidence that the strikers had the support of the Labour movement. West Ham South had been won by Keir Hardie of the Independent Labour Party in 1892. Will Thorne regained the seat for Labour, the year before the strike, and he stood for an educational policy that was in advance of the Union's own position. The West Ham Trades Council was the key to his local support and the base for the teacher strike support. At the time, the local alliance was unusual but it had elements that were to surface again in 1919. Thorne represented the new unionism of the militant manual workers' unions who were often opposed by the older craft unions. Some Labour councillors supported the teachers but they did not like them or their attitudes; it was a question of class interest, protection of the education system and a response to the employer's anti-Unionism. All for one, one for all. The problem which remained was that although individual teachers were socialists or ILP supporters, the Union seemed to the Labour movement to be opportunistic in its appeals for support.

The only clear policy ever shown by the Board of Education up to 1919 and post 1921 was the policy it followed at West Ham. It did practically nothing. The question of inefficiency, one of the grounds for its intervention, was never defined and in this case, never raised by the Board. Both the Labour group and the teachers expected the Board to intervene but it consistently denied that West Ham was breaking its regulations. One surmises that West Ham Council was following a policy which the Board approved and that was breaking the power of the Union and lowering the price the teachers could charge for their labour. The Board seemed to care very little for the quality of education and, as in West Ham, it always seemed to surprise teachers and parents by its tardiness in intervening. The pressure that was building up in Local Authority areas was to continue in the next few years as, due to economies, Exchequer grants-in-aid were effectively reduced and teachers' salaries were the main way in which LEAs could save money. Throughout the West Ham strike it was expected that either other authorities would quickly join in with similar demands or wait until the teachers wer beaten before doing so.[40]

First at Portsmouth and then more significantly at West Ham, teachers had shown that they could organize and fight. Instead of disunity and factionalism, they had created a solidarity between themselves, with teachers in other parts of the country and with the local Trades Council and ILP Councillors.[41] West Ham became a symbol of hope to many teachers and the basis for future action in the later salary campaign.

Notes

1. Durman, William *'Portsmouth Education'*.
2. Bransdon, T. 'Early Education in Portsmouth' in *National Association of Headteachers Conference Souvenir* 1931.
3. *Hampshire Telegraph* Jan. 30, 1892.
4. *Hampshire Telegraph* Feb. 29, 1892.
5. *Hampshire Telegraph* Feb. 29, 1892.
6. *Hampshire Telegraph* Feb. 22, 1892.
7. *Hampshire Telegraph* Feb. 15, 1896.
8. *Hampshire Telegraph* Feb. 22, 1896.
9. *Hampshire Telegraph* Feb. 22, 1896.
10. *Hampshire Telegraph* March 21, 1896.
11. *The Schoolmaster* Feb. 29, 1896.
12. Radice, G. & L. (1974) *'Will Thorne, Constructive Militant'* Allen & Unwin, p. 54.
13. *Schoolmaster* April 20, 1907.
14. *Schoolmaster* April 20, 1907.
15. *Schoolmaster* April 20, 1907.
16. *Schoolmaster* April 27, 1907.
17. Portsmouth was one of these associations. *Schoolmaster* May 4, 1907.
18. One of the worst examples — a single teacher teaching 130 children in a room built for 70 children. *Schoolmaster* May 11, 1907.
19. *Schoolmaster* May 25, 1907.
20. *Schoolmaster* May 25, 1907.
21. *Schoolmaster* June 8, 1907.
22. These Councillors were allied to the local MP, Will Thorne, and influenced by the industrial unionism he represented and his great championing of a free, secular education system. In 1905, he had won support at the TUC on a resolution demanding free meals and medical inspection for all children. Simon (65)p. 286.
23. *Schoolmaster* June 29, 1907.
24. 600 teachers could be an almost complete compliment of new teachers to replace the old. The *Dundee Advertiser* was also carrying this advert.
25. *Schoolmaster* July 13, 1907.
26. *Schoolmaster* July 13, 1907.
27. *Schoolmaster* July 13, 1907.
28. *Schoolmaster* July 13, 1907.
29. On one occasion on the same day as issuing regulations fixing the maximum secondary school class size at 35. *Schoolmaster* July 20, 1907.
30. *Schoolmaster* July 20, 1907 — Chairman "Later it will be our duty to go more carefully into these appointments".
31. *Schoolmaster* July 20, 1907.
32. *Schoolmaster* July 20, 1907.
33. *Schoolmaster* July 27, 1907.
34. August 1907.
35. *Schoolmaster* Aug. 10, 1907.
36. *Schoolmaster* Aug. 10, 1907.
37. NUT Report 1908, pp. LXI.
38. *Schoolmaster* Aug. 10, 1907.
39. Similar difficulties to the West Ham situation were present in different parts of the

country "it is experiences like these which convince the Executive that, short of a considerable sustentation fund, the teachers in no administrative area of the country can be safe" NUT Report 1908, pp. XIV.
40 A Labour Council in Aberdare, S. Wales created a dispute in 1907 again on the issue of unionisation and working conditions. However the same process at West Ham was present at Aberdare — the teachers' ties to the Labour movement were strengthened by contact between the younger, left wing elements.
41 It wasn't a coincidence that a 1908 Annual Conference (NUT) resolution on class size said it was necessary "to secure the cooperation of the Trades Congress, Labour Representation Committees, the ILP, the Cooperative Societies, Trade Unions and any other organisation interested in the welfare of the children to bring about this urgent reform," NUT Report LXXVII.

Chapter 3

Turning the World Upside Down

Rural teachers appear to have been seen by their employers, local farmers, landowners or clergy, as a form of social servant, teachers of the poor, who were themselves drawn from that class and often recruited locally. One of the most interesting features of the early decades of this century is the way in which the rural teachers began to break free of their 'masters' either by demanding and getting a proper wage or by seeking better local schooling. What they were breaking free from was the social paternalism of rural education management, the extra duties demanded of them (by their school managers and the local Church of England vicar) and the poor quality of their schools, which were often dirty, badly lit and heated and with no running water. In the country-wide strike in Herefordshire, before World War I, and in the Burston school strike, the teachers were seen as turning the natural order of the rural areas upside down.

It is not surprising that these teachers should have in some cases felt closer to the agricultural labourers they served than to the farmers, landowners or clergy who excluded them socially. Strange, a teacher in Leintwardine, Herefordshire, had allied himself with the labourers' cause and helped to organize West of England labourers in a Union.[1] Later, John Arnett and Tom Higdon had joined with the East Anglian labourers. Arnett was a member of the Executive of the Eastern Counties Union and survived the disastrous strike in 1910.[2] Higdon joined the Union whilst a schoolmaster at Wood Dalling in Norfolk in 1907,[3] and was to become a major force in the Union organization in branches and on Parish Councils. He was also part of the new socialist revival which took place in the Union after its defeat in 1910.[4]

It was the rural areas which gave the teachers a boost across the country. The first and hardest battle in a newly declared salaries campaign, the Herefordshire strike, was begun in 1913, and the Burston School strike, a local event with a national impact, energised the rural teachers and the growing link with organized labour, in the Trade Unions and the ILP.

Tom Higdon and his wife, Anne Higdon, were at the centre of the labourers' fight in Norfolk and it is no coincidence, that, as teachers, they fought for better schooling as well. In Wood Dalling and after their compulsory transfer, at Burston, they stood for a better education for the labourers' children, and in the records of their fight, we can see the difficulties of the rural teacher. At Wood Dalling, they persistently made the local Attendance Officer bring children into school from farming work. Tom Higdon even pulled boys away from farmers using them in the fields and Mrs Higdon encouraged the boys not to help the local Harriers. They provided dry clothing for the children on rainy days and often sought permission to use the school fire to dry the childrens' clothing.[5] With the aid of the NUT, they had protected the Infants teacher (most probably a supplementary teacher) from a manager's complaint. They constantly asked for visits by the County Medical Officer or the village doctor to the children, especially with the recurrent whooping cough epidemic. They invited the Sanitary and Building Inspectors to the school. The school log book is a record of a running battle undertaken by the teachers against the managers. The managers, were, in the main, local farmers and Tom Higdon provoked them by encouraging the Attendance Officer to visit them and by increasing school expenditure. Trouble came to a head when Higdon, involved in the organization of the local Agricultural Workers' Union, had helped to win a clean sweep of the local Parish Council by the labourers — but the school managers were still dominated by the farmers. Although the school regularly received good reports from the HMI, the Norfolk Education Committee (also mainly farmers or landlords) sustained a charge against the Higdons of referring to the Managers as 'liars'. With some fainthearted help from the NUT legal department, the Higdons were transferred to Burston School in 1911.

In March, 1913, the local farmworkers, whom he was again helping to organize in the surrounding villages,[6] asked him to help in the Parish Council elections and again the labourers won control, expelling the farmers and (most important) humiliating the new Vicar of Burston. The Parish Council was an active one. It removed the Vicar and the Churchwardens from the Charity Committee, kept the farmers from encroaching on public footpaths[7] and agitated for new village housing. Again, the question of rates and representation came to the fore. Higdon argued that new houses were needed and that the Council represented the ratepayers; an argument which was addressed to farmers who suggested otherwise. To Higdon, rents were a form of indirect rates.[8]

Apart from the Parish Council elections, two other issues soured relations between the Higdons and the Managers. Firstly, the Vicar was always trying to pressure the Higdons to be churchgoers not chapelgoers, as an example to the labourers and their children. The Higdons were probably Primitive Methodists. Secondly, the two teachers continued to battle for better school conditions. They were in trouble for closing the school in the whooping cough epidemic and the Managers even wrote to the Education Committee complaining that Mrs Higdon lit the schoolroom fire without their permission. Also 'Faults of lighting, heating, drainage and the Schoolhouse pump'[9] were complained about. Their dismissal this time occurred over a number of charges, all of them scratched together but sufficient for the Education Committee to act upon.[10]

The case of the Higdons illustrates the feudal conditions in which teachers and the other village workers lived, and how socialist teachers and the new agricultural Unionism was seen as a serious threat to the social fabric of the village hierarchy. Each time the teachers complained to the Managers or argued with the Vicar, there is a perceptible sundering of the system. This was to be redoubled by the growth of the Eastern Counties Union and the Parish Council elections.

What made the Burston case reverberate throughout the Teachers' Union and the wider Trade Union Movement was the result of their dismissals. The pupils went on strike after their teachers were given two days to leave the school and a fortnight to leave their tied cottage.[11] A public meeting on the village green resulted in a resolution that the 'parents would not send their children to school before justice was done'.

What happened next can best be illustrated from the minutes of the Norfolk Education Committee. During the course of the next eighteen months, the Committee was inundated by resolutions and appeals from trade union and socialist bodies, including the British Socialist Party, the Norwich ILP branch, the County Association of the NUT, the Norwich and the Lowestoft Trades and Labour Councils, the National Union of Railwaymen (2 branches), the Manchester and Salford Labour party, and 54 branches (and the Executive) of the Agricultural Labourers Union.[12] The latter were the mainstay of the Higdon's support and reveal the organic links that had developed between them and the rural workers.

George Edwards, the Agricultural workers leader, was one of two labour councillors on the County Council (though, in name, at this stage, he was an Advanced Liberal),[13] and in his autobiography, mentions that he felt the teachers had been victimized and was assured of '. . . the devotion of the people to the teachers and . . . that the teachers and the parents of the children were fighting a just battle'.[14] He warned the Council of the consequences of their action in words that were rapidly to come true — 'The whole great Trade Union Movement would take the matter up and then they would probably have another school built'.[15]

The new strike school symbolized the freedom sought by the rural teachers and agricultural workers. It would be independent of the financial and social controls imposed upon them by the farmers and the church; indeed for many of Burston's supporters, the school was the 'first school built by the working classes' and a 'permanent socialist educational institution'. The teachers' role in this was not lost nationally or locally.

Overlapping with the Burston strike, though not so evidently symbolic as Burston, was the beginning of the NUTs national salary campaign. In the large towns and cities, the teachers' Associations had managed with difficulty to force the local education committees into offering better salary scales, yet even there the control by ratepayer councillors of municipal budgets and the declining value of Exchequer grants caused sharp conflicts. In the rural districts, teacher Associations found it extremely difficult to talk to or convince the landlords and farmers on the County Education Committees. Conflict between the teachers and their local employers grew. In many areas teachers were not on salary scales but on fixed wages and they were under extreme pressure from the post-1900 inflation which had grown to 20 per cent by 1912 (9 per cent between 1910 and 1913).

In the past, the Union had tried to influence backward or recalcitrant authorities by 'blacklisting' them in the *Schoolmaster*, a major source of job advertising. Applicants were invited to enquire of the Union if a local authority was in dispute over salaries. This policy was being rendered ineffective by the increasing number of teachers, outside the Union, ineligible to join. Another policy was a recommended list of pro-education candidates for local elections but this, too, was increasingly ineffective due to the homogeneity of mainstream Liberal and Conservative municipal policy or the monopoly of Conservative party control in the shires.

At the Annual Conference in 1913 at Weston-Super-Mare, the Union had adopted a recommended standard scale of salaries for teachers and the Executive had been instructed to start a campaign to achieve it. A Special Salaries Committee was set up, composed of teachers, headteachers and Union officers, which was to act as a catalyst to local Associations. It urged them on, providing facts, cost of living statistics, petitions and recommended procedures in organizing a local campaign. It was well understood in the Union, and a reflection on its history, that:

> the Local or County Associations must be the unit of action, if any good is to accrue, as a full knowledge of the local circumstances and difficulties is the first condition of success. The time and method of action can only be best known to those who are in close touch with the district and with all the local conditions.[16]

This policy reflected the Union's strength, that some local Associations by their strong organization and industry could create precedents or sound examples for other, weaker Associations. The strong encouraged the weak and the role of the central Executive was to funnel experience and tactics. The *Schoolmaster* provided a new 'Enthusiasts Column' with suggestions sent in by readers on tactics and the enrolment of members.[17] All this was very necessary as it was the Union's suspicion, remarked upon during the West Ham strike, that the education authorities were about to combine to further reduce wages.[18] Although the Union proposed to support the local education authorities if they petitioned the government to increase central grants for education provided a proportion of the grant was reserved for improving pay and staffing ratios, the more likely event was an employer combination against the teachers.

The NUT Tenure Committee recognized a further spark to action in the high level of industrial strikes taking place nationally among miners, railwaymen, cotton spinners and dockers. The committee saw in the salary campaign:

> a widespread movement corresponding to the recent unrest in the industrial sphere. Attempts to economise at the expense of the teacher are giving place to agitations on the part of the teachers to secure more adequate salaries and better increments.[19]

Improvements were sometimes very little and hard fought. The only new advantage the Union had was that there was a temporary shortage of teachers after 1910 as the old pupil-teacher recruitment was being phased out and the new secondary school recruits had not yet developed substantially. In some parts of the country there was a considerable fall in new recruits to teaching.[20] The Union also welcomed the concern expressed in Trades Councils and *The Herald* at the overcrowding and bad classroom conditions which prevailed in many places. It had been made clear at Weston-Super-Mare that the teachers had to go out and state their case to the public to enlist their support.[21]

There was also a recognition that this time the Union would choose to strike (or allow teachers to resign) in pursuit of its claims and not, as before, in reaction to employer action — a campaign that would take 'the teachers out when the authorities were not willing to pay them decent salaries'.[22]

The dispute in Herefordshire brought the tension between rates, councillors and the Board of Education in the schools to wide public notice. The overwhelming evidence that members were being 'sweated' in the county left most newspapers with little other than favourable comment to make on the teachers' action. Since 1904, the certificated teachers had sent 'memorials, deputations and direct communications'[23] to the County Council appealing for salary increases. Their situation was grave, combatting inflation and the fact that wages in the county were about one-third below a country-wide average. Many of the school managers had tried to help their schoolteachers over the years without success. This tended to make the Herefordshire clergy, including the Bishop of Hereford, support the teachers. One, the Reverend William Hapton, wrote to Yoxall, the Union Secretary, with his support:

> We have done our utmost for years past to induce the Local Education Authority to deal more liberally with teachers but simply in vain. They are paying now more than 20 pounds per annum less than we were paying teachers on our staff before the Act of 1902 came into operation — and until quite recently were paying 46 pounds per annum less than we paid . . . Anything by which we can influence the Local Education Authority I feel sure we shall do, as we have done since 1905, when they commenced their present underpaid treatment of our staff.[24]

The support from the school managers and therefore the Church was to be important when the Council asked them to evict striking teachers from schoolhouses, which they refused to do.

In 1913, a final appeal was made by the Union to the Council for revised salaries and for a salary scale (newly adopted by the Weston-Super-Mare Conference). Ingeniously, and not without precedent, Herefordshire Local Education Authority had a *standing order which ruled out any discussion of a salary scale*, so the appeal was made impossible. The Council decided to enquire into teachers' salaries in comparable areas as a means of forestalling further teacher action. This inquiry was seen as a delaying tactic by the teachers who then handed in their resignations to the Union, most of which were to be effective from January 1st, 1914 (the headteachers were on 3 months notice and they would join the strike later).

The Union opened a strike headquarters in Hereford, a central position in the County although not itself affected by the impending strike. Initially a hundred resignations were handed in. On November 8th, a further thirty teachers were added to the list. In the following weeks, Union members travelled around Herefordshire encouraging all the non-unionized teachers to join, so that by the middle of November, another sixty-nine teachers gave in their notice. It was reported in the *Schoolmaster* that, in total, 229 teachers struck (or had the intention of doing so in the case of headteachers) in January. This consisted of seventy-nine headmasters, thirty-eight headmistresses, six class masters, thirteen class mistresses and ninety-three other teachers.[25] It is not clear if all these teachers were certificated teachers but it has to be assumed so as the Union did not mention any other type of teacher, although in a rural area one would expect to see a considerable number of pupil-teachers or supplementary teachers. They may have been temporarily protected by the Union with strike pay although they were ineligible to join.

The question at stake in the disputes with Local Education Authorities was often the recognition and very existence of the Union. As was common throughout the salary campaign in the rural and town areas, the Union was barely recognized by the employers. The NUT Secretary sent a letter to the Herefordshire Authority asking to state the Union case before it; in return the Executive was invited to a meeting in the Shirehall in November. The Secretary of the County Association was also invited to a meeting. Both groups attended together but the Authority would not receive the local teachers with the Union Executive. The teachers then left. The Education Committee's tactic was to divide the teachers.

The Union was fairly confident that the places of the striking teachers could not be filled. This must has been a reflection of the shortage of teachers in 1913/1914, the strong strike fund and the determined effort the Union made to advertise its case nationally. Its confidence was well-placed. The Authority was to advertise widely but by January, 1914, had only recruited five teachers. It had tried offering headships to junior staff but they had refused. It had, like West Ham earlier, advertised in Scotland, but the Educational Institute of Scotland, the NUT's equivalent, made strong representations against any Scottish teacher taking a Herefordshire post:

> Any Scottish teacher ... will surely not give away the professional position so staunchly maintained across the Border by applying for a post in Hereford.[26]

Just before the strike was due to start, the salary enquiry set up by the Education Committee reported back. It had been chaired by a Colonel Decies, who was obviously the linchpin of the employers' resistance.

Decies said that the strike had not influenced the report but he then suggested that small increases should be given to some teachers. The Committee had used other rural counties with which to compare its salaries — Cambridgeshire, Worcestershire, Wiltshire, Shropshire, Westmoreland and Buckinghamshire. Not surprisingly it found that in one or the other of these counties, for a male or female headteacher or class teacher, lower wages could be produced which showed Herefordshire in a good light. However, some increases were suggested, on the basis of the 'teacher's service, capability and character' as ascertained by the Authority. Under no circumstances could a salary scale be agreed, though.

Throughout the strike the teachers received a favourable press nationally, and comments made in editorials and articles reveal the watershed the salary campaign was making to a national assessment of the education system. The *Daily News* in an editorial headed 'Sweated Teachers' raised questions about education in Herefordshire which should have been addressed more widely:

> [The Hereford Local Authority] does not want good education; it does not want any real education. It is compelled by law to administer a system of education, and it does it as stingily and badly as it dare. Clearly the appeal to reason and to the sanctity of education cannot affect such bodies. They can only feel coercion. Surely through its control of finance the Board of Education has power to end a gross scandal.[27]

It was only because the spotlight had turned so fully on to Herefordshire that its miserliness had been exposed and its 'cult of economy'[28] accused of endangering efficiency. The other rural areas were escaping the same degree of opprobium though equally deserving as Herefordshire. But the issue of underpaid teachers, cheapness or efficiency and the nation's education system was being raised fully by the campaign and by the actions of the teachers. The *Yorkshire Post*, for example, raised the fundamental issue of financing, pointing out that rates were increasing and grants-in-aid were shrinking and only a new Government policy could help to alter this declining or inverse spiral.[29] The *Birmingham Post* focused on the changes that the Union was making for itself and its class of white collar workers, and it foresaw a new industrial arena for disputes similar to that of the engineering, mining or railway industries. It attached great significance to the fact (albeit in ignorance of West Ham) that:

> This is the first occasion on which such a Union as this resorted to the strike weapon. In the noise of industrial warfare, in the clamour over the wages of artisans, we are inclined to forget the humbler members of the professional classes. For them, too, the battle of existence is growing harder and harder. In many ways it is true to say that they are far worse off than the men of the industrial Unions. But so far they have not attempted combination.[30]

The Observer was interested in the working conditions of the teachers (low pay, poor promotion prospects, no salary scale and often tied to a local authority) and the fact that the strike, and the Union behind it, was successful, whilst the Local Authority was obliged to provide 'adequate educational facilities'. It gave Herefordshire only a week to recruit new teachers or settle with the strikers. It expected the latter.[31]

The question of 'adequate education' should have been pressing to the Education Committee. It had to be pointed out to them, informally by the Board, that they would lose the grant-in-aid (a 'serious financial loss') if they allowed the schools to lack proper staffing or meet far less than the necessary 400 meetings a year.[32] Indeed, the Board's Secretary, in private correspondence, was amazed at the lack of tactical forethought on the part of the Committee and Colonel Decie. The fact that the ratepayers were hardly overtaxed in Herefordshire had become well-known; the rates for education were practically the lowest in the country. The Board felt unable to act directly which is a reflection not on its powers to ensure adequate schooling but its political willingness to intervene in the local milieu of its political allies. Instead the Bishop of Hereford seemed to act as the Board's agent on the spot; he privately corresponded with the Secretary of the Board and arranged conciliatory meetings for the teachers and the Committee.

The Bishop and the Clergy were particularly exercised about the lack of moral control on the children during the strike. About sixty schools were closed and a further ten seriously understaffed. In many villages, the parents and pupils supported the teachers and caused havoc with what few new teachers had been found. The children went on strike in Ross and in several villages, were bribed to attend in Ledbury, and in other schools locked out their new teachers or rioted in the classrooms.[33] In the national papers children were reported as rioting or yelling 'blacklegs' or 'we want our teachers back'. The Committee still pressed on, appointing teachers at higher wages than the strikers, to break the strike.[34] Even so, half the children in Herefordshire were not being educated at all. Colonel Decie tried to get the permission of the Board to agree that the closed schools were unavoidably closed which would not have affected the Grant. The reply was not reassuring, it said only that each case would be judged on its merits, and suggested a round-table conference. By this time even Decie and his fellow councillors could sense that a salary scale would have to be agreed with the NUT.

The face-saving document that was finally produced by the Salaries Committee and agreed by the Education Committee reads throughout as if it were a reasonable and moderate solution. It discusses the scales, the conditions for promotion and the small amount that was outstanding between the teachers and the Council which, in its magnanimity, it had taken over. It does not read as the conclusion to the hard fought and bitter battle it was. The document was agreed by the Committee on February 21st, 1914 and on March 1st, a mass meeting of teachers agreed to the settlement. For many teachers, it had been a three-month strike in which they had to worry not only about their livelihood and futures but their homes as well. They were united, and a powerful council, making some tactical errors, and with new allies won over to the teachers, had lost. The teachers were all reinstated, with the exception of a few whose posts had been filled during the strike.

The latter were placed on a sustentation allowance that lasted for several years.

At the mass meeting the teachers made it clear that the salary scale was inadequate, but the fact of its existence at all and the Union recognition involved led them to agree to the terms, 'for the present'.[35]

The *Schoolmaster* quoted approvingly from a *Daily Chronicle* editorial at the strike's end, which agreed that an immediate social reform was the need to improve education and the teachers' pay and status along with it. It added:

> The status of the rural teachers under the County Councils is generally speaking the worst of all. The strike in Herefordshire has done much to advertise and something to diminish this serious evil.[36]

Rural teachers, badly paid and under-organized, had shown that they could win a strike against a confident, local employer.

The salaries campaign had ended in 1914, with the outbreak of war, with improvements to pay in half the LEAs. Class teachers, male and female, were the main beneficiaries and eighty-eight LEAs now had salary scales. However, within two years, the campaign was re-opened, largely it seems, because of the rapidly rising cost of living and because of the cuts in the quality of the service, particularly through the employment of untrained teachers or 'dilutees'. It was not easy, teachers were patronized again, with employers refusing to see deputations of teachers or even inviting them to resign if they didn't like the pay or conditions. Yet the salary campaign became a cause, a source of ferment and new ideas among the Union's grass-roots, which began to alter the way the teachers saw themselves and their work.

Notes

1 Dunbabin, J.P.D., 'The Incidence and Organization of Agricultural Trades Unionism in the 1870's'. *Agricultural History Review* 107; 16, 1968.
2 Groves, R. (1949). *'Sharpen the Sickle' The History of the Farmworkers' Union*, Porcupine Press, p. 108.
3 Groves, R. ibid. p. 109. He was at an early meeting with George Edwards, its organiser, and was to continue on the Union Executive until 1939 (the year of his death).
4 Groves, R. (1967) *Conrad Noel and the Thaxted Movement*, Merlin Press.
5 Edwards, B. (1974) *'The Burston School Strike'*, Lawrence and Wishart.
6 Twelve new branches according to Tom Higdon in *'The Burston Rebellion'*, National Labour Press.
7 Higdon, T. ibid.

8 Edwards, B. p. 136, (Parish Meeting October 30, 1914).
9 'Casey' of Labour Leader *'The Burston School Strike'*, National Labour Press.
10 A charge of excessive punishment of two Barnardo girls and discourtesy to the Managers, (including not bowing to the Vicar's daughter and giving her a 'cold reception' and not replying to the Vicar's 'good day'!). Edwards, B. p. 28.
11 Higdon, T. op. cit.
12 Norfolk Education Committee Minutes 1915/1916.
13 Edwards, G. (1922) 'From Crow-Scaring to Westminster', N.U.A.W., p. 201.
14 Edwards, G. ibid. p. 187.
15 Edwards, G. ibid., p. 188.
16 NUT Report, 1914.
17 Thompson, D. op. cit. Other devices included deputations to trade unions and cooperative societies, indoor and outdoor meetings and house to house calls, p. 228.
18 NUT Report, 1910.
19 NUT Report, 1913.
20 *Yorkshire Herald* 19 November, 1913
   Leeds 1907   277 teachers entered schools
          1913   30 teachers entered schools
   Gosden, P.H.J.H. (1972) *op cit*. Pupil teacher recruits fell from 11,018 (1906/7) to 1454 (1913/14). p. 209.
21 Thompson, D. (1927) *'Professional Solidarity among the Teachers of England'*, Columbia Univ. Press, p. 227.
22 Thompson, D. p. 227.
23 Thompson, D. p. 232.
24 The *Schoolmaster*, Nov. 8, 1913. When the teachers had written to the Council in 1913 they pointed out that two-thirds of the headmasters received less than £130 and headmistresses £100!
25 *Schoolmaster*, Jan. 3, 1914. The NUT Annual Report 1914 gives the figure of 'nearly 240 teachers'.
26 Reported in the *Schoolmaster*, Jan. 24, 1914.
27 Thompson, D., p. 237.
28 *Daily Mail*, in Thompson, D. p. 236.
29 In Thompson, D. p. 239.
30 The *Schoolmaster*, Nov. 15, 1913. The Post also referred to the way in which some Local Authorities had little to choose but to 'sweat' teachers, caught between little finance and new demands from the Board. The demand that the State involves itself financially with teachers' salaries to stop the 'sweating' case in the *Westminster Gazette*, Feb. 3, 1914.
31 *Observer*, Jan. 25, 1914.
32 PRO ED/241768 Herefordshire Teachers' Strike: Secretary's Private correspondence with certain individuals.
33 Horn, P. *'The Herefordshire School Strike of 1914'* in History of Education Society occasional publications No. 3, Autumn 1977 and Thompson, D. p. 253/4. *Schoolmaster* Feb. 7, 1914.
34 Horn, P. (1977). At Newent, a headteacher (£95 p.a.) and his daughter probably a supplementary teacher (£20) were replaced by a young couple (£160–£170 p.a.).
35 Thompson, D., p. 260.
36 *Schoolmaster*, Feb. 28, 1914.

Chapter 4

The Rhondda and the Teachers

The significance of the Rhondda strike in the development of the National Union of Teachers, and of all elementary schoolteachers, lies in the fact that, for the first time, the Union's recommended salary scale was achieved, not just talked about, and secondly, that to achieve a successful strike and a major pay advance, teachers worked closely with many of the young, socialist miners in the Rhondda labour movement. The result of the strike and the labour alliance was to radically change the leadership of the NUT and to reorganize it fundamentally.

The same conditions prevailed in the Rhondda valley as existed elsewhere — poor conditions of work, the education system in crisis and a divided teaching force. Yet the Rhondda was the home of the new turbulent Miners Federation of Great Britain, and particularly, of the new socialist industrial unionism. The close proximity of the teachers by birth, habitation and living conditions to these militants was a factor in the success of the Rhondda strike.

The de-humanizing work conditions of the miners and the rapid spread of socialist ideas to a well educated working-class caused *The Times* to describe it as 'the industrial storm centre of Great Britain'.[1] The influence of the Central Labour College and the Plebs League, with their courses in Marxist economics and industrial history, was very strong in the South Wales valleys. Will Mainwaring,[2] A.J. Cook,[3] Noah Ablett and Noah Rees were among the leading figures of this new militant group of miners. This group, known as the Unofficial Reform Committee of the South Wales Miners Federation[4] was closely connected with the Plebs League as students and tutors, with the Miner's Lodges and the Trades Councils. The leader of the teachers in the strike was W.G. Cove, who had himself worked for five years as a miner before training as a teacher. The relationship between this group and the teachers can only be deduced from fragments of evidence — the eloquent speeches in support of the strike by A.J. Cook in the Council

Meetings, the public speeches at teachers' strike meetings of Will Mainwaring and A.J. Cook and the materialist outlook, expressed in the writings of W.G. Cove, common to the Plebs League and Unofficial Reform Committee work.

The Plebs League and the Central Labour College had been created from a strike at Ruskin College, Oxford on the issue of an independent Working Class Education. Self-financing classes, a significant number in South Wales, were taught by unpaid tutors in miners' halls, cafes or private houses.[5] The subject was usually Marxist economic theory and the classes were also a major part of the 'advanced' miners' movement, often run under supervision of the local Miners' Lodge: the significance of these classes was recognized elsewhere, viz:

> The sense of antagonism between Capital and Labour has been considerably deepened during recent years by the propaganda of a small but earnest group of men whose teachings are rapidly permeating the entire trade union movement. Advance causes feed on discontent and the indisposition of employers to concede the claims of the workers to a higher standard of life had provided fuel for the propaganda of the Independent Labour party and recently of the enthusiasts of the Central Labour College movement. The influence of the 'advanced' men is growing very rapidly and there's ground for belief that under their leadership attempts of a drastic character will be made by the working classes as a whole to secure direct control by themselves of their particular industries.[6]

Cove is recorded as teaching an Industrial History Class in Abergorky in 1917, and an Industrial History and Economic Class 1917[7] and Gwen Ray, another teachers' leader, taught an English class in the Mid-Rhondda in early 1917[8] (one of 7 miners' classes running that year in the Rhondda by the Central Labour College and the No. 1 Miners' Lodge). Cove had written to *Plebs* in 1916, discussing a previous issue on Education, and expressing his own views on elementary education:

> [it was possible to observe] that the prevailing form of society and the most powerful economic classes in the various epochs have been responsible both for the type of teacher employed and for the particular brand of education given in the schools.
> The problem I have to face in my work as a schoolteacher is how to make the children class conscious under present conditions ... let him get a conception of the struggle for existence by lessons on the development of his class ...[9]

This interest in a working-class education was shared in the Plebs League by miners and teachers, as it was of general concern in the valleys.¹⁰ Mark Starr, a Labour College organizer, reported to *Plebs* in March 1917, on a talk he gave in Aberdare on the Central Labour College and education, in which the issue of the 'relation of the movement to the professional elementary schoolteachers', was raised, a subject of strong local interest.

Cove wrote a *Plebs* pamphlet, with D.W. Thomas (the Secretary of the Upper Rhondda Plebs branch) on '*Helps to the Study of Capital*'. The preface stated: 'We lay no claim to be expert Marxists but we are strongly of the opinion that in order to understand Marx, *Capital* itself must be read'. In the same issue of *Plebs*, he wrote a long, complex article on 'Supply and Demand' — value, price, etc.¹¹ *Plebs* congratulated him on election to the NUT Executive in 1919. Cove was exceptional but not unique — Gwen Ray and other teachers worked closely with the miners in the Plebs League. (The year after [1921] a Rhondda teacher wrote to *Plebs* asking to be put in touch with other 'Plebs schoolteachers':

> Among *Plebs'* readers are doubtless a good many schoolteachers — the great majority of teachers, as we know, are hopelessly ignorant of their economic relationship to capitalist society and I suggest the drawing up of a manifesto showing clearly the anomalous position of 'non-industrial' wage workers. Are we clear in our own minds on the subject? Plebs can help us here).¹²

The way the strike was described and fought suggests a close link between this new industrial unionism, socialist militancy and the teachers.

The Rhondda strike was preceded by a number of significant events in the locality. Firstly, the affiliation of the Rhondda Class Teachers Association with the local Trades and Labour Councils,¹³ the attempted dismissal of W.G. Cove from his teaching post and the dispute between Miss Mainwaring and her headteacher.

The affiliation of the Teachers' Association to the Trades Council in March 1913 was taken partly as a positive response to the principle of 'equal pay for equal work' which the Trades Council was in favour of. The uncertificated teachers were mainly women and therefore were paid less than the certificated teachers and, on average, less than the male uncertificated teachers. The socialist politics of the Trades Councils caused some disquiet amongst the teachers but a column in the *Rhondda Socialist*, written by a class teacher, mentioned a significant increase in membership of the Association after Trades Council affiliation. The *Rhondda Socialist* also recognized the step the teachers had taken:

> a new era is about to dawn for the class teachers of the Rhondda, they have finally recognized the fact that they are workers — some of them slaves on the brink of poverty, others actually in poverty on

the brink of destitution and subject to petty tyranny from those in authority over them.[14]

W.G. Cove, who had become involved in the salary revision and Association work, was recommended for dismissal by his School Management Committee 'for having attended to work other than school work during school hours'.[15] The general feeling seems to be that this was clear victimization. The *Rhondda Leader* mentioned his unique number of testimonials from parents and children. Appeals, testimonials and letters from various Labour organizations and teachers were ignored by the School Committee but the Rural District Council accepted a deputation, consisting of the representatives of the NUT, the Rhondda Class Teachers Association, the Miners and the Railwaymen. One of the miners:

> asked to be acquainted with the decision of the Council so that they might convey the result to their lodges. He answered then that the matter would not be allowed to rest.[16]

By a small margin, the Council allowed Cove to remain at his teaching post.

Miss Mainwaring, a Rhondda teacher[17] became involved in a dispute with her headteacher, arising from a particular incident when he came into her classroom and asked her to change her teaching. Her refusal was supported by the other schoolteachers who threatened to close the school. 'Drastic action' was also threatened by the Rhondda Class Teachers Association, perturbed by the 'dangerous precedent' of this executive action of the headteacher. Miss Mainwaring was eventually transferred.

The mood of the teachers at the time was described by W.G. Cove, in a reflective article twelve years later, as 'sullen and resentful'.[18] The annual meeting of the Rhondda Class Teachers Association, on February 3, 1917, was packed. It voted to elect representatives on to the Trades and Labour Councils, was addressed by a Mid-Rhondda Labour delegate, discussed its attitude to the NUT and resolved to initiate a Salaries Campaign. With public support, it succeeded in persuading the Authority to revise its Salary Scales by the following September.

However, general dissatisfaction with the new scales and with the late arrival of the salary cheques changed the Rhondda Class Teachers Association meeting in November from its proposed business of discussing the new Education Bill to a discussion of the Salary Campaign. This time, W.G. Cove, in an impassioned speech, declared a new Salaries Campaign, based on unity between the various teachers' sections and with the support of the organized Labour movement in the Rhondda. A later mass meeting of certificated and uncertificated teachers was almost unanimous in declaring its intention to strike if the pay demands were not met. At the same time, a deputation of the Action Committee tried to show the Council that the provisions of the new Education Bill for Exchequer grants for teachers' salaries would not therefore affect the local rates. The new salaries would not be a financial burden but would be subsidized by the State. According to the *Schoolmaster*, the Council neither attempted to prove or disprove this argument but stuck to their provisional salary scales.

The Rhondda Class Teachers Association teachers struck on February 28, 1919.[19] Not being eligible for strike pay, their determination seems to have forced the NUT to support them, especially as they were fighting for the NUT salary scale. An NUT executive member, Celfyn Williams, was appointed to the Action Committee and a strike office was opened in Tonypandy. A number of public meetings were held in the valley, at Ferndale, Tonypandy or Porth, addressed by Celfyn Williams and W.G. Cove, and by A.J. Cook and Will Mainwaring. Miners' Lodges and Union branches were addressed by the teachers. The natural allies of the teachers were the young miners, 'especially those who had been to Labour College',[20] but not all the Labour representatives and support were with the teachers. The differences between the new socialist Labour ideas and the old Liberal/Labour ideas were remarked upon by the teachers. Celfyn Williams said:

> it was almost inconceivable to the teachers that direct Labour representatives should decline Trade Union rates of wages to the teachers in their employ.[21]

The 'Labour Teacher' in the *Rhondda Leader* constantly attacked the 'old' Labour councillors, seeing them as '(looking after) the interest of the Ratepayers' Association and the Chambers of Trade',[22] or as:

> lacking in vision and (having) compromised their principles. I cannot see the difference between the colliery proprietor and the coalminer, the brewer and the check-weigher.[23]

The teachers, as W.G. Cove remarked later, had to make 'fearless propaganda among the miners and the public in the Rhondda'.[24] A distrust on the part of the older Labour supporters of the new class of teachers, demanding their rights as fellow workers, and allied to the socialist militants, is evident.[25] (A.J. Cook was elected as a Rhondda councillor during this period, he was a strong supporter of the teachers.) Speakers at the public meetings, which were very well attended, stressed the 'sweated labour' aspects of teaching and how the teachers were changing. Goodwin, a local teacher, said:

> Some teachers had been regarded in the past as smug and self-satisfied individuals ... the teachers now realized that they were

subject to the same economic laws as every member of the community. They had been brought face to face with the fact that they had been wage slaves.[26]

Again and again, the speakers stressed that the strike was for 'trade union rates', a new step for the teachers. Will Mainwaring said:

> The teachers were now beginning to acquire the education which the miners had gained by experience.[27]

The Board of Education intervened in the strike as an arbitrator with agreement on both sides. A Whitehall conference on the 28th and 29th March dealt particularly with the question of the rate support grant. A joint committee with power to settle the dispute was formed, and in the meantime the teachers would return to work. If there was no agreement by April 30th, then the strike would resume.

The question of a return to work concerned a mass meeting at Porth on the 31st March, which lasted four hours. The *Rhondda Leader* describes a 'considerable reluctance ... shown by the teachers to resume work in the absence of more definite assurances and pledges being specified'.[28] A 'Report from South Wales' in the militant *Workers Dreadnought* reflects this concern of the militants: 'It is a disgrace to think that the teachers have been on strike for a month — for what? For the right of having their grievances negotiated upon?'[29]

Two further meetings of the joint salary committee, on the 9th and 14th April, eventually resulted in the agreement of a new salary scale. In many cases, this doubled the teachers' previous salaries — for instance:

Male certificated teachers — pre-strike   £80—£150
                            post-strike   £150–£350
Women certificated teachers — pre-strike   £80–£110
                              post-strike   £140–£300[30]

The success of the strike action was disputed by the Chairman of the Education Committee, who believed that the 'same wage award' would have been given to the teachers if they had stayed at work.

The strike had been won, according to W.G. Cove, because of the 'complete unity of all grades, a readiness to give up our individual opinions and rally as one'.[31]

Yet further demands were made by the uncertificated and supplementary teachers about anomalies, and for the latter, a salary scale. The question of trade union rates was still being fought, though not by the NUT who had sent a letter (from its Secretary, Yoxall) expressing satisfaction with the salary scale. The issue of 'cheap labour' was repeated by the Rhondda Class Teachers Association Secretary, Gwen Ray Evans, in a letter to the Committee, on behalf of the uncertificated and supplementary teachers, in September:

> (These) teachers are not satisfied and did not pretend to be . . . It was generally understood an early application for the revision of the scales would be made . . . especially the serious anomalies.[32]

A.J. Cook, in a later Council meeting, took up this issue:

> They ought to get a certificate of qualification and then they would be able to get the same salary as the certificated teacher. There are many who have been in our employ for many years, some for 21 years, I understand. It is practically impossible for these men to go to College — after serving 29 years. They are efficient and you are going to penalise them because they cannot go to College . . . you want them and you employ them and as long as they are necessary it is the duty of this council to pay them properly.[33]

The success of the Rhondda strike, and its example to other local Associations throughout the country is recognized as a vital step for the Salary Scale and for the development of the Union.[34] The Union Salary Scale had been obtained for the first time ever.

In South Wales, other areas were in dispute (Pontypridd, Pembroke, Merthyr and Aberdare). Indeed, at Merthyr, the teachers refused to accept the *possible* arbitration award agreed in the Rhondda (before it was known), presumably wanting more.

W.G. Cove always maintained that the Rhondda strike was a milestone for the Union. The Rhondda struggle was:

> The spearhead of an offensive that lead to higher salaries and the Burnham Committee . . . it was fought on the slogan 'The Union Scales and nothing but the Union Scales' . . . (when) it was said that the Union Scales were ideal scales to be aimed at, but not necessarily achieved.[35]

More, it represented a new approach to unionism, influenced by the new materialist philosophy of the Rhondda miners. The strike was won because of the 'fighting spirit' and 'complete unity' of the teachers.[36] The descriptive strike speeches of the time, far removed from the modest petitions of some Associations (Lewes, for instance) or the outraged common sense appeals of local branches (West Ham, for instance) are a declaration of class interests and class struggle. The very language of the speeches was one of unionism — 'skilled workmen'[37] (teachers), 'downing tools',[38] 'fellow-workers'[39] (miners) and of 'sound trade union principles'.[40]

In a series of articles in the *Rhondda Leader* at the time, W.G. Cove, analysing the strike and isolating difficulties, expresses this new view of the teachers in more detail:[41]

> I have always thought it was a bad trades unionism to cavil at any good conditions of another body of workers, and that the true attitude for a trade unionist was to fight for the same conditions in his own industry ... Hours are an essential factor in the standard of life as wages, to increase the hours is to lower the standard of life.[42]

He then describes teachers as 'sweated labour', a just term, he believes, when labour produces profit not returned in wages by the employer, the local authority.

After a fortnight, Cove returned to this question of the teacher's labour, in response to the criticism that the Rhondda pay rates were already high:

> Any questioner who asks this question adopts as his standard of values the market price of labour called teaching, that is, he at once turns the teachers into commodities, and begins to ask the very same question as when he asks the price of bacon. Now, I know that all kinds of labour under the present system of production and exchange are turned into commodities, but it is precisely this fact that provides one of the chief indictments of the workers against the present system. How then, I ask, can any one person who allows himself to be a trades unionist and a 'Labour man' consistently with his principles allow a market price of teachers' labour to determine his attitude towards them?
>
> One of the factors determining the market price of labour is the power of the Trades Unions. Trades Unions tend to force up the market price. Relatively speaking, the teachers' unions have been weak. We are now in the Rhondda experiencing a revival of unionism amongst the teachers, which is expressing itself in an effort to raise the market price, and any trade unionist who opposes us is endeavouring to thwart the inevitable expression of a reunified unionism. The market price of a commodity — of the commodity called labour — is the standard of the capitalist employer, and no sound trade unionist can use the standard of a capitalist employer.[43]

This shows the tremendous influence of Marxist economics on W.G. Cove, the main leader and organizer of the strike.[44]

The strike in the Rhondda altered the Union in several ways. W.G. Cove began to exert a significant influence on the Union Executive, after his election in 1920, and on the Annual Conferences. Although he rarely expressed the detailed Marxist analysis of teaching as a commodity as he had in the *Rhondda Leader*, it remained implicit in the policies and outlook he supported. His influence was not due just to his oratorical skills or forceful ideas but rested upon the concrete gains for teachers made in the Rhondda. New industrial policies or discussions held within the Union in 1919 and 1920 reflected the lessons learned in the Rhondda. In debates about strike action, relations with the Labour movement or recruitment of uncertificated teachers, Cove and other Rhondda teachers took a leading role and acted as the new focus for the Left in the Union. The crucible of the Rhondda, which made great changes in the Miners' Union and was the main base of the Plebs League, influenced the way the teachers in that area saw themselves and their work. Those ideas spread outward into the NUT at the time when a number of crucial decisions about the Union were being discussed.

A Socialist analysis of teaching and the Union's programme for education were already in operation among teachers, with ideas drawn from the Fabians or Guild Socialists. The influence of the Rhondda socialists, and particularly Cove, with their brand of syndicalism, created a sharper debate about the nature of professionalism and power which became the focus of the succeeding Union conferences.

The initiative of the Rhondda class teachers in joining together, overcoming the divisions of gender and qualification, became the model for the NUT in 1919.[45] It was to move a long way toward an industrial union structure by extending membership to uncertificated teachers and some way in creating a labour outlook. It moved away from the conservative, patriarchal craft union policy which had dominated the union since the 1870s.

Notes

1 *Times*, Nov. 1916, quoted in Simon (65)p. 334.
2 Later the MP for the Rhondda Valley.
3 The Miner's leader, locally and nationally.
4 Publishers of the *Miners Next Step*, 1912, their manifesto.
5 Millar, J.P.M. (1979) '*The Labour College Movement*', NCLC London, p. 17.
6 Millar, p. 19. '*Commission of Enquiry into Industrial Unrest*', No. 7 Division, Report of the Commission for Wales including Monmouthshire HMSO 1917, p. 112.
7 *Plebs*, Vol. IX, No. 11, Dec. 1917.
8 *Plebs*, Vol. VIII, No. 12, Jan. 1917.
9 *Plebs*, Vol. VIII, No. 10, Nov. 1916.
10 Commission in Millar, p. 17. "Evidence has been brought before us to show that the workers view with alarm the shortage of teachers and the consequent failure of the local authorities to provide proper education for the children".
11 *Plebs*, Vol. X, No. 5, June 1918.
12 *Plebs*, Vol. XIII, No. 3, March 1921. This is exactly the kind of outlook expressed within the new Teachers Labour League, formed with the help of Cove and Ray and other

Plebs teachers (G.R. Coxon in Ashington). A tape recording of Mark Starr discussing these Pleb teachers is in my possession.
13 *Rhondda Socialist*, March 15, 1913. There were a number of T & LC's in the area.
14 *Rhondda Socialist*, March 15, 1913. The Trades Councils were described by the Commission of Enquiry into Industrial Unrest as "centres of educational work from which lectures and classes on political and social subjects have been organized, and secondly ... centres of social and political activity", Simon, p. 335.
15 *Rhondda Leader*, Oct. 10, 1917.
16 *Rhondda Leader*, Oct. 10, 1917.
17 Related, perhaps to Will Mainwaring.
18 *Schoolmaster*, May 14, 1931.
19 1200 teachers in number.
20 *Rhondda Leader*, March 22, 1919.
21 *Rhondda Leader*, March 18, 1919.
22 *Rhondda Leader*, March 8, 1919.
23 *Rhondda Leader*, March 22, 1919.
24 *Schoolmaster*, 1953.
25 The Aberdare dispute of 1908 when teachers had fought, on the issue of tenure, with the Labour council, reveals similar problems. An opportunist relationship (on and off) of the teachers to the local Trades Council — consequently their actions and notices were distrusted.
26 *Rhondda Leader*, March 22, 1919.
27 *Rhondda Leader*, March 29, 1919.
28 *Rhondda Leader*, April 5, 1919.
29 *Workers Dreadnought*, April 2, 1919.
30 *Schoolmaster*, April 19, 1919 and 1953.
31 *Schoolmaster*, May 14, 1931.
32 *Rhondda Leader*, Sept. 27, 1919.
33 *Rhondda Leader*, Oct. 11, 1919. This issue was stilled by the Burnham Report on national provisional scales, produced in December.
34 Tropp, p. 311.
35 *Schoolmaster*, 1953.
36 *Schoolmaster*, May 14, 1931. Cove.
37 *Rhondda Leader*, Nov. 10, 1917.
38 *Rhondda Leader*, March 8, 1919.
39 *Workers Dreadnought*, March 22, 1899.
40 *Rhondda Leader*, March 8, 1919. "Indeed as 'skilled' workmen they should claim the right of cooperating with headteachers in the forming of timetables and syllabuses", *Rhondda Leader*, Nov. 10, 1917.
41 Cove later became the youngest NUT President in 1922 and a Labour MP from 1923–1959.
42 *Rhondda Leader* March 15, 1919 — in response to arguments about the short working week of teachers.
43 *Rhondda Leader*, March 29, 1919.
44 Whether 'Labour Teacher' is the same person, I do not know — but the same influence is present viz 'The right to fix our own value on our own labour' March 8, *Rhondda Leader*.
45 Too great a claim can be made that the strike was a breakthrough. There was little support, even in the thirties, for the struggle against the marriage bar and the fight for equal pay continued in the Rhondda, led by Gwen Ray Evans.

II. 1919

Introduction

The renewed salary campaign by the teachers occurred in a period of strong social conflict in Britain. The social fabric appeared to be either ripped apart by strikes and social protest or to be under close scrutiny in plans for post-war reconstruction. It was a period of rising political and social expectation for the working class. It was also a time of strong expectation for women, campaigning for the vote and equal pay at work.

The language used by the teachers and by central government about education and teachers' work within it changed rapidly. Socialists, industrialists, Conservatives and the coalition government all vied with each other in their appeals to teachers. In turn, teachers who were supporters of these groups made alliances, wrote books or made propaganda for the ideas and plans put forward about educational change. The major and determining feature of this offensive for change was the appeal of socialist ideas and policies to many teachers, and the necessity, on the part of the government, to produce a viable, alternative model of change. There could be no going back to educational servitude.

Fisher, the person brought in by Lloyd George to plan the educational reconstruction, referred several times between 1917 and 1919 to the social danger of a class of restless teachers. Not all teachers were so educationally or socially disaffected as to become 'revolutionary socialists' but that was the fear in the mind of the government.

Both Fisher and the teachers agreed on one thing. The local control over education, run by the ratepayer class by means of a tax on themselves, for the working class, was the major block to reform. Fisher, for tactical and strategic reasons, appealed to the teachers directly — they were to be the new guardians of quality in the education service. But he was not the only one to make an appeal — socialist writers and educators all wrote about teachers in the new social order.

This debate within education was mirrored by a wider debate about white-collar workers generally. Brain-workers or 'intellectual workers' were seen by Tawney and others as a third party, neither worker nor employer, and the crucial issue was their future class alliance. Socialist proposals to this new 'intellectual proletariat', as they were described, were based on their key role in the regeneration of society and emphasized the progressive aspect of their expertise, professionalism and service ethic. On the other hand, they were to be seen by progressive Conservatives (Fisher and *The Times* among them) as a relatively autonomous group, a Third Party, removed by ideology, strong boundary definition in work and appeals to status.

In retrospect, the year 1919 can be seen as crucial to the choices the discontented teacher was to make. In theoretical terms, it was a choice between other workers or an employer's caste, the third party. In political terms, it was a decision about whether to join the Labour Party or not.

Chapter 5

A Collegiate Civil Service?

The period between 1917 and 1919 was one of great intellectual and social ferment for teachers and other workers; while the main question was one of class identity, expressed in terms of political action and a new social policy, there were contradictions among the teachers in the process of decline and expansion. The conflict between a National Union of Teachers representing an elite of certificated teachers and headteachers, and other teachers who were either uncertificated or supplementary, was coming to a conclusion. The NUT was moving sharply from a craft union basis toward an industrial union structure, accepting the uncertificated teachers in its ranks. At the same time as the local pay scales seem to have been replaced by a hard-fought national salary scale, the question of equal pay for women teachers, who were often in the majority in the disputes and strikes, began to be raised increasingly within the Union and indeed eventually caused a secession from it by the National Federation of Women Teachers (NFWT). As the political and industrial identity of the elementary teachers appeared to be resolving itself in 1919, with more and more teachers taking an active industrial approach to unionism and supporting Labour, the teachers' unity was threatened by the Union's inability to resolve the question of equal pay satisfactorily.

The major contradiction between employer and employee was debated again within or around the question of professionalism and vocation. *The Times Educational Supplement*, newly arrived on the scene, in its own leaders or comment or in the full reporting of Fisher's speeches increasingly counterpointed a responsible, professional association to an active, industrial model union. Throughout 1919, each strike and each speech of the NUT militants was opposed by a rhetoric of reconstruction and new responsibility. It was not a question of power and participation for teachers, it argued, but of responsibility and a new professionalism in a reconstructed service.

In its report for 1918/1919, the Salaries Committee of the NUT described this period as unprecedented in the history of the union. Teachers were on strike in Accrington, Bacup, Carmarthenshire, Dewsbury, Ebbw Vale, Gateshead, Grimsby, Rhondda, Rowley Regis, Ryde and Stockton-on-Tees. It added however that strikes were a last resort and that 'frank and free conferences between representatives of both sides were becoming more common'. It also added:

> it is most important to remember that successful action in one part of the country has its reaction in other parts, and that every improvement in salaries or conditions in one place makes similar improvement easier to secure in another.[1]

In May 1918, 240 certificated teachers in Carmarthenshire had gone on strike, supported, according to the *Daily Herald*, by all 'Trades Unionists and Labour organizations' around the district. Irish teachers had a one-day general strike in 98 per cent of the schools, aided by a cycling corps of pickets, and won a substantial war bonus in November. In early 1919, five hundred elementary *and* secondary teachers handed in their strike notices to Merthyr Local Education Authority. The Authority offered to pay the result of the Rhondda teachers arbitration award to the Merthyr teachers but they refused it. A compromise without a strike was achieved — the pay award doubling what Merthyr originally offered.[2] There was considerable unrest in the West Riding of Yorkshire, especially in Mexborough.[3] In Sunderland and Middlesborough, notices were handed in — by 700 teachers in Sunderland.[4] In April, all Pembrokeshire elementary schools were closed and a public meeting called upon the Education Committee to negotiate with the teachers.[5] A strike was threatened in Worcestershire,[6] in Peterborough and Bristol.[7]

At issue in these strikes was not just pay, the war bonus, but the economies in the service, the use of untrained teachers and the increased workloads. In sum, the management and direction of the education service, locally and nationally. The great advantage to the teachers in this contest was their shortage. The entrants into teaching had declined from 12,000 a year in 1906 to 7,000 in 1917.[8] Areas like London were increasingly using untrained people in nursery classes or as supply teachers, known by the name 'guinea girls'.[9] According to Fisher, before the war 9,000 teachers left teaching annually and now there were only 6,000 new entrants to replace them.[10] Of these new entrants, trained, certificated staff were declining — from 1913/14 to the autumn of 1916, male students in training colleges declined from 4,242 to 700.[11] Teachers felt that the war was being used to increase the number of cheaper, untrained teachers in areas where they had been successfully resisted by the local teacher associations before. *The Times Educational Supplement* asked that the teachers, for their own good really, should allow 'fairly well-educated women' into the schools and that they should be trained on the job. At the same time, they could not be paid much less than the teachers or they would go into the factories. It even suggested they would stay on after the War.[12]

The rapid deterioration of the education service, teachers' strikes and industrial union organization and the sharp movement towards the Labour Party or trade union alliances, were a major cause of concern to the Lloyd George coalition government. The question of post-war reconstruction and a stable society had to be planned in a situation of war and domestic crisis in which trade union power was on the offensive. Increasingly the position of teachers in the post-war period was seen as pivotal to the future of a reliable education service and a reconstructed state. This was not just a question of the Government, and then Fisher, the new President of the Board of Education, planning and connecting people to their vision of education, it was also the main idea of the Left. The Labour Movement was surging forward — locally and nationally. The publication by the Labour Party, in 1918, of their socialist programme, *Labour and the New Social Order* laid great stress on education as the means by which other social changes could occur. The Labour Party looked to teachers for support and help in constructing the 'New Social Order'.

The movement towards a forward union policy on salaries and conditions by the National Union of Teachers and the drift towards the Labour Party have been mentioned. It will be noted that within the Union there was a strong reaction to Labour Party affiliation; arguments came from the Church and voluntary teachers' sections, the rural teachers, Conservative Party members on the Executive and those who argued for civil service status or a professional register. Their support was strong. It was to these people that Fisher and *The Times Educational Supplement* addressed their arguments. Yet there is no clear division in the Union between the Left and Right — towards Labour and partisanship or professionalism and neutrality. The whole tenor of the period is one where great changes in society were envisaged — both sides were planning a new deal. For many teachers it must have been a question of which post-war utopia was possible and many Labour teachers used the term 'professional' constantly. It is to this debate, a watershed for teachers and many other working- or middle-class workers, called brain-workers[13] or 'intellectual workers'[14] or the black-coated proletariat[15] or craft professionals[16] by observers, which I now turn.

Fisher argued in August 1917 to the Cabinet that the expenditure on teacher supply and conditions was necessary to improve the 'quality' of teachers and remove discontent — 'inasmuch as at present revolutionary movements were to no small degree fermented by discontented school teachers'.[17]

In a letter to the Chancellor of the Exchequer, Austen Chamberlain, in November 1919, he again referred to teachers as a social danger:

> You will readily appreciate the influence of the teachers in the country and the effect which a discontented body of over 160,000 teachers may easily have in keeping alive increasing social and industrial unrest.[18]

Fisher moved forward in two ways. He set up a departmental enquiry into teacher pay scales in 1917 and on its recommendation in February 1918, introduced a system of percentage grants to Local Education Authorities to help with the remuneration of teachers. He also created the 1918 Superannuation Act for teachers which was a non-contributory pension scheme similar to the Civil Service scheme. Lastly, he eventually created the 'Standing Joint Committee' (on a Provisional Minimum Scale of Salaries for Teachers in Public Elementary Schools), later known as the Burnham Committee.[19]

Throughout this period, from 1917 to 1918, Fisher made speeches throughout the country in support of his Education Bill. Then, and in 1919, he argued strongly for a new deal for teachers and in return, a new set of responsibilities and attitudes *from* teachers. After some consideration, Fisher rejected the argument that teachers should be civil servants and later tried to persuade teachers that they could become one of the liberal professions. Whatever he argued, his private comments to colleagues in the Cabinet that the teacher was a social danger should also be borne in mind (something he later avoided doing in his autobiography).[20]

In his autobiography Fisher writes of his rejection of the proposal that teachers should be civil servants, appointed and paid by the State — his main grounds were that this would be deleterious to educational freedom and experimentation and would create too large a burden for the Board of Education. A Report[21] to the Secretary of the Board of Education on the 31st January, 1917, six weeks after Fisher's appointment as President of the Board, suggests other reasons, which in this period of educational and teacher unrest, have a more likely validity.

The Report started with the difficulties of the 'civil service solution'. If the whole cost of the teachers' salaries were paid by the Exchequer, then the teachers would ask for parity with the highest local salary scale, yet this 'levelling-up' as it would be in most cases, would annoy the 'strong sections' of the NUT in areas like London, who were not keen on the civil service solution anyway. The certificated teachers, the 'best qualified', were unevenly distributed across the country.[22] How could the State re-distribute them? Similarly uniformity between teaching grades would be a difficulty, and the Board would have to take powers of staff dismissal. This last point becomes important in the Report — the State would have to guarantee employment as well as judge competence. The high visibility of the State as the teachers' employer would lead to *direct* agitation for salary increases and 'The State Department of Education would necessarily appear from time to time . . . as an obstacle to educational progress.'[23] Agreeing with the version in Fisher's memoirs that a State teaching force is inimical to the traditions of 'English Education' and its securing of freedom, the writers felt that 'certain Local Education Authorities' had been a greater threat to freedom than either the Board or its Inspectors. But:

> The decisive consideration seems to me to be that the teaching profession as a whole is now both much more conscious of its unity and its rights and much more powerful than it was in the days of 'payment by results'.[24]

The tone of the Report is that the State would have to find ways of solving the teacher problem other than making them civil servants. It would not only become enmeshed in arbitration between teachers, it would be openly a target for the powerful, conscious unity of the teachers. The State would have to act, in particular ways and general direction, as the teachers' employer. If Fisher were concerned about the social danger of teachers, this was an option that would not reduce his concern and did not appear feasible. Other ways had to be explored.

It is of some interest that the idea of being part of the civil service was treated favourably by an element within teaching. Goldstone, in an article in *The Times Educational Supplement (TES)*, suggested that teachers wanted the move from municipal control to reduce the variation between salary scales, increase fixed tenure and improve pensions.[25] (It was this article that seems to have been used by the Board Secretary in his report on civil service status). The following week, a correspondent from *The Times* stated that teachers were increasingly in favour of civil service status:

> The present discontent of a very large number of teachers has led them to consider desirable at least one of the present Civil Service conditions which is a hindrance to the effectiveness of the teaching profession. That condition is fixity of tenure . . . There is precisely the same sort of distrust between teachers and their employers that initiates the relations between employer and employed all over the country.[26]

The supporters of this proposal seem likely to have been rural teachers, faced with powerful local employers, and looking towards the pay and working conditions available in the urban areas. C.W. Crook confirmed this view when, a year later in his *TES* column, he thought 'the large associations and particularly London, were against, the smaller ones in favour'.[27] Although it was never directly offered as an option for teachers it seemed to have provided a convenient way of solving the rural and country town teachers' problems. It little mattered that it might well involve dissolving the Union or giving up their freedom to act politically (which was dubious anyway),[28] as these were the conditions of civil service membership, current at the time.

The Reconstruction aims of the Government included a significant place for education. This was a reflection of the State of the education service during the War and its pivotal position in a renewed society. War, to Fisher, had given the State the great opportunity to remodel the education system. He used this opportunity to argue in the Cabinet for the previously shelved plans of the Board to expand the education system. The new Education Act of 1918 abolished all pre-fourteen years school exceptions (ending the half-time system in the textile industry), extended the public provision of higher education and planned a system of continuation schools (after elementary school-leaving age); it also provided for the creation of nursery schools and public scholarships in secondary education.

Fisher argued consistently for a new, patriotic teaching force, one capable of working the new investment in 'human capital', and capable of making better connections with the business world. Teachers would be vital, he argued during the Education Bill readings, in the production of good citizens, in the creation of the civic spirit. Fisher's vision was long-term — the creation of a societal harmony, of investment in skill and education and discussion between capital and labour.[29] This was not the position or concern of many of the local education authorities, of the Treasury or of some employers.[30]

The creation of 'an efficient and devoted corps of teachers'[31] for Fisher came to involve a number of overlapping points, on professionalism and responsibility in the Union, the revival of the Teachers' Registration Council, and service to the State. All serve to change the direction he privately felt teachers were taking by 1918. A comprehensive report of a speech he gave to a local association of the NUT in Sheffield in 1918 illustrates his strategy.[32]

He argued that the State had developed a direct interest in the remuneration and position of the teaching profession though they were still employed and paid by Local Education Authorities. He detailed the 'direct interest' — the Superannuation Act, the fixing of salary minima and a Parliamentary grant toward teacher salary costs. The system might have had faults but it was changed now:

> Don't let us, because here and there we may find a Local Education Authority which does not rise to the height of its responsibilities, do not let us condemn the system...³³

This statement is ironic as up and down the country, disputes, negotiations and resignations were in full swing. But it is essential to his argument. Now the State *guaranteed* the fair treatment of the teacher, it expected new results. Fisher laid stress, here and elsewhere, on the need for unity in the teaching profession — a new flexibility towards work in teaching implied movement between different branches of teaching (particularly between elementary and secondary schooling).

In return, he criticized the National Union of Teachers. It was effective in looking after the material interests of teachers but this was no longer necessary now the State safeguarded the profession. It should instead concentrate its activities on the 'spiritual and intellectual interests of the teacher's work'.³⁴ What he meant by that was a humanistic spirit of enquiry and patriotism, of appreciation not criticism, that should distinguish teaching and teachers. The profession would become more interesting and varied and full of opportunity for its members.

At the same time, the State now expected teachers to perform a civic service:

> analogous ... to the functions performed by members of the Civil Service and just as the State does not tolerate any perfunctory discharge of duties on the part of its Civil Servants, so the State will expect, and will receive from the teaching profession a measure of unstinted and zealous service on behalf of the childhood of the country.³⁵

In effect, Fisher argued that a new direction was now in force in the education system, the Union could dismantle its politicking and trade union actions, and that the State would safeguard teachers. They would be unified, concerned with their craft skills and intellectual development and give a recognized public service of quality.

His audience was not just at Sheffield but nationally, and at Hamilton House, the NUT headquarters. During the same period as numerous salary disputes and the continuing discussions about Labour policy and trade union action (a direction Fisher was concerned about) he offered teachers another vision — of peace and tranquillity, of status without struggle, of craft and skill unhampered by social poverty.

As his Parliamentary Secretary stated in a letter to the *TES*:

whatever might be the drawbacks of the teaching profession, the possibilities of valuable service to the State which it provided were very great.[36]

Service in the future was to be in aiding industrial competition and in the continuation of a patriotic and civic-minded curriculum.[37] For these two aims, competition and civic spirit, different teachers would be needed — not teachers choosing the partisanship of labour.

Fisher mentioned the unity of the profession and suggested that the Teachers' Registration Council was the body all parts of the profession could gather within. The ideal of a profession is one which was expressed early in the NUT history — never defined, it always implied escape from the petty tyrannies of school managers, the Church and the Inspectorate; a path to freedom and a way out. An earlier Teachers' Registration Council had ended in 1908 because of the implacable hostility of the NUT — it involved a two-column register, the first, Column A, a list of all certificated elementary teachers, supplied by the Board of Education, and the second, Column B, by application and a fee of one guinea, of secondary teachers with a degree. Not unity of the profession as seen by the NUT, nor any kind of move toward self-government, but government from the Board of Education which controlled it — a paradoxical and unsatisfactory situation which continued in the new Teachers' Registration Council (TRC), in the years following the demise of its predecessor. The power the teachers wanted was control over access to teaching, in other words, control over qualification. The State controlled certification and altered (diluted) the conditions of entry to suit supply, allowing uncertificated teachers to increase in number and inventing supplementary teachers — which in turn, decreased the market value of the certificate, the teacher's wage. As the Board refused to give any official recognition or standing to the new Register, it also failed to recruit well.[38]

The Register always involved talk of responsibilities but these lay mainly on the teacher. Talk of a 'collegiate spirit', 'professional standards', a 'vocation', 'honour', 'regulation and responsibility' and 'sacrifice'[39] were so much hot air. The illusion of self-government did not fool the elementary teachers, what they required was not in the TRC.

Yet, in 1918 to 1919, the Council was being promoted heavily, by Fisher, by the *TES* and by some members of the NUT. As the Union became more politically and industrially active, it became opposed by people who ascribed all the new virtues and requirements of teachers to the Council. As one was partisan, the other was for unity, as one was a section of teachers, the other was for all. Never mind that the NUT existed in fact and deed, and the Council was a shadow, it was the idea of a Council and the ideal of the required teacher that was being pushed for the support of the public but more importantly, the teachers. *The Times* had a leading article, one of the first, that argued for a united profession, not a Labour-affiliated NUT, built on the TRC, though:

> outside the fact (of its existence) is apparently unknown, and, inside, it is often forgotten.[40]

This did not stop *The Times* describing it as the only body capable of promoting the new education reform programmes, and if finance was a problem, the Treasury, with Fisher's help, might support it, without, of course, prejudicing its independence.

On February 22nd that year, the day after the Register had been published with the names of relatively few teachers on it, the *TES* made an 'urgent appeal to all teachers', though it meant all *qualified* teachers (thereby excluding a large number of elementary teachers), to join the Council.

From 1917 onwards, the *TES* constantly argued that a new profession of teaching had come into existence. Present conditions of work and pay were poor and discontent was widespread, it acknowledged, yet a bold policy, 'Mr Fisher's opportunity', could save the situation.[41] This editorial policy, 'the noble teaching profession' was formed at the same time as the meeting in Birmingham of the Union militants on salary action and labour affiliation, in January 1917. The policy began when it looked to the *TES* that the Government, to increase teacher supply, was likely to sanction the return of large numbers of supplementary or pupil-teachers,[42] but with Fisher its call for a 'new profession' approach was answered. In *The Times*' view, teacher supply was indistinguishable from the registration of teachers, the Teachers' Registration Council, and the creation of a National Teaching Service. This was a forward policy, one in tune with Fisher and the Reconstruction committee, and its audience was teachers *and* the educational administrators. In harmony, together eligible for registration, teachers and administrators would fight for reform.

Always expressing sympathy for the actions of the Union, and allowing its officers, Crook and Goldstone, a Union Note Column in the *TES*, it tried to bypass the effect of the Union pressure. Not until August 1918 did its irritation at the continuing increase in militant action and rhetoric by Union associations tell. Its argument had become one in which dignity in discussion with Local Authority employers and not threats would allow the Government to safeguard the teachers' position. Strikes would only 'harden the hearts' of the Councils and the Government.[43]

The appeal to teachers was built around a rhetoric of 'noble and dignified' 'vocation' 'responsibilities' and 'patriotism'.[44] Whenever possible in editorials or reports of speeches by Fisher or others with the same argument, the *TES* argued the 'new profession' line.

Lord Haldane, the Lord Chancellor and a person close to Fisher, who had argued since 1913 within the Government for a new Education Act and a national system of education to 'stabilize democracy'[45] and to counter 'intense economic competition' from abroad,[46] was also reported. He followed, or preceded, the *TES* line — democracy and education, a national organized profession and greater social status and salaries for teachers.[47]

Yet, it was a special kind of unity wanted by Fisher, Haldane and the *TES*. It would include university lecturers, public schoolteachers, and secondary teachers but only the *certificated* elementary teacher. It would exclude, and in practice the Register did so, the uncertificated teachers. These teachers were in the forefront of the fight for an industrial union policy, Trades council membership and in favour of equal pay in teaching. As the Union considered admission of uncertificated teachers into membership throughout 1918, and, as local associations of teachers united to fight local employers, the *TES* made it clear that they were not just excluding the uncertificated but a policy and a direction.

It was cant for the Board of Education to publish, in its Departmental Committee Report on salary scales:[48]

> We may, however, look forward to a time when admission to the profession will be limited to persons who have reached accepted standards of education and training, a result which will be of great benefit to national education

when the Board always controlled entry qualifications into teaching and had moved them to match any problems of teacher supply; it was just this situation that the Union policy of professional control was meant to be against. In this way, then, the policy of *The Times* and the Board was contrary to Union policy — it did not treat the Union as a basis for teacher unity but tried to create another basis, the Register, and its view of unity would actually disunite the teachers even more by excluding a large section.

With the support of some teachers,[49] The Teachers' Registration Council spent several years, aided by *The Times*, trying to convince the rest of the teachers that if only they joined together, they would by this act 'recognize' themselves and make it inevitable that the Government would recognize them as 'the body to decide the qualifications and technical ability necessary to become a teacher'.[50] Calls for unity in the profession were, then, increasingly opposed to the actions of the Union members to create unity through action and policy. The stronger their determination to control, to finally wrest some power from their employers, the louder became the claims for a unity based on the Register, on vocation, neutrality and professional responsibility. The State, through Fisher, offered just enough in the way of 'safeguarding' and reviving old plans for education[51] to 'head off' teachers joining, or actively leading, an insurgent labour movement — Fisher's fear.

Notes

1 Salaries Committee, Annual Report, NUT, 1919.
2 *Daily Herald*, March 31, 1919.
3 *Daily Herald*, April 1, 1919.
4 *Daily Herald*, April 5, 1919.
5 *Daily Herald*, April 12, 1919.
6 *Daily Herald*, April 27, 1919.
7 *Daily Herald*, May 20, 1919.
8 *Times Educational Supplement*, Jan. 18, 1917.
9 *Times Educational Supplement*, Jan. 18, 1917.
10 Sherington, p. 84.
11 Sherington, p. 49.
12 *Times Educational Supplement*, Jan. 18, 1917 — 'London, The Supply of Teachers'.
13 Tawney, R.H. (1921) '*The Acquisitive Society*' Bell.
14 William MacDonald (1923) '*The Intellectual Worker*' Cape.
15 *Daily Herald*, April 21, 1919.
16 *Times Educational Supplement*, April 24, 1919.
17 Sherington, p. 127.
18 Sherington, p. 146.
19 Tropp, p. 212–213 and Ward, L.O. 'H.A.L. Fisher and the Teachers' in *Brit. Journal of Educ. Studies*, 1981.
20 H.A.L. Fisher (1940) *An Unfinished Autobiography*, OUP.
21 School Teachers as Civil Servants 1916–1932, PRO ED/24 1736.
22 Per thousand pupils; London 22·4 certificated teachers to 6 uncertificated; Portsmouth 21·6 to 2·2 and Preston 10·7 to 10·1. PRO ED/24 1736.
23 PRO ED/24 1736.
24 PRO ED/24 1736.
25 *Times Educational Supplement*, Jan. 11, 1917.
26 *The Times*, Jan. 25, 1917.
27 *Times Educational Supplement*, Sept. 19, 1918.
28 A point made by Howard 'Unrest Amongst Teachers', *Socialist Review*, Jan//Mar. 1920. He referred to the idea as selling the teacher's birthright for a 'mess of pottage'.
29 *Times Educational Supplement*, Feb. 7, 1918. Speech at Hanley, Staffs.
30 *Daily Herald*, Feb. 23, 1918. Memorandum on Education, Federation of British Industries.
31 *Times Educational Supplement*, March 1, 1917.
32 *Times Educational Supplement*, Dec. 12, 1918.
33 *Times Educational Supplement*, Dec. 12, 1918.
34 *Times Educational Supplement*, Dec. 18, 1918.

35 *Times Educational Supplement*, Dec. 18, 1918.
36 Herbert Lewis, Feb. 27, *Times Educational Supplement*, 1919.
37 Fisher, *Times Educational Supplement*, March 8, 1917.
38 Baron G. 'The Teachers' Registration Movement' *BJES*, Vol. 2, 1953.
39 J.L. Paton, 'The Teachers Register and its Possibilities' *Contemporary Review*, Aug. 1912.
40 Reported in the *Times Educational Supplement*, 25 Jan. 1917.
41 *Times Educational Supplement*, Jan. 25, Feb. 22 and April 12, 1917, April 19, 1917.
42 *Times Educational Supplement*, Jan. 25, 1917.
43 *Times Educational Supplement*, Feb. 1, 1917.
44 *Times Educational Supplement*, Sept. 27, 1917.
45 Sherington, p. 23–6, 1913.
46 Sherington, p. 57, March 1916.
47 *Times Educational Supplement*, Jan. 31, 1918, speech in Glasgow.
48 *Times Educational Supplement*, Feb. 7, 1918.
49 Crook and Bentliff, Conservative ex-Presidents of the NUT.
50 TRC Advert, *Schoolmaster* March 6, 1920. 'Why you should become a Registered Teacher' by Walter Bentliff ex-NUT President.
51 Sherington's view is that the 1918 Act was a revision of Haldane's 1913 proposals.

Chapter 6

Working with the Grain: Teachers and Socialism

Teachers were attracted to the Labour Party and to socialist ideas and plans in significant numbers between 1915 and 1925. It was not just a question of the Conservative party being seen as the party of economy and anti-elementary education nor the failure of the Coalition Government's Education Act. Socialist ideas, from the Fabians to the syndicalists, had percolated discussions among teachers about the role of elementary education and the elementary teachers and their relation to the State. The contradiction between teachers and their employers is a constant in conference debates and *Schoolmaster* correspondence from the inception of the Union. For many teachers, ideas from the Fabians or guild socialists had been grafted on to the analysis of this contradiction and key words like 'professional self-government' began to alter in meaning and consequently in proposed operation as they became suffused with socialist terminology about the State, social responsibility, unity of the working class and the nature of work.

The influence of socialist writers like Sydney and Beatrice Webb, G.D.H. Cole, H.G. Wells, R.H. Tawney, and significantly in this period, a writer like A.S. Neill (who joined the socialism of the guild socialists to a detailed if idiosyncratic intervention in the New Education discussion) was important to teachers. Although ideas and programmes differed, they jointly offered a new vision of teaching as a major service in the reconstruction of society, the antithesis of the teachers' conditions of work at the time. Other white-collar workers were influenced by this new role for the social service sector in a socialist society and their placement within a category defined as the 'intellectual' working class. The very strength of these ideas can be gauged by reference to Fisher's ideas on professionalism and service to the State. Winning the ideological battle over teachers' class identity was a matter of some concern to elements of the employing class within the central state. The 'hearts and minds' of State employees, re-defined as of value to the stable working of society, were at stake.

The Labour party had radically re-organized its constitution and its character in 1918. It was now possible to join as an individual and not either as a part of a union membership or within a socialist society, like the Independent Labour Party. The old federation of trade unions, socialist societies and Trades and Labour Councils, joined together to maintain a Labour presence in Parliament, was now becoming a socialist party, organized in branches throughout the country. Francis Williams, in his Labour Party history, described it as a 'new moral force' in British politics. It deliberately widened its appeal to 'producers whether by hand or brain'[1] and aimed to recruit them by means of mass individual membership. Its programme *'Labour and the New Social Order'* was one of national ownership of basic industries. It appealed to all the community to involve themselves in the creation of a new social order by the application of science and rationality to the running of every branch of society, by planned cooperation and the 'widest possible participation in power'.[2] It argued for a legal basic wage and a system of public work programmes, including schools.[3]

The Daily Herald[4] regularly reported meetings of Trades Councils and their local actions on education provision, on recruitment of teachers' associations or the progress of the Burston inquiry. Teachers' strikes were always reported in the paper and the local Trades Councils concern for 'uncertificated teachers' regularly mentioned[5], as was equal pay, NUT conferences and militarism in schools. By 1919, reports of the teachers' disputes and strikes were appearing weekly. *The Daily Herald*, representing the more active or even syndicalist policy of militant trade unionism, stated clearly its position on teachers in social reform, and, in doing so, the appeal to teachers of Labour:

> ...The educational policy of the capitalist parties neglects the fact that all education rests upon the teacher. While we continue to pay our teachers as if they were errand boys, and to expect them to teach impossibly large classes in impossibly ill-equipped and ugly buildings, while we deny to them all real liberty of teaching and of thought, and train them at colleges which are a laughing stock and a sham, how can we expect educational results? The teachers themselves must be the potent force in the regeneration of the educational system, and the Labour Party will use all its strength to secure for the teachers, men and women alike, the fullest measure of justice and recognition.[6]

Instead of being the servants of a penny-pinching system, Labour offered to teachers the chance to help, indeed be the 'potent force' in educational regeneration. Not only would Labour help with the question of salaries but with much more: the question of participation and control.

Working with the Grain: Teachers and Socialism

The attraction of the Labour programme *Labour and the New Social Order* and the practical support teachers' associations received from Trades Councils and Labour councillors was only one part of the relationship between teachers and Labour.

Socialist thinkers like H.G. Wells had earlier stressed the place that teachers would hold under socialism. Whether teachers should be regarded as middle-class or 'brain-workers', Wells in '*New Worlds for Old*' appealed to them directly. Socialism was a moral and intellectual process and it was just the enterprise that could help the middle-classes overcome their depression, financial worries and lack of courage.[7] Indeed, Wells placed teachers at the heart of this new moral purpose. Teachers (widely defined to include not only schoolteachers, but books, discussion groups and universities) could 'collectively' renew the 'collective mind'.[8] Constructive socialism needed teachers:

> The most creative profession of all . . . that great calling which with each generation renews the world's circle of ideas.

Instead of being the exploited, isolated servants of local employers, their purpose was to renew the national culture; socialism would depend on them. This element of attraction may not have converted many teachers but those it did would obviously see teaching in a new light — useful, essential, dynamic, etc.[9]

Wells was keen that his readers understood exactly what difference socialism would bring to their lives, and the elementary teacher was one of his two examples. His Utopian vision altered and improved the school layout and provision, even the responsiveness of the children; it mentions the improved salary, pensions and insurance. It involved the notion of vocation:

> . . . under Socialist conditions, it cannot be too clearly understood that all the reasons the contemporary Trade Unionist finds against extra work and unfair work will have disappeared.[10]

He adds further information about quality housing, gardens and electric power. The vision is of interest — it is a secular, enhanced version, a 'modern' version, of the teachers' aims in organizing together: a good education service, benefits to children, release from poverty and a public service or vocation were all represented in this new form.

The collectivist or administrative socialism of the Fabians, the Webbs in particular, was improving the educational facilities in London since the 1890s and it was Sydney Webb who drafted the outline of the Labour programme *Labour and the New Social Order*, with its new role for education. In a long address to teachers, published as a Fabian Tract, *The Teacher in*

Politics, he argued for a natural alliance between the Labour Party and the teaching profession;[11] a different appeal, almost classless in approach, Webb argues for a natural technical expertise partnership in a democracy between the teachers and administration which goes further than questions of socialism or indeed politics at all. In order, Webb praises the 'ubiquitous' Union, the Teachers' Registration Council, and the campaign for salary scales and decent conditions of service, but it is to the service function he turns with emphasis.[12] Webb explained his theory of democracy as an interaction between two representative groups — the consumers and the producers (or professions). The State acts as an arbitrator and decision-maker; between them 'they decide only what comes before them'.[13] His point is that teachers should, and do, act on behalf of all the community in insisting on *effective access*[14] to the whole field of education. (According to the 1918 Conference, this phrase should mean a socially equal national system not just a question of access — it is certainly ambiguous here). The Labour Party was the natural party of education:

> It is the newly reconstituted party of the workers 'by hand or by brain' — not the Conservative or Liberal Party — that nowadays supplies the Minister of Education with the driving force of educational reforms.[15]

It is the Labour Party that supported teachers in demanding educational advance and improved conditions of service.

His appeal to the teachers is that they should provide the programme of reform to the Labour Party and give authoritative criticism to their proposals. The 'Teaching Profession' as a whole should answer the multitude of questions he asks of them (on nursery education, staff duties, school room design, etc.) — it should be 'promoting changes in the public organization of the State'.[16] He sees the engine of this advice as Professional Advisory Committees to all the Education Authorities.

Again, this reaffirms for the Union, in its policy, and for teachers generally, the place, a professional place perhaps, in the counsels of the State on educational matters. Although this is not a Wellsian socialist vision that is offered, it is a practical administrative socialism that showed teachers *exactly* how their counsels would fit in. This was a bargain to be struck with the Labour Party, a Party expected into power soon in post-war Britain.[17]

It has already been argued that syndicalism was a major force in the Labour alliance with teachers that led to the successful strike in the Rhondda. This strike was not only a major step forward for the alliance in South Wales but nationally - its effect ran throughout the Union in 1919. Its leading figures, particularly W.G. Cove, were to play a major part in Union counsels from that time on. But the Rhondda strike was specific — it had a mixture of teacher-miner cooperation, a forward syndicalist policy in the Miners' Union (MFGH) and the involvement of Plebs League tutors. Its effect was great but the syndicalism or industrial unionism that created it — was it peculiar to the South Wales valleys?

Two years before the strike, G.D. Bell of the Teachers' Labour League and a member of the Union Executive, had, during the Executive debate on Labour affiliation, referred to the question of syndicalism.[18] He denied that there was any conflict of interest between the professional and the trade union approach to teaching. For him, the medical profession was:

> The best example of syndicalism that existed in this country, it absolutely owned and controlled the medical service of this country.[19]

Syndicalism was the term used in the Union by its left wing, Bell and later, Cove, to discuss not only industrial action by all teachers but industrial control. Although it was also referred to as self-government and easily moved into other shades of meaning used by their opponents (the Conservative 'professionals') its use was specific — through strikes and direct action (a point sometimes under-emphasized), control over the industry would be obtained. It also was part of a movement that expected other workers in other industries to be part of that forward movement. It had a strong critique of the role of the State and, as Bob Holton describes it, it:

> asserted the primary importance of working class self-reliance at the point of production free from coercive bureaucratic apparatus.[20]

This was a sense, congruent with professional control, in which it was used by Bell and Cove. It was well known in the Union as to their advocacy of this philosophy and was bandied about in Conference debates.

A popular (and weaker) version of syndicalism was the development of guild socialism. This did not refer directly to industrial action but concentrated upon the question of practical worker control. The idea of guild socialism was expounded in the journal, *New Age*.[21] After 1911, this journal addressed itself to 'workers of hand and brain' in arguing for workers' corporations controlling and managing their industries. During the course of the War, the actual workers' control of the shop stewards movement and the ideas of guild socialism, in some cases, came very close together; it influenced the miners' Federation 1919 demand for public ownership and workers' control.[22]

Guild socialism was felt by its adherents to be qualitatively different to the 'collectivist' strand of socialism, exemplified by the Webbs, and the independent labour representation strand, seen in the Independent Labour Party. It based itself on a denunciation of a capitalist system which saw workers as no more than 'living' tools in the production process, deserving no consideration or freedom. Work being central to life, the workers could never be fully satisfied nor able to fully serve the community until they controlled the means of production in the workplace by self-government. This self-government would operate through Guilds, based on trade unions, and a policy of 'encroaching control'. This policy was not the same as joint workers' control, as seen in the works committee or in 'Whitleyism' but exclusive control at the point of production. The guild would join with consumers when deciding on the choice and quantity of a commodity to be produced. Guild socialism involved, as one of the conditions necessary for its successful operation, joining all workers, including supervisory and professional personnel, into a single union per industry.

The appeal of guild socialism in the Union was again its congruency to professional self-government. On the question of practical control over industry, it appealed directly to the 'brain-workers' or management and supervisory staff. No workers' control could be effective without them. Cole, in 1920, discussing the National Guilds' League, talks of its appeal to professional workers, such as teachers:

> it has concentrated its propaganda work entirely upon the question of industrial and professional self-government.[23]

Cole argued that it was foolish to refuse to recognize the importance of the 'technical and professional elements'[24] or to see them as entirely the 'adherents of capitalism'.[25] These workers were underpaid and exploited and yet were under pressure to make a new class alliance. For Cole, the 'middle section'[26] of society, the professional, managerial and staff grades, were being asked to decide whether to join up with the capitalist class or the working class — to maintain or overthrow the social order. This choice:

> does not, of course, present itself, in the same form to all the members of the grades and classes in question.[27]

Yet, because the employers 'tyrannize' and refuse to negotiate or 'recognize' these workers:

> it is usually not long before an association . . . begins to consider the propriety of an alliance with the working class, or before its members as individuals begin to vote Labour or link up with the Labour Party . . .[28]

The drive towards Labour was both political and economic (i.e., the rising cost of living). Cole could easily be describing the movement of teachers in this section but he is also thinking of journalists, clerks, local government workers and so on. Even in 1913, Cove was describing guild socialism as self-government:

> in fact, they are to resemble in their main characteristics the self-governing professions, the doctors and lawyers, of the present.[29]

In a description which echoes Webb (in *The Teacher and Politics*), Cole argued that:

> The internal management and control of each industry or service must be placed, as a trust on behalf of the community, in the hands of the worker engaged in it; but he holds no less strongly that full provision must be made for the representation and safeguarding of the consumer's point of view.[30]

Again, socialism was equated with self-government and with workers' control. Later in the book, the equation is made directly between teachers and their administration of the education system, subject, of course, to the 'ownership' of education, on behalf of the consumers, parents and children, by the State.[31]

An entire chapter in *Guild Socialism Restated* was given over to an analysis of how it would work in education. The teachers are portrayed as exploited wage slaves and their only salvation is — a 'fully self-governing profession',[32] freeing education from capitalism. This would be an education guild, highly democratic, capable of allowing schools to organize their own educational direction and controlling qualification and entry (though probably delegating this responsibility). The guild would meet locally and nationally, with the consumers, on cultural councils, within a cooperative relationship.

As Cole perceptively pointed out, the success of these ideas in the post-war period is that they were 'working with the grain'[33] of Union developments. Certainly in the NUT, guild socialism became another source of justification for Labour affiliation and socialism because it was attached to teacher aims — solving the main contradiction of their relations with employers.

W.W. Hill, a member of the Guild's League and an NUT member (later, Editor of the *Schoolmaster*) proposed a conference amendment on self-government at the 1919 Annual Conference that was passed by a large majority.[34]

The idea of an education guild became popular with teachers.[35] Its best propagandist was A.S. Neill, a teacher who, in this period, exemplifies these different, seemingly conflicting, strands of teacher thought.

Throughout his first book, *A Dominie's Log*,[26] Neill illustrates the difficulties a socialist class-teacher had during this period of turmoil, written as it was halfway through the war and at the beginning of the resurgence of the Union's salary campaign. Expressing fully his antipathy towards Inspectors, dull teachers, his local employers and a backward Union (The Educational Institute of Scotland) he revealed the contradictions of his work.

Neill was influenced by George Bernard Shaw, H.G. Wells,[37] and William Morris (in particular, *News from Nowhere*) but it was the journal of the guild socialists, *New Age*, he praised highly:

> if the teachers are masters of the situation I wish every teacher in Scotland would get the *New Age* each week ... The magazine is pulsating with life and youth ... it is the only fearless journal I know.[38]

Throughout, it is the tension between the practical conditions in which he worked and the socialist ideals in the classroom that is the main thrust of the book. The school, a small village school with a single classroom, was controlled by a School Board (the Boards continued to exist in Scotland after 1902). He described the Board members as 'a few low idealed semi-illiterate farmers and pig dealers'.[39] They had the 'haziest notion of the meaning of education'[40] and one or two of them were usually in dispute with the teacher. His own school was:

> always filthy because the ashed playground is undrained. Broken windows stand for months; the plaster of the ceiling came down months ago and the lathes are still showing. The School Board does not worry; its avowed object is to keep down the rates at any price of meanness (some members are big ratepayers). The sanitary arrangements are a disgrace to a long suffering nation. Nothing is done.[41]

Regularly visited by Inspectors, who seemed to be more concerned with discipline than anything else, he objected to being reported on without being able to reply, but most of all, he objected to the fact that 'the School Board gets not a single world of criticism'.[42]

In his curricular work he was definitely opposing the views or rather attitudes of the Board members and the other farmers, not only in the way they treated children but the range of experience he gave to the children. Some of his lessons were based on topics such as profit or capital and he encouraged them to think out their views of the topic. Neill argues that he was not indoctrinating them but making them heretics rather than socialists — 'I am trying to form minds that will question and destroy and rebuild'[43] 'Whose side are you on?' asked a pupil, meaning the people or the capitalist class. Neill replied 'I am with the majority'.[44]

So, the visionary socialism of Morris and Wells and the practical approach of the *New Age* helped Neill to create a way of working in his classroom and a way of criticizing the teacher's conditions of employment. The guild would release teachers from the tyranny of the farmer/ratepayer and the Inspectors, to become free to really 'educate'. The guild would:

> replace the Scotch Education Department. It will draw up its own scheme of instruction, fix the salaries of its members, appoint its own Inspectors, build its own schools. It will be directly responsible to the State which will remain the supreme authority.[45]

Neill expressed clearly the mixture of socialism, trade unionism, humanistic educational enterprise and professional control which weaves in and out of these arguments among teachers. He was a socialist but had little faith in teachers because of their lack of action; he argued for an education guild but compared it to 'Law and Medicine'; he saw the State as the ultimate authority but in a way divorced from its past actions and representatives in the School Boards and Education Department. Yet it is clear what the conditions were which provoked Neill and other teachers to seek an alternative organization, to construct a new education system. It was a rallying call against ignorance associated with the control of a social class. This control was open and not covert. As the teachers, like Neill, resisted and organized and voted against this social control, we see elements within the State altering the aims of education, evaluating teachers' aims and appealing to them.

Although Neill is a single, well-known case and not 'representative', his influence was widespread — he connected the economic aspirations of the teachers as a collective force to their educational aims. Years later, William Howard, in an article on teacher discontent and 'sweated labour', in the Independent Labour Party (ILP) journal, *Socialist Review*, while disagreeing with the idea of a Guild, said that:

> An ever increasing number (of teachers) are looking hopefully to the day when they will replace the Board of Education with a guild of their own as adumbrated by my friend, A.S. Neill, in *The Dominies Log*.[46]

In fact Howard, trying to point out to his audience of ILP'ers[47] the reasons for teacher discontent (and himself a teacher) summarizes the appeal of visionary socialism to education and vice versa. It is this appeal which is a significant, though by no means only, factor in the growing support of teachers for Labour affiliation and socialist ideas. The appeal is addressed here to the public:

> (who) must be trained to appreciate the necessity of education not merely as a means to the enhancement of the beauty and dignity of

life itself. They must be brought to see that without that vision which education can give, life is a truncated thing and its horizon circumscribed. And let me add, without that vision Socialism as an established reality is but a dream.[48]

For many years there had been close contacts between some local Associations and trades councils, and individual teachers had played important roles in the development of those contacts and with organizing for the ILP, or writing for the new socialist journals. But the pace of this friendship quickened in the salaries campaign. The local Associations looked for allies locally in their fights for bonuses or over work conditions. The *Daily Herald* constantly refers to the sympathetic help offered by the labour movement locally and the joint meetings held. The ILP Conference in 1916 made 'an emphatic protest against the actions of many Education Authorities in curtailing expenditure on education'.[49]

The salaries campaign, the war, the influence of socialist and trade union ideas, all brought the NUT into an informal, undeclared alliance with the Labour movement. This alliance had become more than the identity of interests that Beatrice Webb had noted:

> in more ways than one the NUT has identified itself with the needs of the wage-earning class family and with the educational aspirations of the most enlightened of the manual workers[50]

It was now a search for a social and political identity for teachers which increasingly looked towards Labour arguments and example.

A central figure in this move to the Labour Party was Alderman Michael Conway, the President of the Bradford NUT. He was not only a significant factor in the referendum to join the Labour Party but he was known as the representative of a Local Authority, Bradford, where an alliance of teachers and organized labour had created great improvements in the education service. It was not some distant socialist future he represented but the practical improvements that were possible immediately.

Conway was a leading member in Yorkshire of the ILP.[51] From the time of the School Boards, the ILP had fought, through its representatives, for a better education system for children and teachers. In Bradford, the ILP member of the School Board was Margaret MacMillan and her influence on Bradford, the ILP, and teachers was strong.[52] She became the pioneer in Bradford and elsewhere of school clinics, nurses and baths and the founder of a school meals service.[53] Within the ILP, at the national conferences, and in the Labour Party, these practical policies were influential, especially when addressed by McMillan herself.[54]

The school meal service was run by Bradford teachers, who looked after the health of children and the dining halls.[55] This was the kind of action that the teachers in Bradford were capable of taking because of their power within the labour alliance. The Bradford teachers had organized their own Bradford Teachers' Association, as a local rival to the NUT, some time previously. This Association had a policy, developed from the ILP, of having teacher representation on the City Council. They avoided the problem that teachers were forbidden by law to serve as elected representatives on a council which employed them, by financing a scheme whereby a teacher could leave school and have his or her salary paid for by other teachers to allow them to stand for election.[56] The Secretary of the Bradford Teachers' Association (which later merged with the NUT) and its first elected Council Member was the ILP member, Michael Conway.[57]

It was no coincidence that the Bradford Charter, calling for 'universal, free, compulsory, secondary education', and including higher salaries for teachers and better medical and sports facilities, came from a meeting called by Bradford Trades Council, nor that Conway was a Trades Council delegate, nor that it would be adopted by the ILP conference in 1917 (and the 1917 Labour Party Conference).[58]

The issue of a Labour Party alliance was bound up with the renewed salaries campaign, after 1916, as the 'industrial' militants in the NUT were also prominent national or local Labour workers. The rank and file of the Union, in many local Associations, was pushing hard in 1917 for a more active policy in the Union for strike action, and the issue of a Labour alliance was inextricably interwoven with this movement.

In 1917, a demand was made of the Executive that a Special Conference be called on salaries; although willing to allow a session at the Easter Conference, they did not agree to a special conference. The demand in the local Associations, promoted in particular by Grimsby, was that the old salary policy of 'memorials, deputations and conferences' was insufficient — they proposed that the Union scale of salaries be implemented nationally by a system of government grants to each local authority.

A meeting was called on January 13th, 1917 in Birmingham and representatives of 230 local associations were present.[59] It proposed a number of resolutions on the supply of teachers, the Union scale and the Board of Education, and a deputation to the Board. It also raised questions about the strength of the sustentation fund and, most significantly, asked that the Executive should seek affiliation with the local and national Labour movement.[60] This last point caused some excitement in the Press — and seemed to act as a spur for the creation of alternative possibilities by H.A.L. Fisher and the *TES*.[61] In its Trade Union and Labour Notes, *The Daily Herald* commented:

> The interests of the teachers in publicly-owned schools are absolutely identical with those of the wage-earners, and we hope that the

NUT will see the need of following the lead of this semi-official conference by initiating a national salaries campaign and by linking up once and for all with the Trade Union Movement.[62]

Mr Tasker, speaking for the deputation to the Executive on the sustentation fund and Labour affiliation, had two main arguments. The first was that:

> they should take a lesson from the miners, the cotton operatives, the engineers, and the railway people but the first thing they had to do was to build up a sustentation fund.[63]

Secondly, he made a clear distinction between the controlling classes of the education system and the schools for the worker's child. The previous neglect of the education of the workers' children and the forward, progressive policy the Labour movement was promoting for educational reform made it clear who the teachers' natural allies were: '. . . it was unanimously agreed that teachers had more in common with the workers than any other party . . .'[64] In discussion with the Executive after his speech, Mr Tasker further explained the views of the Birmingham meeting — that affiliation was a vital and pressing task for the NUT; that strong measures were needed; that a trade union policy had to be thought out, not just drifted into:

> If you refer to the history of all Trade Unions you will find that they first of all build up their organisation, and then choose their own time for fighting. They do not fight when it suits the masters, but when convenient to themselves. We must formulate our strong measures, and as soon as we feel ready and fit for fighting, with all our machinery well planned; then we should launch out.[65]

That this deputation unsettled the Executive can be seen in its resolve at the meeting (on February 3rd) to adopt a motion to the effect that a Special Committee of the Executive be appointed to consider for future policy whether:

> a) to become with the development of the work of the Teacher's Registration Council, a self-governing profession b) to become a branch of the Civil Service c) to affiliate with the Labour Party without the surrender of our political freedom d) to affiliate completely with the Labour Party, involving the limitation of political representation within that party.[66]

Generally it appears that the Executive felt that teaching was in a state of flux, that decisions had to be made about future policy straightaway, and that they should not just drift along. Each of the options was discussed briefly and questions about their mutual exclusiveness was asked. It was felt by one speaker that a self-governing profession and Labour affiliation — (a) and (c) — were not alternatives but could be a single policy.

A meeting of Local and County Associations was held in the Memorial Hall, London on the 11/12 April, 1917. The affiliation motion was moved. One of the chief proponents of the affiliation, G.D. Bell, an executive member, spoke in favour of it with the argument that there was no difference between professionalism and trade unionism — indeed:

> The medical profession was the best example of syndicalism that existed in this country.[67]

So there was no discrepancy for him between developing the Teachers' Registration Council and joining the Labour Party. C.W. Crook, a Conservative member of the Executive, produced an argument for the first time in public which he would use throughout the forthcoming debates — that is, two issues were mixed in this proposal, that of increased salaries and that of compulsory Labour Party membership. He concentrated on the issue of political freedom — nothing would be more certain to ruin the Union than demanding Labour allegiance before joining the Union.[68] A referendum was proposed and passed.

In the weeks following the publication and circulation of the memorandum the correspondence columns of the *Schoolmaster* were regularly filled with arguments for and against the Labour Party alliance and rarely concerned with the question of civil service status.

Four groups of writers regularly supported the alliance option: the country teachers, the changed voter, Labour Party educational policy supporters and the Teachers' Labour League. Several letters came from country areas, like Shropshire and Cornwall, complaining of the penury which the present Union policy had not altered:

> there are tens of thousands of teachers up and down the country, and many even in this remote corner, who for a long time past have been dissatisfied with the lack of vigour shown by our leaders.[69]

A few letters mentioned the change of political allegiances amongst teachers due to the educational crisis. 'Pity' said:

> my pre-war political opinions would have prevented consideration of the suggested Union with the Labour Party but now I shall certainly vote for it, in order that we may use the only weapon, force, that will cause this wealthy Metropolitan County Authority to treat its teachers with justice. . .[70]

'Ground Ginger' agreed with 'Pity':

> ... after the treatment we have suffered at the hands of one or another I am now a 'Labourite' and I am anxious for the time to come to record my vote as such.[71]

Others like 'Simplex' asked what benefits the Union ever received from past Conservative and Liberal ministers.[72] Maskelyne, one of the main proposers of affiliation, was generally referred to as a 'life-long Conservative'.

The Teachers' Labour League, chaired by G.D. Bell, campaigned on a straightforward Marxist ticket for Labour affiliation, arguing that teachers taught the children of the exploited working-class and should join with this class politically. Members spoke at meetings throughout the country.

The Conservative response, notably by C.W. Crook, was to argue for the policy of freedom in political and religious thought which had protected the unity of the teachers in the past, and that affiliation to Labour would cause difficulties with parents about the neutrality of their teaching. Conservative writers would often refer to education as a vocation or calling, above politics. An example of the kinds of argument used is illustrated here from a meeting of the Leicestershire NUT.

Alderman Michael Conway from Bradford spoke for the affiliation and T. Taylor, the Mayor of Stourbridge and an NUT Executive member, spoke against. Conway made a distinction between the opportunistic Union policy in the past and the trend toward combination — its demands were not enforceable:

> The NUT had been living on aspirations for a long time. In Bradford there were 40,000 organised workers behind the teachers when they made a move and they were getting today the largest bonus in the country and had been getting it for eighteen months.[73]

He also said that teachers were from the working-class and the Labour programme on education was superior to that of the NUT. He proposed that:

> The first step to be adopted was affiliation with the Local Trades Council and getting rid of the idea that the teachers were too snobbish to ally themselves with other workers. The next step was to recommend the NUT Executive to affiliate with the Trades Union Congress and leave the question of affiliation with the Labour Party for political action for a future time.[74]

Mr Taylor made three main points. Firstly, that teachers were not like railwaymen — their strikes did not paralyse. The NUT had therefore been as successful as possible in the circumstances. Secondly, that the fine Labour education programme was merely a vote-catcher: the rank and file were still backward on education. Thirdly, to alter the Union political policy was a policy of desperation — Labour was not yet in power.

The affiliation debate was fairly confusing as it was not clear what exactly was meant, nor were the other options, civil servant status and self-government, any clearer. During the course of the debate the Labour Party altered its constitution to allow individuals to join, not just unions or societies, which tended to undermine the necessity for the Union as a whole to affiliate. Also Fisher, while not participating directly in the debate for affiliation, kept raising proposals for the future of teaching during the debates on his Education Bill. He promised them:

> the establishment on a sound basis of an efficient and devoted corps of teachers as a public necessity, less obvious perhaps, but no less imperative than the maintenance of the fighting forces of the Crown.[75]

His call for a 'noble and dignified teaching profession'[76] was echoed by the new *TES* which preached a similar ideology. In one of a series of calls throughout 1917 for a new profession, unified around the Teachers' Registration Council, the *TES* argued a position very similar to Crook and the NUT anti-Labour Party lobby.[77]

> What is needed is a profession as firmly based in popular estimation as the medical and legal professions . . . a profession it must be, open in all its branches to talent, character and personality, and it must offer something more than a bare living wage to its humblest member.[78]

Again, in the following month, the *TES* said:

> so important do we regard that unification at the present time, when we are on the verge of a great national system, that we do not hesitate to make an urgent appeal to all teachers who have the interests of the nation at heart to place their names on the Register.[79]

The actual referendum became lost in this war of position between the left and right on the place of teachers in society and the kind of society they would work in. When the vote was counted and a two-thirds majority was given for non-affiliation, the debate continued among teachers even if *The Times* and its *Supplement* and Fisher quietened down.

The changes that had occurred among the teachers can be seen in the debate on a Whitley Committee for the education service which was proposed by the Union executive at the Easter Conference in 1919. (Whitley Committees were really Joint Industrial Councils for the promotion of industrial harmony and a forum for collective bargaining — often rejected by the large, well-organized industries, like shipbuilding, but welcomed by the less well-organized industries).

Steer, for the Executive, said that teachers must be taken into partnership with rate payer representatives. An immediate amendment, from W.W. Hill (a guild socialist) claimed that the profession should be organized on a self-governing basis, with full partnership in administration. He cited the power of doctors and lawyers in validating their own entry qualifications and the miners and railway workers who were fighting for joint control in their industries. Michael Conway, supporting him, declared for joint control to:

> discuss things on equal terms with Board of Education and Local Authorities.[80]

Several teachers spoke in favour of joint control and:

> a Rhondda delegate spoke of the educational progress made in the Rhondda Valley under the control of the workers.[81]

Although Powell, the Chairman of the Salaries Committee, described it in a hostile way, as 'frank syndicalism' it was carried amid 'considerable enthusiasm'.

So, Whitley Committees were seen in the Union, according to the new Conference policy, as a means of joint administrative control of the industry. The same year, G.D.H. Cole, an opponent of the Whitley Committees republished his book, *The World of Labour*, with an introduction which described Whitley Committees as offering only a share in the profits, but not substantially altering the question of control and ownership. His own guild socialist view was that control meant:

> The democratisation of the actual management of industry and the securing for the organised workers of a real measure of control over the conditions of their work.[82]

He noted Hill's success in his book, produced the following year, *Chaos and Order in Industry* because it was precisely a syndicalist, a guild socialist amendment, that the Union had passed in the full knowledge of its origin.

It was not Whitley Committees but joint control the teachers wanted but they would seek this under the convenient flag of Whitleyism. Indeed, local teacher Associations, as in London, even laid out the rules, in their opinion, on which the employers' side should be selected — these suggested that the side should have no education officials but only elected representatives.[83] The *TES* correspondent noted that at this large meeting of the London Teachers Association the 'younger members' had taken over and also moved for strike action.

Whitley Committees were springing up throughout the country, Goldstone remarked in his Union Notes column,[84] but they had metamorphosed into 'joint advisory committees'. However, in London and in his example, Leeds, the elementary teachers had shared the employee side in amicable arrangements with secondary teachers, deliberate steps to a union-based unity. Goldstone argued for a committee brief that would include recommendations on school organization, salaries and curricular matters, and that it should have the status of a standing committee to the Executive Committee, not reporting only to a sub-committee.[85]

Hill argued the case for professional self-government in a long article in the *Schoolmaster* the following March. From his point of view, the movement was away from the State livery of the elementary teacher and externally imposed restrictions (the Board, Inspectors, etc.) and towards '. . . professional control over purely professional affairs and joint control with the authorities in administration'.[86] It would be responsible for its own training and qualifications, and:

> The profession would act in conjunction with public authorities in managing the schools. Together, the teachers and representatives of the public would decide the curricula, the conditions of employment of teachers, the size of classes, the type of building and equipment.[87]

The Whitley Committee could become the means of achieving this state of affairs and the Teachers' Registration Council, if it wished, could look after the question of qualifications, etc. The Burnham Committee on salaries, while not statutory, was an example of Whitleyism. Nothing less than a transformation, that was Hill's view of professional self-government — right down into the schools, with a staff committee of enterprising teachers.

The 1920 Conference saw Cove and Hill try again to extend the notion of Whitley Committees, or rather subvert them, into a call for self-government and full local and national partnership with administration. An Executive resolution referred to Whitley Committees as a necessary *step* to joint control and that their formation be expedited. Cove argued for a policy of immediate control; he said they would not be given control only consultation and the Whitley Committee was not a first step but the only step. Again, like the doctors and lawyers, Cove added, certainly like the aims of the miners and railwaymen, they wanted self-government and 'joint executive control'. Cove gave the advanced industrial argument:

> Whitley Committees were being rejected in the industrial world because it was recognised that they were based upon the principle of identity of interest between capital and labour when in reality there

was no such interest (applause). Whitley Committees were merely the means by which the workers were being sidetracked from the real thing they were after.[88]

Teachers wanted the power to appoint their own inspectors and directors and to beat the continued power of denominational interests.

However, Powell, in replying, as in the previous year, proved to the Conference that Whitley Committees were wanted — in the country areas. What was being rejected by the syndicalist urban wing of teachers was treated as a major breakthrough in the rural county areas. This time, the resolution in favour of Whitley Committees was passed.

A letter in the *Schoolmaster* soon after this debate argued Hill's point — teaching was important now but will probably not be soon. Their only hope was self-government, to become a free body of workers and in doing so to defeat the State, the enemy of the teacher, who wanted them to produce a citizen according to its plan. A self-governing profession would educate not indoctrinate and open the schools to a searching criticism.[89]

It is impossible to appreciate this movement solely by reference back to the Union's earlier claims for professional status or even a Register with control over entry. This was now part of the 1919 confidence and militancy of the general working class movement, still moving forward, creating plans for a new social order, influenced enormously by socialism and particularly syndicalist and guild socialist ideas.

Teachers were creating a new political and social identity for themselves, some in alliance with Labour, some adopting the new ideas from the State, but always driven by the need to alter the conditions of, and control over, their work.

Notes

1 F. Williams (1947) *'Fifty Years March'* Odhams, p. 283.
2 F. Williams (1947) *'Fifty Years March'* Odhams, p. 281.
3 The 1918 Conference Res. on Education (The Bradford Charter) — 'a genuine nationalisation of education' 'The recognition of the teaching profession *without* distinction of grade, as one of the most valuable to the community', in *'Teacher in Politics'*, Webb.
4 *Daily Herald*, 1917–1919 Hastings T.C., March 10, 1917; Grays T.C., Feb. 16, 1918.
5 *The Daily Herald* and the Herald Leagues reflected a wide range of Left wing opinion — syndicalists, guild socialists and Christian Socialists — yet they were united by the notion of reform through action and saw the State as functioning — on behalf of capital. Holton, B. (70) *'British Syndicalism 1900–1914'*, Pluto.
6 *Daily Herald*, Nov. 30, 1918. The Teacher's Charter.
7 Wells, H.G. (1908) *'New Worlds for Old'* Constable.

8. Wells, H.G. (1908) '*New Worlds for Old*', p. 283.
9. It certainly influenced A.S. Neill, *Domine's Log*, p. 102 — see later.
10. Wells, H.G. p. 312 nb. Wells was consistent. Letter in *Schoolmaster* 1920, May 29th 'Teachers are treated meanly, overworked, underpaid — insufficiently respected. Cheap teachers mean a jerry-built social system. To sweat your teachers is to prepare a revolution.'
11. S. Webb (1918) '*The Teacher in Politics*' Sept. 1918, Fab. Tract, 187.
12. The Webbs' concern for the educational service was well-known but at the turn of the century their attitude to teachers was 'curiously ambivalent' (Brennan, E.J. '75' *Education for National Efficiency*' Athlone Press) (p. 44). Webb managed to persuade the Conservative Government in 1903 not to break up London into boroughs 'unduly dominated by the elementary schoolteachers thanks to their disproportionate representation on borough councils'. This has similarities to B. Webb 'professional egoism in the teacher which tends to impair the social value of his service'. Sept. 25, 1915 *New Statesman*.
13. Webb, p. 8.
14. Access and scholarships are nearer to Webb's ideas at turn of century. Simon, (65), p. 206–7; p. 238; p. 253–4.
15. Webb, p. 9.
16. Webb, p. 13. Webb was a friend of Haldane.
17. The '*Teacher in Politics*' is a direct application to teachers of the general theory outlined by Sydney and Beatrice Webb in '*The History of Trade Unionism*' (1894 and 1920) (Longmans). They had great faith in Labour's ability to harness the astounding post war growth in white collar unionism (the black-coated proletariat) and to direct these associations of producers into a direct participation in management and towards a reconstruction of society. Webb's part in drafting '*Labour and the New Social Order*' was to appeal directly to the brainworkers and the 1920 Edition mentioned the 'considerable accession' of professionals into the Labour Party after the 1918 change in membership rules.
18. *Schoolmaster*, April 21, 1917.
19. *Schoolmaster*, April 21, 1917.
20. Holton, B. (1976) '*British Syndicalism 1900–1914*' Pluto. The relationship between syndicalism and guild socialism is discussed in Holton, R.J. 'Syndicalist Theories of the State' in *Sociological Review*, Vol. 28, No. 1, 1980.
21. Also, in the writings of G.D.H. Cole (e.g. '*The World of Labour*' 1918, Bell 4th Ed. 1919), and the journal, *The Guildsman*.
22. G.D.H. Cole (1966 Ed.) '*A Short History of the Brit. Working Class Movement 1789–1947*' Allen and Unwin, p. 405. Glass, S.T. (1966) '*The Responsible Society — The Ideas of English Guild Socialism*', Longmans.
23. Cole, (1920) '*Chaos and Order in Industry*' Methuen, p. 52 and this point is made in Wright, A.W. (1979) '*G.D.H. Cole and Socialist Democracy*', Clarendon Press, p. 87.
24. Cole (1920), p. 48.
25. Cole (1920), p. 48.
26. Cole (1920), p. 235.
27. Cole (1920), p. 235.
28. Cole (1920), p. 236.
29. Cole '*World of Labour*' p. 363.
30. Cole (1920) '*Guild Socialism — Restated*' Parsons, p. 39.
31. Cole (1920), p. 99 ibid.

32 Cole (1920), p. 100 ibid.
33 Cole *Chaos and Order*, p. 54.
34 Mentioned by Cole in '*Guild Socialism Restated*'.
35 William Howard 'The Unrest Amongst Teachers' *Socialist Review*, Jan/Mar. 1920.
36 A.S. Neill (1916) '*A Dominies Log*', Herbert Jenkins.
37 Neill quotes Wells statement about teachers — 'The most creative profession of all' from '*New Worlds for Old*'.
38 Neill, p. 102 ibid.
39 Neill, p. 124 ibid.
40 Neill, p. 124 ibid.
41 Neill, p. 133 ibid.
42 Neill, p. 133 ibid.
43 Neill, p. 92 ibid.
44 Neill, p. 105 ibid.
45 Neill, p. 125 ibid. Neill continued this argument in '*A Dominie Dismissed*' (1917) Herbert Jenkins, about the Guild, the 'polite Trade Union' ('blackleg proof') but he always recognized the teacher as a servant of capitalism. The Guild would break their relationship. He was aware also that in a strike the teachers would need to align themselves with the citizens.
46 Howard, W. (1920) Unrest amongst Teachers *Socialist Review*, March 1920.
47 The I.L.P. was an active Socialist component of the Labour Party and with its paper *The Labour Leader* was a supporter of the National Guilds League.
48 Howard, '*Unrest Amongst Teachers*'.
49 Simon, (65), p. 347.
50 Webb, B. 'Supplement on Teachers' Organisations' in *New Statesman*, Sept. 25, 1915.
51 That the I.L.P. had an attraction for teachers can be shown by research into the shareholders of the I.L.P. newspapers. Both the *Woolwich Pioneer* and the *Merthyr Pioneer* had representation from teachers in appreciable numbers. Hopkin, D. 'The membership of the Independent Labour Party 1904–1910' in *International Review of Social History*, Vol. XX, 1975.
52 Simon (65) McMillan had been elected in 1894 during a large public campaign, in which she was at the forefront, against half-time education.
53 Simon (65) Her interests in education were based on provision for the healthy child but included the curriculum, teacher training etc.
54 Simon, (65), p. 284–5.
55 Simon, (65), p. 284n.
56 Bradford, E.C. (1970) '*Education in Bradford since 1870*', Bradford, p. 232.
57 Conway became NUT President in 1924 and Lord Mayor in 1927. He was to be a member of the Labour Party Advisory Committee on education created in 1918 and chaired by F.W. Goldstone (the Labour MP and later Secretary of the NUT).
58 The strong links between Bradford trade unions, the Trades Council and the I.L.P. is explained and described in Reynolds, J. and Laybourn, K. 'The Emergence of the Independent Labour Party in Bradford' in *International Review of Social History*, Vol. XX, 1975.
59 Approximately 45,000 teachers.
60 *Schoolmaster*, Feb. 10, 1917, p. 172.
61 *The Times Educational Supplement*, Jan. 25. 'A Trade Union for Education' — unity of all educators interests. *The Times Educational Supplement*, March 1 'To my fellow teachers' H.A.L. Fisher — teachers as an important group/teachers as important as defence.

62 *Daily Herald*, Jan. 27, 1917. This issue had begun to appear in the *Schoolmaster* correspondence column and in reports of local salary meetings.
63 *Schoolmaster*, Feb. 10, 1917, p. 172.
64 *Schoolmaster*, Feb. 10, 1917, p. 172.
65 *Schoolmaster*, Feb. 10, 1917, p. 174.
66 *Schoolmaster*, Feb. 17, 1917, p. 207.
67 *Schoolmaster*, April 2, 1917.
68 One of the opponents of the Bell affiliation line was a West Ham member, Whitlock — he did so as a member of the British Socialist Party and regarded unwillingly attracted teachers as a future 'drag on the wheel of the LP', *Schoolmaster*, April 21, 1917.
69 *Schoolmaster*, Nov. 24, 1917. Radcliffe, Cornwall.
70 *Schoolmaster*, Nov. 3, 1917. 'Pity', Middlesex.
71 *Schoolmaster*, Dec. 1, 1917. 'Ground Ginger'.
72 *Schoolmaster*, Dec. 8, 1917. 'Simplex'. A letter from John Megins, Bethnal Green, March 23, 1918. 'As a life-long Liberal and a Liberal agent, I welcome the suggestion of alliance with the L.P. because after deep thought I appreciate that Liberalism and Conservatism have done precious little for education ... it is Labour, and Labour alone that will ultimately give us a new social order'.
73 *Schoolmaster*, Nov. 10, 1917.
74 *Schoolmaster*, Nov. 10, 1917.
75 *The Times Educational Supplement*, March 1, 1917.
76 *The Times Educational Supplement*, April 19, 1917.
77 By 1918, C.W. Crook was a regular columnist in *The Times Educational Supplement*, in a section called National Union Notes.
78 *The Times Educational Supplement*. The Call for Teachers, Jan. 25, 1917.
79 *The Times Educational Supplement*. New Register, Feb. 22, 1917.
80 *The Times Educational Supplement*, May 1, 1919.
81 *The Times Educational Supplement*, May 1, 1919.
82 Cole, *World of Labour*. Introd. 1919 Ed. p. XV. Others have argued that the Whitley Committees were deliberately proposed to take power away from the shopfloor and towards the management/union top hierarchy; a response in other words, to the shop stewards movement. An adviser to the Lloyd George War Cabinet, Sir Lyndon Macassey, in charge of dilution on the Clyde and elsewhere, openly made this point in his book, '*Labour Policy, False and True*' — quoted in Hutt, A. (1942 Ed.). '*British Trade Unionism*' Lawrence and Wishart (p. 81).
83 *The Times Educational Supplement*, May 8, 1919.
84 *The Times Educational Supplement*, May 15, 1919. On May 1, 1919 *The Times Educational Supplement*, Goldstone made his view of the self-government proposal clear, '...[it] is a repetition in the realm of education of the demand which the miners and other bodies of organised workers are putting forward in respect of their several industries'.
85 Probably nearer to S. Webb (*Teacher in Politics*) notion of Prof. Advisory Committees, except these would be only teachers — yet conveying the 'responsible judgement' to authorities — not to *decide* but to advise.
86 *Schoolmaster*, March 13, 1920.
87 *Schoolmaster*, March 13, 1920.
88 *Schoolmaster*, April 10, 1920 — An insight into the intertwining of syndicalist arguments and their perspective on the TRC, seen in this light, is the fact that since 1916 W.W. Hill, and 1920, W.G. Cove, had been members of the TRC [1922 official list].
89 *Schoolmaster*, May 1, 1920 article on Consultative Committees.

III. THE TEST OF ECONOMY, LOYALTY AND UNITY

No sooner was a national agreement on pay recommended by Fisher's creation, the Burnham Committee, than the wave of progress the teachers were riding began to ebb. Local Education Authorities, especially the rural or small town Authorities, began to use the post-war reaction to the social discontent and the need for economies, to pay teachers a local wage, determined by the authorities. From 1920 to 1925 the NUT was engaged in defending the national award from reactionary local authorities and an apparently ambivalent central government.

The civic rights of teachers were also under attack. Left-wing teachers were faced with expulsion from teaching and a new 'peace' curriculum, a post-war legacy, was treated as seditious by those wanting a 'patriotic' curriculum. Moves were made to make the teachers take oaths of allegiance to the state and to make them civil servants. A new professional service appeal from the Board of Education and a policy of condemning left-wing teachers was used instead.

The new industrial union model was soon in difficulties as new splits occurred among the teachers. The men teachers began to secede, to recreate the older craft union policy, this time based explicitly on the gendered role of the schoolmaster. Many women teachers seceded from the NUT to form their own feminist union, with new ways of working together, to fight for equal pay.

Chapter 7

Brothers and Sisters in the Struggle

Fisher was uncertain about national salary scales which his own officials at the Board of Education warned him would lead to a 'state teacher corps'. He decided to follow his own government's Trade Board policy and create a standing committee on a 'provisional minimum scale', the Burnham Committee (named after its first chair, Lord Burnham, owner of the *Daily Telegraph*). The Union accepted the proposals made by this committee in January 1920 with great difficulty. The difficulties were based on teacher worries if they earned more than the minimum proposed and also whether acceptance implied losing the right to strike. Urban teachers, with a tradition of collective bargaining and relatively high pay, did not like Burnham, rural teachers did. Debates at the special conference in January strongly suggest that many teachers felt laws of supply and demand and their own action would force each authority to compete with its neighbour to provide better than the recommended minimum salaries. Leading militants, like Cove, argued that accepting 'Burnham' would mean a straitjacket for the teachers while their employers were unbound.

It is well to recognize that the four 'standard scales' (ranging from urban to rural areas and decreasing in value) produced by the Burnham Committee later in the year appear to double teachers' pay, yet if the wartime cost of living rise is taken into account (Tropp says this was 164 per cent) then the salary award (about 159 per cent) represented a slight cut. Still, the award was accepted in November by a majority of two to one.

When the counter attack on the teachers' salaries came, it was part of a generally recognized attack on the insurgent working class, its rising unionism and pay claims. The rapid rise of unemployment in the last few months of 1921, the falling wage rates, dropping to the nationally agreed minima and below, and the pressure on the Trade Boards to disband or reduce their statutory minima all increased the pressure in 1921 on the organized working class. By 1921, Britain was in a slump and the cost of living fell.[1]

The Committee on National Expenditure, created by Lloyd George, and with the industrialist Sir Eric Geddes as Chairman, had attacked the growing expenditure on education in late 1920 and the Board of Education followed by trying to stop new local authority agreements accepting the Burnham scales. By the time of the first report of the Geddes Committee on the 10th February 1922, teachers had held protest meetings throughout the country, mainly because the cuts had preceded many authorities' decisions to accept the scales — so teachers were still on the 'provisional minimum' agreed in 1919 and not yet on the new scales. The *Daily Herald* reported in January 1922 that 170 local associations had backed a Union call for resistance to projected cuts in salaries and some local associations were beginning to use their right to a special levy (under their own local constitution) to take contributions to strike funds.[2] A week later, a further 46 associations had backed the Union position.

To rumours of impending cuts due from the Geddes Committee were added details from the Board of Education's discussions with Yoxall, the Union Secretary. The Geddes Committee made initial expenditure cuts of £75 million — in education, they would amount to £16 million. Among other recommendations, the Committee asked that the new non-contributory teachers' pension, created by Act of Parliament in 1918, should now include a 5 per cent contribution from teachers and a reduction on the Burnham scales commensurate with the lowered cost of living since 1920. The Committee had two main areas in which to cut spending — teacher salaries and the number of pupils per teacher. The school entry age limit was to be raised to six years, urban teacher : pupil ratios were to be moved from 1 : 32 to 1 : 50 pupils, and schools with less than 100 pupils should be closed. These proposals were to be promoted by a system of cash limits on the local authorities. They summarized their section on education:

> (The reduction of expenditure) can only be done by raising the lower age limit, by putting more pupils under one teacher, and paying the teachers less, and we think the teachers and education authorities should be asked to face this fact.[3]

The publication of this Report was the signal for an outbreak of public meetings and statements by teachers in local Associations and on the NUT executive. It was also a signifier of the new wave of attacks about to be made by the Local Education Authorities on teachers' pay and conditions. Elementary education and teachers' pay became once again a most important local and national issue, but this time, full-scale attacks on teachers were made — their power was seen as diminished. The rest of the working-class were under severe economic and social pressure and unable to support the teachers as before.

In London, the effect of the Geddes proposals was, according to the London County Council Education Committee, to reduce its teachers in elementary schools by 6,200 and in secondary schools by 1,500. Local authorities, such as Swansea,[4] began to cut teachers' salaries and in those areas where above-scale payments were being made, due to past campaigns, they were also being reduced; in Tottenham, all the teachers received their notice (800 of them), after the Board of Education refused to pay the local grant because of the high scales.[5] Long-standing uncertificated teachers were often in this position, and the NUT held a special conference for them in which this issue was discussed.[6] Some local authorities began to sack some of their teachers, particularly the married women teachers — Bridlington, Isleworth and Heston, Macclesfield, Durham and Dover were reported to be doing this.[7]

The Workers' Educational Association held meetings in support of the 1918 Act and against the cuts, as did the Cooperative Union and the Institute of Working Men's Clubs. The by-election at Camberwell, won by C.G. Ammon, was, he said, a result of the proposed Geddes cuts and the high turnout for Labour by teachers.[8] The Schoolteachers' Superannuation Bill, which was the proposal to include a 5 per cent contribution from teachers towards their pension, derived from Geddes, was, in the main, the only direct Geddes proposal in education to survive from the Government. This was passed after a deal of acrimony about their betrayal, by the NUT.

The real attack was continuing throughout the country. It had two main thrusts, both economic and aimed at reducing educational expenditure on working-class schools and at by-passing teacher power. Salary scales were under attack constantly by the LEAs and cheap, untrained labour was allowed into teaching. Fisher had proposed the latter in Parliament as:

> suitable women without certificates or academic qualifications will be eligible as assistants in infant schools.[9]

The London County Council, later that year, decided to introduce 100 young women to teach nursery classes in their schools. The day on which twenty of these women were sent to schools, and were then sent back by the headteachers, a breakaway section of the NUT, the National Union of Women Teachers, held a large meeting of over a thousand teachers outside County Hall in protest. They wore badges inscribed 'we won't teach blacklegs' and 'no unqualified teachers for children'.[10] This Union had, earlier in the year, reported to the *Daily Herald* that:

> Inspectors are approaching student teachers in the London schools and suggesting to them that they should give up the idea of becoming trained certificated teachers and that they should enter the LCC

schools as supplementary teachers i.e. as teachers with no recognised qualifications or status.[11]

The Superannuation Bill was only the most obvious and public part of a State counter-attack on services, conditions and union power in elementary education. What the Geddes proposal did was to allow the more reactionary local authorities to move back on the offensive after the LEA unity on the Burnham Committee in 1919–1922, to regain their previous education policy — running a cheap, shoestring service. Other authorities, on the surface staying within the Burnham agreement, were trying to recruit cheaper labour even though it was untrained. The move to increased quality of educational provision was being replaced by the earlier prevailing 'cheap' policy.

Other local authorities defended the salary scales against the Geddes proposals and the Board of Education was still threatening recalcitrant Local Education Authorities with grant withdrawal on the grounds of inefficiency if proposed local economies were continued.[12] Many of the Local Education Authorities did not wish to create again the conditions for local competition between themselves over salaries and recruitment.

A writer to the *Daily Herald* in July 1922 explains the processes at work that year in the country. In his opinion, the Burnham scales would not be attacked directly but indirectly. By creating a pool of unemployed teachers, teacher would be divided from teacher, and the teacher reserve would have to 'blackleg' or demand the withdrawal of the Burnham scale to be re-employed at a cheaper salary:

> The older men in responsible posts are being sacked, men below them are given their posts, while their vacancies are either left unfilled or filled by cheap labour in the form of non-graduate, non-trained young lads who are out of work in other professions . . .[13]

In other words, the left-over of State intervention, the Burnham Committee, was to be broken by that element of the State now dominant in reaction, the Treasury and its businessmen allies, using market forces. Herbert Morrison, in a debate by the London County Council, reported in the *Daily Herald*, said that:

> behind (this recruitment of unqualified teachers) was a move to flood the profession and then to cut salaries.[14]

A Burnham Committee meeting on November 28th, was the scene of a successful attempt by the local authorities to impose a 'voluntary' reduction of 5 per cent on the teachers' salaries.[15] The teachers eventually accepted this reduction partly out of fear of further cuts and in an atmosphere created by the press of anti-teacher bitterness.[16]

Although the teachers had bound themselves to accept the Burnham scales and not to strike, local authorities, and not only the rural ones, were cutting wage-awards and employing untrained teachers.

The reaction, then, was threefold: a direct cut taken at national level on the Burnham Committee, a refusal by some local authorities to adopt the recommended scales, and pressure by the Board of Education on local authorities to economize. Large classes were one result of this policy, another was the employment of the unqualified teacher — not only in the infant schools but increasingly in the senior and special schools. Sainsbury noted the trend in London towards a reduction in the numbers and composition of the teaching staff:

> The LCC proposes ... to bring the number of unqualified teachers in infants' schools up to 600 during the next three years (1923–1926).[17]

So, as the 1920s progressed there was a series of hard-fought strikes by the NUT against local authorities still not operating the Burnham scales, or economising on teacher salaries. This period saw a partial reconciliation of the two contradictory State policies with regard to education and the teachers. The system was to return to its original basis, to be as cheap and efficient as possible, and the teachers were to be continually encouraged to be patriotic and responsible (the remainder of Fisher's policy). The economic cuts of Geddes encouraged local authorities to pursue their own policies, secure in the knowledge that the Board of Education would find it hard to resist policies which lay in line with a national economy campaign. In Southampton and in Lowestoft, the Union had to fight hard to stop two local authorities reneging on Burnham and a flood of others waiting to try the same tactic. Although the teachers had been placed under great pressure to accept 'voluntary cuts' in their salaries, no such pressure seems to have been applied to local authorities (until 1925) to accept the Burnham Award.

In Southampton for example, the local authority was still paying its teachers on the Provisional Minimum Scale although in 1921 the authority agreed that the Burnham Scale 3 was the appropriate scale for the area. The local teachers' Association had written to the Education Committee in January, 1922 a year after the decision to defer the acceptance of Scale 3 for the area. The *Hampshire Advertiser* records that local councillors complained of the cost, of higher rates and the unlikelihood of any increase in teacher efficiency.[18] A local ratepayer's group stiffened their resolve after they organized a public meeting which complained of the financial burden of the rates and that teachers already had a 'living wage'. The Southampton councillors decided in March to reduce the local rate from 3s. to 2s. 9d. in the pound which meant that they intended to cut 5 per cent from the teachers' salaries — that is, instead of paying them more (the Scale 3) they intended to cut their present salary (the Provisional Minimum Scale) by 5 per cent. The local Southampton and District Teachers' Association was probably not either well organized or part of the forward movement in the Union. Its President complained to a special meeting of the teachers that they were:

> being paid on the lowest scale in England today. Teachers in all the surrounding areas were being paid on higher scales . . . (They were) underpaid before the War; our salaries were greatly reduced during the War, and since the War, and the agreement arrived at should be honoured.[19]

The conciliatory policy of the Staff and Salaries Sub-Committee and the Education Committee towards Burnham arbitration was unacceptable to the Council. The *Advertiser* reported that the Council had 'repeatedly and emphatically resolved against'[20] the Scale 3 Award and reprimanded the Education Committee for bringing the matter up again! The Council meeting on February 25th agreed to the cuts proposal and, to save £15,000, gave notice to its teachers terminating their employment and offering re-appointment from October 1st on terms involving a *20 per cent* cut on the Minimum Scale.[21] Notices to 620 teachers were given out. A dispute arose, but with the Council in some confusion, never quite sure which was the most effective economy to operate. Finally, it began to recruit teachers from elsewhere. They received over 600 applications for posts, over half of which were from unqualified teachers. A further sign of the changing climate was the action of the new male teacher association, the National Association of Schoolmasters, reported in the Herald, which said:

> pay the Burnham Scale with modified increments to men teachers, the Association would (then) recommend to its members to restart work forthwith.[22]

It was possible to conclude from the subsequent attack on the small NAS that the Union was under some pressure from the NAS argument that economies were likely in many areas because of the increased level of women teachers' salaries. Cove argued later that:

> My great point was that the teachers' salaries could be saved only by the maintenance of a contract (that is, the Burnham Agreement) . . .

and that if the contract was broken for women it would inevitably be broken for men.[23]

In some areas the NAS argument actively led councillors to cut wages. At Southampton, the Board of Education threatened the Council with loss of grant and eventually, after fourteen weeks, it gave in and teachers returned to work with a scale 3 grading, to be given over a period of three years.

Local disputes continued. Gateshead had a two-and-a-half month-long strike which was again won by the teachers but no sooner was a dispute won before another LEA would attempt to economize on teacher's wages. Herefordshire offered to cut women teachers' wages more than men's even though the women were on a lower scale. The Board itself was demanding local economies, not on the pay award but on 'excess' teachers, closure of small schools, early retirement of teachers and the dismissal of married women teachers.

The major stalking horse for a reduction in wages became Lowestoft Council. The Union became extremely worried that if Lowestoft won, other councils would follow. The Burnham agreement could not be sustained, even with some LEA support, if it was possible to hire cheaper teachers throughout the country. Also, to create a 'cheaper' teacher, the unity of teachers had to be broken.

The question of unionization and its effect on the employers' right to manage was the issue. The authority could not undertake the policy it wished to unless the power of the teachers was dismissed. So, the right to organize and the right to control were both clearly at stake at Lowestoft — as the members of the Council made clear. The backbone of the strike in Lowestoft were the women teachers who were under great employer pressure, and social pressure, particularly from men in the community, to give up part of their wages. The victory at Lowestoft was partly due to them and their steadfastness.

In December 1972, the Lowestoft Education Committee had decided to make an overall cut of 10 per cent on its teachers' salary bill. This was not a 10 per cent cut in wages for every teacher, but more or less depending upon the teacher's position on the scale. The 'voluntary' cut of 5 per cent agreed nationally was not sufficient for Lowestoft and the decision to repudiate the Burnham Agreement was taken.

The Authority sent notices to its teachers asking them to sign new contracts by March 31st, with payment reduced by approximately 10 per cent, otherwise their employment would be terminated. This was reported by the Lowestoft newspaper, *The Journal*, as involving sixteen schools and 200 teachers, though later, it was claimed that 163 teachers, including Headteachers, had been dismissed and that this was all the teachers in Lowestoft.

The Authority argued that the 'present scale is too high for existing conditions'[24], and that they only adopted the scale under duress. In the same edition of *The Journal*, the NUT's continuing position was made clear:

> The N.U.T. cannot waive its settled policy of refusing to recognize the right of an individual authority to make a breach in a national agreement, properly arrived at . . .

The position of the Lowestoft Education Committee was that it signed the Burnham Agreement under duress, or at least members of the Committee, including the current Chairman, Mr H.C. Adams, argued that they were under duress — if they did not sign, the Board of Education would remove their grant. The question of duress was fully argued out in a Town Council meeting on Friday, March 30th. The Town Clerk and other members of the Council, including an ex-chairman of the Education Committee argued that there was no duress. Indeed the Town Clerk said that the idea of duress was 'an absolute fiction' and went on to say that:

> if the Education Committee did not know when adopting the scale that they had a free hand, they were sadly lacking in their public duty. It was their business to know.[25]

This was also the argument of the Lowestoft Teachers' Association. In an advertisement placed alongside the Council Report and headed 'The Crisis in the Schools, open letter to Ratepayers', they attacked the idea of a 'mistake' or 'compulsion':

> Rarely has a more damaging admission been made by a public body for the official documents containing the scales and the schedules make it abundantly clear that such a mistake could not be made by anyone who took the trouble to read the documents for himself.[26]

Whether or not the question of compulsion was an excuse for the Lowestoft action, the councillors felt themselves to be under sufficient economic pressure to break the high level of teacher remuneration. There is constant reference to the economic depression, the increasing burden of sea defence, the recent bad fishing seasons and unemployment. It was said by one councillor, representing a ward where 90 per cent were on relief from the Guardians or the Labour Exchange, that no other town was suffering as Lowestoft was. These Conservative, Liberal or Ratepayer councillors, in the main, saw teachers' salaries as indisputably high, a burden on the rates, yet capable of being reduced in a way that sea-wall capital expenditure, say, wasn't. Their obligation was to the ratepayers — no one else — and only to a minimum efficiency in local services.

Mr H.C. Adams, a councillor for some twenty years by 1923, was a leading figure in the action taken against the teachers. He had been the Chairman of the Finance Committee and had taken the Chairmanship of the Education Committee in the period immediately before the action. Judging by newspaper reports of public and council meetings, Adams was an extremely powerful figure on the council, a councillor with strong opinions and a decisive factor in the strike. He had won the consent of the Council for the Education Committee to have full delegated powers from the Council for 12 months from early March and for the Council not to question its actions in the dispute except over the question of financial detail. So, Adams was the prime mover against the teachers and represented the local employers' 'active' policy of reducing salaries and creating a cheaper education service.

The Council meeting on March 30th was acrimonious. It had been called under special orders by several councillors and aldermen trying to provide for a new procedure for negotiating with the teachers. These people, supported in effect by the Town Clerk, argued that Lowestoft schools were good and efficient, the teachers were tried and trusted and that both parties had entered into an agreement fairly and it should be a point of honour to continue it. The possibility of recruiting teachers who were under-qualified whilst the old teachers were supported by parents was not a pleasing prospect for these councillors. These councillors were not radicals or great allies of the teachers but were a party of moderates, disliking the Burnham Agreement but after it was ratified, sticking to it. There was a general resentment against the teachers expressed in the debate and particularly against women teachers — Adams said at one point:

> no similar class of the community was enjoying the benefits enjoyed by the teachers. Two ladies walked up the town the other day, and he looked at them. Single ladies with no responsibilities. They carried over £600 of the ratepayers' money per year.[27]

Another member, a moderate for sticking to Burnham, even though it was a 'bad bargain', said of the teachers that:

> many businessmen would like to receive for their income the salaries that some of the teachers got.[28]

So, the Council of householders, businessmen and shopkeepers were no friends of the education service except if it was cheap. The obstacle to cheapness was the teachers and their organization, the NUT. Members wanted a compromise and no strike or lockout yet this would involve them breaking the Burnham Scale, the national agreement. There was little fear of the Board of Education, almost invisible in their deliberations, but a greater fear of the Union. This was the organization keeping up their rates.

Although Adams, as Chairman of the Education Committee, tried to unite the councillors by talking of further meetings with the Lowestoft teachers, it was obvious that the councillors had been superseded in a 'palace' or town hall revolution. Adams controlled the discussion — attacking the Town Clerk, refusing compromise, and gaining new powers in the creation of a selection committee to appoint new teachers. Alderman Notley, asking for compromise and reason, asked that the Burnham arbitration procedures be used: . . . 'The teachers must not be allowed to leave the town. Let them be met'. Adams replied, 'Not with the NUT'.[29]

The Union was seen as the problem. Lowestoft teachers were reasonable. The NUT was the barrier to a solution of the pay dispute. Again, Adams said that any proposal from the teachers would be considered but, 'the teachers' union advised them not to offer any concession whatever'.[30] At the end of the meeting Adams very astutely offered to suspend the appointment of new teachers if the Council passed a vote of confidence in the Education Committee. This was passed and the meeting closed. This apparent attempt at unity and a compromise with the teachers was broken three days later in a meeting of the Education Committee. Adams made it clear, mainly to a councillor who was a teacher representative, that although they were willing to listen to any new teacher proposals, the ultimatum (on contract termination) would not be withdrawn.

In other words, the Committee intended to negotiate only about exactly how the 10 per cent could be cut, not whether there should be a cut of this magnitude at all. It was stated again that the teachers were being forced into a strike by the Union. One councillor protested that they had always been willing to talk to the teachers:

> They were willing to meet the teachers but they were not willing to meet the officials of the Union, who were out for trouble. If the teachers were left alone they would meet the committee and there would be no difficulty in compromising. It was not the teachers they were fighting. Every teacher he had spoken to said 'It is not a question of money: I might give way but my Union will not allow me to'.[31]

In retrospect, it is difficult to imagine that this councillor, like the other members of the committee, did not believe this view, unless his speech was intended to unite the worried councillors on the committee. It is a view similar to that expressed in West Ham and the North Riding and in other disputes; a view of a subservient class of employees, a feudal class, loyal and trustworthy, in penury yet inexplicably, earning more and acting in ways 'out of their class'. The Union is an outsider in this relationship and is a powerful but interfering element in a straightforward situation. The teachers are misguided and the Union needs to be eliminated from the situation for peace to prevail. Peace is defined by the councillors as the situation in which their views and power continue to be dominant.

A large public meeting was held in the Regent Theatre on April 13th. Packed out and with hundreds more outside, [32] it was a presentation by the teachers of their side of the dispute. The Chairman of the Education Committee was vilified throughout the evening, with audience approval, and eventually, forbidden to address the meeting. In many ways, the dispute was seen as Adam's lockout. The Education Committee policy of the preceding three months was identified as his policy, and one speaker talked of the 'astounding amount of power invested in one man'.[33] His method of negotiating was described as 'surrender your case before you come, and we will talk'.[34]

One councillor spoke in favour of the teachers and against the Council or Adam's policy, arguing for the Burnham Scale and the now 5 per cent 'voluntary' cut, and suggesting that, with the strike pay of the teachers paid by the NUT, a quick agreement would result in *savings* for the Council. A further speaker, Fred Mander, an NUT Executive member (and later General Secretary) tried to divide the Education Committee by attacking Adams and quoting from statements made by him referring to 'teacher double-dealing' and yet speaking of honest but misguided councillors.

Whether it was Adam's lockout or not, the accounts read as if, by general assent, he spearheaded the attack on the teachers.

In his eagerness, he created a massive opposition from the parents, united the teachers and irritated the churches. The parents voted overwhelmingly at the Regent Theatre meeting to register their 'independent protest' at the dismissals and for the Council to dismiss Adams from his Chairman's post. The teachers were solid for the strike even though by April, Adams had appointed 125 new teachers who, he claimed, were better qualified and cheaper than their predecessors (and who would now benefit from increased book and equipment capitation allowances), and even though Adams had tried to divide the certificated from the uncertificated teachers by his intention to treat the latter 'favourably'.[35] The Church of England incumbents in Lowestoft had withdrawn their support from the Education Committee when it tried, unilaterally, to break the Burnham Settlement and later began to dismiss teachers in the council schools against the wishes of the Managers who were often vicars or rectors and later still, allowed thousands of children on to the streets.

Though Mr Adams was unlikely to care, he had also alienated the Labour movement. The Trades and Labour Council in Lowestoft had protested to the Town Clerk in early March about the actions of the Education Committee. It was an ex-councillor for Labour, John Joplin Jnr, who moved the unanimous resolution at the Regent Theatre — the meeting which Mr Adams left, driving slowly 'through the hostile crowds, with a headteacher on each footboard of his car and a posse of police as bodyguard'.[36] Mrs Godfrey, a Labour Party parent, became one of the strongest supporters of the teachers — at the same meeting, she had said that if the parents didn't strike, the children would!

The connections between the farmworkers' union in Norfolk and Suffolk, some village schoolteachers and the organized Labour movement in Norwich, Ipswich and Lowestoft were strong. It was not only Tom Higdon at Burston, the centre of the teacher-farmworker alliance, who was connected with the East Anglian Labour and Socialist movement but other teachers like Arnett and Leadbetter. George Edwards, the farmworker's leader and a local Labour MP said at the Mayday meeting in Lowestoft:

> I want to tell you teachers that you have the entire sympathy of the Agricultural Workers' Union, we are with you and we have been watching your great struggle. They had no bigger sympathizers in the recent agricultural struggle than the teachers, because they knew of the necessity of their cause.[37]

Sympathy and support for the teachers then came from the Lowestoft parents, organized by the Labour party, and the wider Labour movement in Suffolk which already recognized a common struggle against the same class of employers — the farmers or businessmen and shopkeepers, the people who ran the councils, from parish to borough level.

The Monday night following the parents' meeting, Adams held a public meeting in the Regent Theatre to explain the case for the Education Committee. The meeting was described in the *Lowestoft Journal* as one of 'considerable uproar'. It was full of teachers and friends who shouted and whistled throughout.[38] Adams addressed the crowd, whenever he could, in a combative and confident manner. As the evening wore on, his explanation of the Education Committee's course of action, the point of being under duress and his consistent opposition to the Burnham scales, degenerated into an exchange of insults and persistent denigration of the moderate councillors, who were, in his opinion, turncoats. Later, he called his opposition Bolshevites which caused 'furious uproar' and then offered to name teachers who had volunteered to the committee a willingness to accept the 10 per cent. Again, uproar. Yet, a motion of confidence in the Council's action was passed or at least, declared 'even' although many declared it was a majority of six-to-one against.

Some time in the week following this meeting, the Education Committee had a closed session in which the names of the appointed teachers were read out by Adams and approving comments made about their qualifications. The list of teachers Adams attempted to keep secret, even from other councillors.

The following day, a specially convened Town Council meeting was called by four moderate councillors who tried to pass a resolution calling on the authority to accept the Burnham scale but allowing for a special committee which would enquire if circumstances in Lowestoft allowed for a further financial reduction. In other words, this was an attempt at a face-saving compromise. However, Adams was set on greater things — the lockout was having a national impact — he said:

> They had lighted a fire in Lowestoft last December which has raised a blaze throughout the country.[39]

Two new developments in the strike were mentioned. One, that children were being encouraged to strike if they had 'blackleg' teachers, and two, that the Union had succeeded in convincing a number of these teachers about the inadvisability of working in Lowestoft.

The reference to a childrens' strike was the result of fourteen meetings held by teachers and parents throughout Lowestoft that week, at which parents had explained their desire to keep their children away as a sign of solidarity with the teachers. One such mass meeting resolved, after the teachers had withdrawn, that they would 'abstain from sending the children to school until the old teachers are reinstated in their former positions'.[40] The Journal also reported that numerous petitions had been sent to the Town Hall, sometimes taken by 'mothers with sundry forceful expressions'.

The childrens' strike on Tuesday, 1st May when the new teachers started work, was a mixed affair. There were many school-refusers that day and a large march through the town by a thousand or so children, organized by Joplin and Godfrey of the Labour Party, yet many of the schools were open with most of their normal complement. *The Journal* reported that the schoolchildren attending were often unruly and the police were in attendance at one school. Many parents were anxious about their children and the new teachers and were reported as needing a good deal of persuading about leaving their children.

The march through Lowestoft was an exuberant affair. Parents lined the streets, traffic was halted, flags waved, the children shouted 'ditties' about Adams or shouted 'no settlement, no school'. In reply to the shouted question, 'when are you going back?' the reply came, 'never, till we get our teachers back'.

As we have seen, the teachers in the schools had been described by Adams to the Education Committee as often better qualified and certainly cheaper than the striking teachers. At a Committee meeting the day before the schools re-opened, it appeared that a number of the new teachers had not arrived in Lowestoft. It was Adam's opinion that the Union had 'pressured' them, in one case, with actual violence, not to join the 'blackleg' teachers.[41] A figure of 48 teachers out of an appointment list of 125 was mentioned as having been lost due to Union pressure. It came out at the meeting that one of these new teachers:

> had not been in the profession for twenty years . . . He was a Headmaster until 1903 then took up farming which had proved disastrous and he had turned his attention to his old profession.[42]

The secretive action of Adams in controlling the list of teachers and their qualifications lead to widespread suspicion that they were under-qualified or low quality or even, it was said, that they included criminals.

The strike teachers and their parent supporters held another large public meeting at the Regent Theatre that week. Great play was made of the solid united action of the teachers, the lack of justice in the action taken against them, that Adams was a 'danger to the town' and that success would come to the teachers, slowly but surely. When Fred Mander used that phrase, it came from his confidence that the authority would lose their grant given by the Board for an 'efficient' education system. This would happen after inspection and not immediately.

W.G. Cove spoke from the platform and his speech illustrates a continuing theme of this study — the popular appeal made by teachers who defended vigorously 'professional' standards. He argued that:

> schools were going to be started with imported blackleg labour, and it was said that the NUT would be defeated by these imported blackleg teachers but he told them that the struggle would not cease before the NUT had been victorious (applause). He declared that a body of men and women who had not the professional spirit in them, a body of men and women acting contrary to the interests of the great community to which they belonged, a body of men and women who were prepared to let down their brothers and sisters in the struggle, who had no sense of comradeship . . . men and women who did not feel that the highest interests of the children were at stake in this struggle were not fit to teach in the Lowestoft Elementary Schools (applause).[43]

The sense of struggle, unionism, defence of education and children and a professional spirit are inseparable in Cove's view of teaching and teachers.

There is no distinction between unionism and professionalism, one is the organized defence of the other. There is a clear community addressed and that is the working-class parents and children on whose behalf the teachers worked. Strikes were the active defence of the worker's education system and an extension of a classroom professional responsibility. For Cove, the NUT was the highest expression of an active professionalism. It stood for unity not individualism, comradeship not selfishness, a principled defence of education, and the 'highest professional interests'.[44] This active industrial policy taken in defence of teachers and education was of popular appeal. It was not the call of a privileged elite for the maintenance of privileges — it was a conscious alliance with working-class parents, aided by the growing active element within both sides of the Labour Party.

In a superb extension of Cove's argument, that was both a propaganda coup and a practical cementation of the alliance, the NUT, aided by the Labour movement (particularly John Joplin Jnr), created a number of Welfare Centres. These were in fact strike schools where the strike children were taught by the striking teachers.[45] For the remainder of the strike, between a quarter and a third of the Lowestoft elementary children were being taught in three centres (approximately 1,500 children), even though the authority prosecuted parents for the non-attendance of their children at the Council's schools and threatened to deprive scholarship children of their scholarships. As in the Burston strike, the parents and teachers 'clubbed' together to pay the fines and the children continued to attend the Welfare Centres. In November 1923, the Board of Education Inspectors thoroughly inspected the Council Schools and the Welfare Centres. The report on the schools was, in the NUT's words, sufficiently unfavourable to lead the Board of Education to *suspend the grant*.[46] On the other hand, the good report on the Welfare Centres, was a propaganda victory. As reported in *The Schoolmaster*, the Inspectors had noted that:

> ... in no fewer than nine (elementary) departments (out of twenty-five), there has been a serious deterioration of efficiency since that date, and a perceptible deterioration in three others, while no improvement is visible at any school ... much reason to fear (by the Board) a progressive deterioration in the general efficiency of the educational provision for Lowestoft.[47]

The *Schoolmaster* also reported on the curriculum of the Welfare Centres; this had steadily developed to incorporate swimming and cooking facilities, and the use of cinema films in the curriculum. A main event became the organization of a summer camp.

The pressure on the Council and the Education Committee increased after the unfavourable Inspectors' report and the *Daily Herald* was suggesting on the 7th January that the Board grants were being suspended and that the burden of financing the schools would fall fully on to the ratepayers. Adams led a delegation to the Board to complain about the inspections' findings and to provide explanations but to no avail. By February, it was obvious the Council would have to negotiate directly with the NUT. A Special Council Meeting on February 8th appointed a Negotiating Committee drawn from the Council and from the Education Committee members. Several members of the Committee met an NUT delegation on February 15th. After two hours discussion, agreement was reached, and the Committee members then withdrew to confer with the remainder of the Committee in an adjoining room in the Council Chamber. After another hour's discussion, the terms were approved by the negotiators by a majority vote. The terms of the settlement were entirely the demands of the NUT; reinstatement of the 163 teachers to their old posts, the Burnham scale 2 minus the 5 per cent abatement and back pay for the 'locked-out' teachers. The ultramontanes on the Education Committee met the following Monday, February 18th, and voted against the settlement, by twelve votes to six — a sign that unlike previous NUT disputes, the Education Committee was in the hands of the financial retrenchers, such as Adams, rather than educationalists who were often out of step with their Conservative Councils.

The Council had begun to dissociate itself from the policy of the Education Committee; the almost united front had been seriously weakened by the threatened loss of grant. It could face a lockout of 163 teachers, 1,500 pupils gone from its schools, a poorer quality education in the schools and mass meetings of parents, but not the grant loss. This would affect their finances and their businesses. It voted on the Thursday to accept the terms of settlement by twenty-three votes to sixteen.

So, the Union remained intact after the assault by Adams. It had withstood an eleven-month strike that threatened not only the livelihoods of its local members but the start of a major counter-attack by some authorities on the Burnham scales. As the Burnham settlement was not binding, the result of a defeat in Lowestoft would surely have lost all the rural areas and country towns from the salary scales and back to the pre-war standards. It couldn't have defeated a council so determined to win if it weren't for the absolute unity of the 'locked-out' teachers. The *Schoolmaster's* columns were full of praise for the fact that, in times of great unemployment for teachers, not a single teacher had broken ranks. The Education Committee had tried to divide the certificated from the uncertificated, the men from the women, the class teachers from the headteachers, and failed. The symbol of the unity shown there was not lost on a Union which had overcome previous divisions among certificated teachers but was now faced by new divisions between male and female, with new associations created for each sex. As an NUT ex-president, Miss Conway noted the teachers consisted of 120 women and 47 men; the latter were offered good pay and conditions if they broke with the women but their strike unity prevailed. Lowestoft became important in the 1920s not only for the significant way in which recalcitrant local authorities were dissuaded from leaving the Burnham settlement and those who remained in it stayed there, but as a symbol of industrial unity.

However, although the slide into local wage bargaining (or rather non-bargaining) was stopped at Lowestoft, there were places in England that still did not pay Burnham Scales and the Union was unable to force them. Again, it was the mainly Southern rural counties — in a belt from Worcestershire to Berkshire and Oxfordshire and on to Suffolk — and small country towns within those areas or the West Country — like Maidenhead, Barnstaple or Falmouth. These areas, twenty-one in all, paid teachers on the Provisional Minimum Scale, two years after Burnham, but it appears that the West Country (Cornwall, Devon and Penzance) paid their teachers the Provisional Minimum Scale *minus* three-and-a-quarter per cent.

By 1926, the Burnham scales were made compulsory, although odd disputes still occurred as Essex did not adopt the Burnham scales until 1926, and Carmarthen not until 1927. The final local problem was at Abertillery in 1928 when teacher salaries were again the focus of public expenditure cuts.

Lowestoft was the new symbol, replacing the Rhondda, of a united industrial union, overcoming divisions between teachers and resisting the employers. There was no contradiction in their minds between unionism and professionalism. There was one big union, attacking the problems of the child and the teacher, allied overtly or implicitly with the working class, and bound by an ideology of professional skill.[48]

An advantage to the teachers, which was unexpected, was the way in which the Burnham Scales were not tied to the cost of living, and were created in a period of high prices. They were attached to a national 'normal' cost of living standard which, luckily for them, was not reached through the 1920s. The value of their Award rose, in effect, as prices, the cost of living index, fell.[49]

In the 1920s, Union action and not the Board or Education defended the Burnham Settlement. It was only partially successful but the forces against it were formidable. Government lip-service to a formal agreement between teachers and employers was being eroded by employment policies and national pay cuts. In a period of diminishing industrial working-class strength, the Union succeeded in keeping the relative gains of an earlier period of militancy. In effect, the attention of its members was drawn more and more to the Labour Party — the party of education which was not yet in office for any considerable period. The battle with the employers was not just betwen teachers and councillors but more and more with the major employer, the supplier of major Exchequer grants and the operator of a Treasury policy which moved and shifted teacher pay: the Board of Education and the Government. The Labour party was seen as an effective way of influencing the Government — the new social order in education could be voted in. This was an extension of the borrowing of socialist ideas and the creation of local Labour teacher alliances. It was a recognition that ultimately teacher control over education and the education service had to be a political not just an industrial policy.

Notes

1 The alliance that Fisher had recognized between a forward education policy and commercial and business interests began to break up. The pressure for cuts in the public services became paramount in decision-making.
2 *Daily Herald*, Jan. 25, 1922 — Cornwall and Twickenham mentioned.
   Daily Herald, Jan. 16, 1922.
3 *Daily Herald*, Feb. 11, 1922.
4 *Daily Herald*, Feb. 16, 1922.
5 *Daily Herald*, May 3, 1922.
6 *Daily Herald*, Feb. 23, 1922.
7 *Daily Herald*, March 1, May 13, June 29 and Oct. 16, 1922.
8 *Daily Herald*, Feb. 21, 1922 and Simon Vol. 3, p. 47. Turned Tory 4,000 majority to Labour 1,000 out of 10,000 total.
9 *Daily Herald*, April 28, 1922.
10 *Daily Herald*, Sept. 27, 1922.
11 *Daily Herald*, June 16, 1922.
12 *Daily Herald* (Southampton) July 6 and (Wiltshire) July 22. There was also the beginning of a concern about the left in the Union by AEC representatives. Percy Jackson (W. Yorkshire) warned the Panel that if it broke up without agreement, 'I think we shall have done more for revolution and Bolshevism and all that means than any body of men sat down at this moment face to face'. Barnes, S. 'Individual, Local and National Bargaining for Teachers' Salaries in England and Wales'. Ph.D., London, 1959, p. 225.
13 *Daily Herald*, July 21, 1922.
14 *Daily Herald*, Nov. 1, 1922.
15 A special NUT conference accepted this further cut.
16 Simon (74), p. 50 and Tropp, p. 220 — ref. *Daily Mail*.
17 NUT Annual Report 1923.
18 *Hampshire Advertiser*, Jan. 7, 1922. In March, (Advertiser, April 1) 1200 summonses for non-payment of rates were made in Southampton.
19 *Hampshire Advertiser*, Feb. 11, 1922.
20 *Hampshire Advertiser*, Feb. 18, 1922.
21 NUT Annual Report, 1923.
   Hampshire Advertiser, March 11, 1922. Report of NUT meeting.

22 *Daily Herald*, April 6, 1922.
23 *Daily Herald*, June 9, 1922.
24 *Lowestoft Journal*, Feb. 17, 1923.
25 *Lowestoft Journal*, March 31, 1923.
26 *Lowestoft Journal*, March 31, 1923.
27 *Lowestoft Journal*, March 31, 1923.
28 *Lowestoft Journal*, March 31, 1923.
29 *Lowestoft Journal*, March 31, 1923.
30 *Lowestoft Journal*, March 31, 1923.
31 *Lowestoft Journal*, March 31, 1923.
32 *Lowestoft Journal*, April 21, 1923.
33 *Lowestoft Journal*, April 21, 1923.
34 *Lowestoft Journal*, April 21, 1923.
35 *Lowestoft Journal*, Feb. 24, 1923.
36 *Lowestoft Journal*, April 21, 1923.
37 *Lowestoft Journal*, May 12, 1923.
38 *Lowestoft Journal*, April 21, 1923. Outside the meeting Mrs Godfrey exhorted people to contribute to the relief of the farm labourers' wives and children and a large sum was collected.
39 *Lowestoft Journal*, April 28, 1923.
40 *Lowestoft Journal*, April 28, 1923.
41 *Lowestoft Journal*, May 5, 1923. This was denied by the local NUT officer who threatened Adams with legal action if he repeated the slanders outside the Education Committee.
42 *Lowestoft Journal*, May 5, 1923.
43 *Lowestoft Journal*, May 5, 1923.
44 Cove, *Lowestoft Journal*, May 5, 1925.
45 These strike schools were to be an inspiration to socialist teachers and were described in depth by the Teachers' Labour League in their journal.
46 NUT Annual Report 1924. Salaries Committee.
47 *Schoolmaster*, Jan. 11th, 1924.
48 *Schoolmaster*, March 14, 1924. At an Executive Committee meeting Mander talked of the 'unparalleled example of loyalty, fortitude and devotion to the principles of unionism' and Papineau (Salaries Committee Chairman) of the 'splendid professional enthusiasm of the Lowestoft teachers. They had given an example of real united opposition without suggestion of divisions either of sex or section'. The meeting passed a resolution citing the 'practical example of effective unionism' of the teachers.
49 In the Thirties however, a further cut of 10% was imposed (1931). According to Branson, N. and Weidenfeld M. (1971) *'Britain in the 1930's'* Weidenfeld and Nicolson, teachers' salaries were cut the most severely of all in the public sector and as much as workers in the most depressed industries.

Chapter 8

'A Reasonable Independence'

On 20th February, 1922, C.G. Ammon won Camberwell for Labour in a by-election. This was seen as a considerable blow to the Lloyd George Coalition Government. It followed another major by-election victory for Labour at Manchester three days earlier. In each case, an important factor in the Labour victory was the threat of the Geddes 'axe' on education, and the large turn-out of teachers canvassing for the Labour candidates. Philip Snowden, in conversation with Lloyd George, is quoted as pointing out this support:

> All the schoolmasters and schoolmistresses have been working like blacks for the Labour man.[1]

These by-elections were the start of the unofficial alliance by the teachers with the Labour Party, the party of education. They were also the basis for a revival of interest by the governing parties, especially the Tories, in the social danger the teacher represented. Lloyd George already held this opinion, which Fisher had offered him several years before. Lord Riddell, a newspaper owner, was to express this view in the same exchange with Snowden and Lloyd George — Riddell, resisting the Geddes cuts, said:

> If you cut down the teachers' salaries, the results will be to turn them into Bolsheviks. I look upon adequate payment for teachers as an insurance, as well as an act of justice . . . (He added later): If you don't take care, you will have the next generation educated by disgruntled people who will inculcate ideas prejudicial to the stability of the country.[2]

It is with these two elements of the same contradiction that this chapter is concerned: the move of the teachers to the left and the ways the governing elite tried to stop them. This movement between these two forces is a major

117

feature of the 1920s. It appears in by-election victories, Labour Party statements, purges of individuals and a determined attempt to influence the school curriculum, away from the teacher's own perceived views. The counter attack on the teachers and their Labour movement alliances came at a time when these alliances were not really consummated. Apart from a capable and eloquent minority, the leftward trend among the teachers was a voting trend only, born out of a general natural sympathy and a sharing of ideas that existed between working-class parents, teachers and the Labour Party. The alliance was never officially recognized in NUT membership of the Labour Party or of the Trades Union Congress.

The Conservative Party at all levels started to be concerned at the teachers' move to the Labour Party. Locally and nationally the teachers' action was seen as a major threat to the status quo. In view of the correspondence generated between MPs and the President of the Board of Education and letters of complaint written by the shires, two files were started at the Board. One, entitled *Teachers and the Oath of Allegiance* began in 1922 and the other, *Drift of teachers towards the Labour Party* in 1923[3]; both these files are important indicators to the state of feeling, public and private, of the new connection between teachers and Labour. As the decade moved on, the file not only contained the inquiries or condemnations from the shires but Special Branch reports on radical teachers, and the public speeches made by Lord Eustace Percy, the Board of Education President, on the dangers of socialist teachers. Percy was under considerable pressure to sack Labour Party teachers and he chose instead to try and isolate them from other teachers and parents. In Parliament, the first shot came from Gideon Murray, MP, who asked that:

> in view of the fact that schoolteachers are paid public servants and are pensioned by the State, he will consider the desirability of arranging that they take the oath of allegiance upon appointment.[4]

The idea of the oath of allegiance closely resembles an earlier option discussed at the Board on controlling the conduct of teachers. The Civil Servant option was rejected because it would make clear the links between the State and the teacher. The same argument was to be used by the Board against the oath of allegiance, although there was a consistent pressure, from Murray onwards, from the Conservative MPs and associations for an oath. The involvement of some teachers in the General Strike of 1926 prompted Colonel Vaughan Morgan, MP for Fulham East, to write to Percy, referring to constituents' concern for the youth of the country in these teachers' hands and asking for an oath. Later that year, a Society for the Promotion of Duty and Discipline unsuccessfully tried to promote a Parliamentary bill making it compulsory for state schoolteachers to take an oath of allegiance.

The most interesting correspondence on the issue came between Percy and a persistent supporter of this idea, Colonel Sir Charles Yate. Yate had written to the *Morning Post* in February 1926 and January 1927, suggesting an oath of allegiance for teachers, prompted by the socialist teachers of the Teachers' Labour League. He wrote to Percy in January 1927 and Percy replied with some impatience to the idea — he wrote that it would only create a 'class of insincere Vicars of Bray' continuing:

> But if we are going to try to counteract modern subversive activities by administering Oaths of Allegiance we shall need a very different kind of Oath from anything which has yet been contemplated. The subversive propaganda of the present day is concerned with the class war and with attacks on religion. We all know from everyday experience that the holding or propagation of such opinions is generally regarded as quite compatible with professions of loyalty to the King. An Oath of Allegiance to His Majesty is, therefore, from this point of view quite beside the point.

The sophistication of Percy's response to the 'law and order' section of his own Party was formidable, for he then went on to agree that:

> the fact of compulsion in Education does put a heavy responsibility on the state but what could be worse from your point of view than to encourage a conception that teachers are servants of a Government in the same way as Civil Servants and, therefore, must teach in their schools precisely what any future Labour Government may tell them to teach?

Essentially his view was taken from the experience of teachers in Eton and Harrow — they were not servants but semi-autonomous. Percy continued with the view he was to express in a number of major speeches in 1927 and 1928:

> I still believe that the best safeguard against such irregularities is to give teachers a sense of reasonable independence and not to subordinate them too much either to a Central or to a Local Authority.[5]

This was not a laissez-faire policy. On the contrary, it was a difference with Yate and others about means and ends. Percy had written back to Vaughan Morgan in 1926 that he would deal effectively with any teacher who could be shown to be inculcating views of a 'partisan political character'.[6] It was Percy's view, similar to that of Baldwin in whose Government he served, that the State should not intervene openly and widely in ways that would ultimately endanger its own policies. Rather than an oath of allegiance, he encouraged his own Party activists with the idea that he would act if there was evidence, and spent time, in public speeches, promoting the isolation of the Teachers' Labour League. He also, in ways that might not have been obvious to him considering their poor personal relations, continued Fisher's policy of encouraging a responsible professionalism. This was to be the bulwark against subversive teaching and an oath of allegiance, and taken with a regard for the problems raised by 'structural' controls between the State and the teachers which could be used effectively by a Labour Government. Percy's sophistication of response to the radicalization of teachers was opposed by the backwoods Tories and extreme right-wing bodies yet it was in line with the policies of the Baldwin Administration and, according to Percy, derived from Lord Lugard's view of colonial administration. It was consistent with the decentralization of the education system occurring since Fisher's time yet still with a concern for 'real tactical control' from Whitehall. For Percy, Lugard's view of 'indirect rule' was very 'applicable to teachers'.[7] There was no statutory control over them, it had to be by judiciously applied external pressure. Conservative Members of Parliament and Conservative Associations were given short shrift by Percy; the long correspondence throughout 1927 between Percy and Yate (and involving Samuel at the Treasury and Austen Chamberlain at the Home Office) must have been unsatisfactory to Yate. Percy even rejected a call for a religious and loyalty test for teachers from his own Conservative Party Headquarters, describing the idea of the test as causing 'a great deal more embarrassment than it is worth'.[8]

Giving a loyalty oath to teachers was only one possibility open to the Government. There was another — having an education policy. The Conservative Party seemed unaware of its lack of an education policy for the state schools. Percy remarked, in his memoirs, that the rising tide of concern for 'equality of opportunity' had hardly risen above the level of municipal politics. Neville Chamberlain had said to him in 1924 that Conservative public opinion was in favour of economies in education.[9] Economies in education seemed to be *the* Conservative policy. The *Westminster Gazette* commented in October 1924 that there was the clearest possible connection between the actual Tory education policy and the teachers' lack of zeal for the Tories.[10] It was this apathy that on the same day made the Conservative Party conference pass unanimously a motion demanding new policies to attract schoolteachers to the Party 'on account of the tremendous influence they hold over the rising generation'.[11] It was in this context of an increasingly confident Labour Party attracting large numbers of teachers, and a Conservative Party (as the main governing party) becoming concerned about this process on schools and society, that C.W. Crook sent a letter to the Tory Headquarters, addressed to Colonel Jessel. Crook was an ex-President of the NUT, Conservative Member of Parliament in East Ham North and honorary secretary of the Conservative teachers' advisory committee. He had been the main opponent within the Union of the move to Labour Party affiliation in 1917. His letter argued that the Labour affiliation movement had died down after 1917 but ;

> the action of the Government in imposing a 5% levy for superannuation, in not enforcing the Burnham Scales and in not taking action to prevent the breach of a National agreement in Lowestoft has given the movement a very strong impetus.[12]

He added that although he was an official NUT-sponsored MP, his own constituency now had a 'Teachers' Labour Association' which opposed him and that, nationally, this association would be a strong menace to the Conservative Party at the election just called by Baldwin.

Within days, Colonel Jessel and other members of the Unionist Central Office met with a group of Conservative teachers. Three complaints surfaced in the discussion between them and appear in a memorandum written after the meeting. Firstly, the Board of Education should have *insisted* that Lowestoft Council pay their allocated Burnham Scale; secondly, that Local Education Authorities were making considerable cuts to their staffings, particularly of women teachers and thirdly, that the Burnham Committee was under great pressure from the Board of Education to substantially reduce the salary awards.[13] A deputation to Baldwin was arranged for 20th November, 1923.

Biographers of Baldwin make little or no mention of his attitude to state education at this time; it most probably reflected Chamberlain's view, expressed to Percy. In the President of the Board of Education's papers, preceding the reports of the deputation's meeting with Baldwin, it was suggested that Baldwin wished to dismantle the Burnham Committee, and to place it in 'harness'. The Parliamentary Private Secretary to Baldwin sent a note to the President that he had warned him that:

> the NUT generally and Sir James Yoxall (NUT Gen. Sec.) particularly were very close to joining the Labour party and he remarked that such a move would not suit Sir James Yoxall's game at all.[14]

So Baldwin, in his knowledge of Yoxall and his lack of concern for elementary education saw little threat to either the Conservative Party or the State from teachers moving to the Labour Party. Indeed, after the deputation, his views remained unchanged. During the election campaign, Baldwin made public speeches calling for cuts in teachers' salaries, on the basis that they were fixed in totally different circumstances and should be reviewed.[15] Only later did he change his approach to the teachers.

The deputation consisted of Jessel, Ray (vice-chairman of the LCC Education Committee), Crook, Major Ernest Gray (a Union stalwart and NUT-sponsored Conservative MP from 1895 to 1906 and 1918 to 1922), Sainsbury (a Chelsea Alderman and President of the NUT in 1923) and Benchley, a retired headteacher. Crook argued in the same vein as in his letter to Jessel but added that, in the Union:

> our present Vice President is a strong Labour man; our present ex-President is a strong Labour man and I suppose now we have practically a majority of Labour men on our Executive.[16]

This movement was unthinkable before the war, he added, and was a danger to the teachers and the state.

Sainsbury chided the Government for not allowing the nineteen authorities who were willing to pay above the Burnham scale to do so, but concentrated mainly on the Lowestoft strike. Sainsbury said that most of the striking teachers were Conservatives but as a result of the strike, they had all worked for the Labour Party at the municipal elections and elected five out of eight councillors. It was happening in Devonshire, Hereford, Huntingdon, Lindsay (in Lincolnshire)[17] and in Sheffield:

> every teacher in Sheffield turned away from the Conservative Party and a Conservative teacher was run as a Labour candidate and got returned at the top of the poll.[18]

Sainsbury complained of the letter from the Board of Education to the Burnham committee demanding large reductions in expenditure. In that case, he said, it cannot be a Whitley Committee if the negotiations are preceded by the demands of economy. Returning to Lowestoft again, he said:

> we have Lowestoft teachers going into every district in England, the rural districts included, to preach what the doctrine of Lowestoft means. It means that Lowestoft does not recognise the standard scales and therefore no standard scales may in future be recognised. It means that Lowestoft is departing . . . and therefore everybody can do the same.

Gray mentioned the landslide to Labour and the lack of enforcement by the Board of the scales, yet it intervened to stop payment above the scale. Ray, from the LCC, complained about the Labour Group which constantly found ways to express their sympathy with the teaching profession over the dismissal of married women teachers and the introduction of untrained infant assistants, etc.

Baldwin's response was unimpressive considering the air of desperation that united the deputation and their plea to Baldwin to reassure the teachers in some way, even by producing a Conservative manifesto on Education. He thought that teachers joining a single Party was, for them and the country, 'hopelessly bad'.[19]

According to Brian Simon[20] Baldwin's electoral defeat was the beginning of a new attitude by the Conservative Party towards teachers: teachers were to be taken account of in the politics of education; they had to face up to the loss of the education vote in the country. This point is further confirmed in the Board of Education's files on the teachers in the following correspondence between Wood, the part-time President of the Board in 1923 and Edward Cadogan, who had just lost his Parliamentary seat at Reading. He wrote to Wood, complaining about Baldwin's speech on salary cuts for teachers which he believed lost him the election, and added that a great number of teachers would be against the Conservatives if the economies continued. Wood replied that he was constantly thinking about the danger of teachers going over to the Labour party, but shortage of money left him powerless to act. Cadogan replied the next day that teachers were a special sector:

> They hold very considerable influence among their contemporaries and the influence that they have over the coming generation is incalculable.[21]

So, to 'take account' of the teachers began to take several forms, and not, as is perhaps implied by Simon, a dialogue between the teachers and the Government. For the remainder of the 1920s, there was direct Special Branch reporting on the Teachers Labour League, at home and abroad (in its Teachers' International meetings) from the Home Office to the Board of Education; a constant attempt to divide the radical teachers of the Teachers' Labour League or Labour Party teachers away from other teachers; and the encouragement of local attempts to intimidate teachers not teaching the right things, that is, 'unpatriotic' teaching. Ways of dealing with the radical teachers took effect within a developing framework of de-centralization and 'indirect rule' which we glimpsed in the writings of Percy and Baldwin. They were part of the 'real tactical control' options. These were actions taken not just because the Conservatives were losing teachers' votes to Labour but because of the powerful effect the teachers had on the young. In other words, there was a continuation of the Fisher/Lloyd George approach to the teachers: they were a social danger if not treated carefully. The difference in approach lay not in their agreement about a responsible profession but in the opportunity, denied to Fisher/Lloyd George, to isolate and contain radical teachers. The working-class movement was in retreat from

Servants of the State

1921, and flight from 1926. Professionalism could now be enhanced with an 'autonomy' fostered under 'indirect rule' but the dangerous elements could be isolated. It was the opportunity to express what Simon called the 'assumption that the State machine belonged to conservatism'[22] and the fear of the instability to the State a radicalized teaching force could create.

Membership of the Labour Party was seen as evidence of subversion of the state by some Conservative MPs and Education Committees, aided by a constant stream of vituperation from the *Morning Post* and *Daily Mail*. When Gideon Murray had asked his question on the oath of allegiance in May 1922, he named a teacher who in his opinion was undermining the patriotism of pupils and goodwill towards the British constitution. He complained of:

> ... the conduct of Mr H. Moore, a teacher at Isleworth County School, who ... walks out of the room when the National Anthem is played; will not permit the boys to use capital letters for King, Empire, etc. and asks them whether they are Socialists.[23]

This kind of allegation against teachers became quite common, reported in the *Post* or *Mail* or *Daily Herald*, and could lead to suspensions and inquiries. Although Percy might try to reassure the Tory shire committees and the backbench MPs by talking of a small minority of teachers, they saw Labour Party membership as synonymous with school subversion. His well publicized speech in Leicester that:

> a danger that threatened education was that some people seemed anxious to use the schools not for the purpose of teaching and of inculcating knowledge and the love of knowledge but for the purpose of propaganda[24]

became in the context of the period less a warning to a few (the Communist teachers he was receiving reports on), than an encouragement to the many Conservative councillors, MPs and school governors to check their teachers. Judging from reported comments, Conservative associations were in a near frenzy of rooting out subversive teachers. Letters in the two Board of Education files came from the National Citizens' Union, The British Womens' Patriotic League, The Somerset Womens' Unionist Association and The Imperial Fascisti as well as from several newspaper reports. The impossible had to be achieved: Lady Askwith of the Ladies Imperial Club quoted a *Workers' Weekly* report that teachers could be class conscious by teaching them little known facts not opinions, and declared that 'that must be stopped'.

So far, the alliance between teachers and the Labour movement has been treated as a question of redefining professionalism through the influence of socialist and syndicalist ideas and the clear attachment of many teachers to the Labour Party, seen as the party of education. The exception to this political perspective has been the Burston School strike, which turned a political alliance into an educational programme, a working-class curriculum.[25]

The earlier concern, expressed by W.R. Lawson[26] about the growing secular power of teachers, was realized by the growing examples of teachers acting against the 'militaristic' approach to the curriculum in the war and post-war periods. The concern for future generations and the stability of the State expressed by Conservative Party members was founded on the translation by socialist and pacifist teachers of social ideals to educational practice. Many teachers separated their political and educational work until a change to a Labour Government became possible, others either began a new critical approach in their classrooms or were accused, by their enemies, of doing so. What is so extraordinary about this period is that the people complaining of 'propaganda' or 'sedition' in schools were those who were implicated in their present social conservatism — the local squires, businessmen or vicars!

John Langdon-Davies, in his book *Militarism in Education*[27] argued that, in 1919, schools were becoming Prussianized. He cites evidence of the work of the Navy League (concerned with armaments and the value of imperialism) and the general encouragement of patriotism in schools through Empire Day, lantern lectures and prize essay competitions. He cites one particular case, drawn from a National Council for Civil Liberties report. A teacher in a boys' school in Chester refused to give a Trafalgar Day lesson based on a Navy League pamphlet in 1917. The pamphlet consisted of 'atrocity' stories, bragging about the 'starving' of Germany, and denouncing Lloyd George and other 'Little Navyites'. This pamphlet was presumably distributed by the Local Education Authority because that teacher's refusal to teach from the pamphlet led to her being ordered to resign in order to avoid dismissal. A Conservative MP, C.B. Stanton, asked the Board of Education in 1916 to make sure that schoolteachers who subscribed to 'anti-British' ideas were dismissed. The *Herald* editorialized about this statement, seeing it as part of a general movement, like Langdon-Davies, to militarize children and dismiss teachers throughout the country.[28] Conscientious objectors were dismissed from teaching or not appointed, even when there was a shortage. The Lord Mayor of London was proposing to start a national organization of cadets from the age of nine; in this he was supported by the Director of Education at Leicester (quoted in Langdon-Davies) who encouraged teachers to create a new kind of training, like cadets, based on obedience — 'the first and final element' of discipline. The *Herald*, at that time the main paper of the Left, argued not for a socialist dogmatism in schools but for fair-mindedness, seeing two sides of the question and so on. It is this reasonable approach that would have attracted teachers wishing to break the monopoly of 'militaristic' and 'capitalist' sentiments expressed in their schools.

An observer at the time described the pressure on teachers as affecting them by:

> denying promotion, removal to a new school, forced resignation and removal and other incidents which do not make a dramatic record but are quite effective.[29]

As examples of the latter, he mentions the growing power of the inspectorate and the powers of heads and governors to keep control over the teachers. Certainly many teachers who were opposed to or did not participate in the war were dismissed, and were penalized officially until 1924. Conscientious objectors in London and other places were granted a forced leave without pay, and even if medically unfit were dismissed.[30] Starr was of the opinion that the post-war period saw teachers moving more towards social history and away from jingoistic nationalism. Percy, in his memoirs, describes this as:

> (. . . a flight from reality). War has become an unthinkable horror; the earlier reaction against mere 'drum and trumpet' history, for instance, had been heightened by the nightmare of four years of trench warfare. That obsession will have to be reckoned with by the future social historians and in the 'twenties it operated nowhere more dangerously than on the teaching profession. This was after all the truth about war, not the panache of Agincourt or Ramillies or Salamanca; and the thoughts of children must be deliberately directed away from that horror to the serenities of the League of Nations.[31]

The movement toward a social history which he deplores as childishness (in his memoirs), does not reflect the urgency of the issue addressed to him in the 1920s. The pressure of creating a loyalist and patriotic curriculum was redoubled after the General Strike in 1926. Even Lord Burnham, as President of the Royal Society for St George, led a deputation to Percy on the necessity for systematic training in patriotism.[32] In February 1922, and later in March 1923, a 'Seditious Teachings Bill' was tabled in Parliament by Conservative MPs (including Neville Chamberlain) whose purpose was to 'prevent the teachings of seditious or anarchial doctrines or methods to the young' on pain of a substantial fine or three months imprisonment.[33] Starr mentions internal resolutions within the Conservative Party to make the flying of the Union Jack compulsory in schools.

Yet evidence exists that political and religious selection, very similar to that existing at the turn of the century, continued in schools. They were still controlled by Conservative or Liberal politicians or in Church Schools by local Church of England vicars. These people had no compunction in excluding socialist, pacifist or 'nonconformist' teachers. For instance, at a Conservative Party Conference in 1926, the emphasis on political opinion and not qualification was stressed. A delegate, Mrs Gower of Pontypool, declared that:

> by quiet and private efforts she had secured a position in her district in which 75 per cent of the teachers were Church and Conservative and 80 per cent members of the Junior Imperial League.[34]

Another delegate, Sir Mervyn Peel, was reported as saying he always asked any teaching applicant if he were a socialist, and never voted for a socialist teacher. An item in the *Schoolmaster* included a verbatim report of interview questions for headship of a British school. They included:

> What are you — a Methodist, Baptist or what? Are you a Bolshevik? Would you salute the Union Jack? Would you sing the National Anthem and stand bareheaded when you sing?[35]

And again, in 1925, it reported that the managers of a Church of England school in Derbyshire asked a headship candidate:

> Have you any socialist leanings? I've heard you have. We do not want any socialistic teaching in this school. This is a Tory village and the parents of the children are all Tories and we want them bringing up (sic) in the faith of their fathers.[36]

In Church schools it was still common for the vicar to be the major influence in appointing teachers and expecting that they would act as unpaid church assistants in choir training and organ playing.[37] Only rarely was the contradiction between the claim to a national freedom in education and its actual controllers revealed. For instance, Captain Gee, MP, writing to *The Times*, complained of the move of teachers to the Labour Party and accused Labour authorities of employing only socialist teachers.[38] It was later revealed, Starr records, that in his own constituency his local Conservative Party had sent free tickets to teachers for their pupils to 'A Conservative Victory — Children's Tea and Entertainment'.[39]

Faced in the 1920s with a resurgence of political and economic power by their employers, socialist teachers must have taken a very circumspect line, avoiding public declarations of political allegiance and even denying it outright, or made certain that their classroom work was good and clearly 'fair-minded' in operation. This was vital, as the national press regularly made reference in the period to teachers who were in the Labour Party and to complaints made against them about their teaching. In some papers, like the *Morning Post* or *Daily Mail*, it was often sufficient for a mention of a teacher's actions, such as speaking on a Labour platform, for an editorial comment to fume at the Bolshevization of education.[40] So, references to obscure council or by-election victories, made by teachers in the Labour Party, were not accidental but part of a major drive to divorce them from working-class parents. For instance, a Richmond headteacher speaking publicly in support of a local Labour candidate, had a Council meeting discussing his work and searching for evidence of indoctrination during school hours; no evidence was found, it was later mentioned, but the *interrogation* was made.[41] The *Daily News* mentions, as in passing, that a local headteacher, Shepherd, won Darlington for the Labour Party. *The Times* was probably the most detailed in its reports of Labour teachers, especially in fully reporting the meetings of the Teachers' Labour League and identifying clearly its speakers and place of origin, and always following these reports, days later, by noting Conservative protest meetings about the Teachers' Labour League. It gave several columns to Percy's speeches on the dangers of socialist teachers and the virtues of the rest and encouraged the creation of a Conservative Teachers' Group.

The dangers of being active trade unionists and Labour Party workers or voters must have been very clear to teachers in the 1920s. The newspapers clearly detailed the difficulties they would face if most of the local employing authorities were in a position to act as they would wish on this type of teacher.

When Charles Trevelyan, the ex-President of the Board of Education for Labour asked the Board in 1926 to define and explain the rules on the political activity of teachers, the memorandum produced in the Board to aid Percy's reply said initially that teachers had the same constitutional freedoms as other citizens. A paragraph added to the Departmental memo, however, takes a different view:

> ... There can be little doubt that notice given by the employers ... to the teacher on the ground that these activities were detrimental to the proper discharge of his duties would be held, in the absence of mala fides, to be good.[42]

This view prevailed in advice offered by the Board in the next decade.[43] In effect this was an attempt to apply Civil Service conditions of employment to teachers without the necessity of directly employing them. It allowed a new post-1926 political straitjacket to be applied to teachers. The civil servants had legislative action taken to enforce this neutralization of their class alliances in the 1927 Trade Union Act[44] but the teachers had, instead, a legal opinion added to the considerable social and economic power already wielded by their employers in a period of teacher unemployment.[45]

Dan Griffiths, a conscientious objector in the war, and later a candidate for the NUT Executive, was a Labour Party parliamentary candidate in Stroud. In 1921, a 'deputation of women' laid a complaint against the Education Committee in Llanelly. At the time he was a teacher in New Dock School and was a part-time tutor for the Plebs League, writing for the journal *Plebs* ('Revolution — How?', May 1919) and working as a day school tutor, (*Plebs* May 1924). He was accused of bringing *The Communist* and the *Daily Herald* into school, of discontinuing morning prayers and breaking some other school rules.[46] A special Education Committee was called a month later to receive the deputation, which was asked to produce charges in writing. Griffiths attended with the NUT solicitor. The charge failed as the deputation would not write down their allegations. A local councillor, obviously sympathetic to Griffiths, said there was nothing to prevent other teachers from taking in the *Daily Mail* to school! The Conservative MP, Major Boyd Carpenter, repeated the parents' charges and had to make a public apology.

Other attempts to dismiss teachers for their Labour Party membership were not so easily dismissed.[47] Miss Spurrell, a certificated teacher and Labour Party candidate for Totnes, was viciously attacked in a letter in the *Kingsbridge Gazette*, a local paper standing, as it often reminded its readers, for 'God, King and Country'. Spurrell was accused of teaching atheism, revolution and communism. An appeal was made for parents to write to the local MP to complain. The letter described the other local teachers as being in one of the 'finest professions', the irony of which would not have been lost on Devon teachers on less than the provisional minimum scale. Spurrell contacted the NUT solicitor, who wrote to the letter writer and the publisher asking them to withdraw. A writ for libel was issued.

Spurrell was described in court as a teacher for 21 years and a Wesleyan Methodist School Superintendent. Two headteachers of the school in which she had previously worked for 13 years gave evidence that she was a Christian and a good teacher. From her testimony, it is clear that Spurrell was a radical, Christian Socialist, working for a fundamental change in society through the Labour Party. She was not a communist yet her accusers made great play of her faith in the Red Flag and her singing of the Internationale. One of her election addresses included the paragraph:

> We are out to make rebels; we are a revolutionary party, do not forget it. We are out for revolution.[48]

It was obvious this revolution was as much a spiritual as a material revolution for her; she emphasized 'class love' not class war.

The main point of the defendant's submission was that it was impossible to hold these beliefs (that is, in revolution) and membership of the Labour Party without affecting the children — their QC put this position expressly to the jury:

> When a lady in public service, paid out of public rates came forward at an election, was heard by others to express opinions which were anathema and detestable to them, they were entitled to take objection to such opinions. In the case of a schoolteacher who put herself forward as vitally interested in the reform of civilization and admitted being a revolutionary, how could it be that she should keep herself free from politics in her teaching of children under her charge.[49]

And there was a further point. Labour Party membership in itself was evidence that indoctrination was taking place, which a ratepayer had every right to wish to discontinue by forcing the teacher's dismissal.

The Lord Chief Justice, extremely annoyed at the unwillingness of the defendants to appear in the witness box, was clearly impressed by the divorce of the political from the educational in that Spurrell had campaigned widely on a socialist platform, yet she had taken part in every Empire Day celebration, according to her headteacher. She was a devout Christian and an efficient teacher to examination level.[50] High damages and costs were awarded to her against the publisher and the correspondent of the *Kingsbridge Gazette*.

Spurrell's case illustrates how open to attack and even dismissal the Labour teachers were in the towns and in the country. They were seen as a threat to entrenched interests and more, as usurping a right to teach children values — once Conservative, now Socialist. Yet these teachers had to be most circumspect in their private and public behaviour and in their classroom teaching. They were, in one sense, marked individuals.[51] Spurrell's case proved that without evidence of classroom misdemeanour it should have been hard to dismiss teachers. This jars however with the legal advice offered by the Board a year later, to Trevelyan, which suggests that political prominence alone was a sufficient ground for teacher dismissal. The 1926 strike heralded a further reaction which allowed communist teachers, if not Labour Party teachers, to be sacked purely on the grounds that they were communist.

While the legal situation may not have been clear, the results of the dismissal cases in the remainder of the 1920s must have been very clear to teachers. There was a very good chance that in some areas, attempts were to be made to dismiss teachers if they were Labour supporters or candidates,

'A Reasonable Independence'

and in other areas, after 1926, if they were communists they were unlikely to be appointed or to keep their job.

After 1926, several teachers were sacked and their teaching certificate withdrawn. The General Strike over, many workers were not re-employed and in its aftermath, teachers who helped the local Strike Committees were victimized.

In Blackburn, on May 13th, Norah Brown addressed a crowd of 400–500 people on the subject of the TUC betrayal of the miners. She was fined under the Emergency Regulations as likely to 'cause disaffection amongst the civilian population'.[52] Her husband, the secretary of the local Communist party and a schoolteacher, was dismissed on the day the summons was served on his wife. Her prosecutor was a Governor of his school, Blackburn Grammar. The headmaster learnt that he was a Communist from a parent, and warned Brown that he had no right, as a teacher, to 'political opinions' and that he should not have sat on a public platform with Philip Snowden (later the Labour Chancellor of the Exchequer). He was also told that his probationary year completed, he would be dismissed through reasons other than for being a Communist.[53] A local parent, Hargreaves, wrote a letter, headed 'The Blackburn Communist' to the *Blackburn Times* asking if a teacher had been found guilty of 'teaching Communism' and had been banned from his School Debating Society because of 'communist activity'. He suggested that school governors should not concern themselves solely with qualifications but with 'character'. A correspondence between Brown and Hargreaves followed; Hargreaves was supported by a letter (Bolshevism in Schools) from the secretary of the Primrose League (a right-wing Conservative organization) describing the penetration of elementary schools by Moscow.[54] Parents were encouraged to find out the active communist teachers. As Brown makes clear, the issue at stake was simple; he was dismissed not for his teaching skill (described by the Head as good) nor for acting illegally but simply for *being* a Communist.

Marjorie Pollitt, (wife of Harry Pollitt, later General Secretary of the Communist Party) was a schoolteacher and Communist. She taught a class of fifty 12-year-old girls at St Johns Road Elementary School in Hoxton.[55] During the General Strike she was convicted under The Emergency Powers Act for publishing false information in the Communist *Workers Bulletin*. Her name had been used as nominal editor. Both the District School Inspector and her Headmistress supported her continuing right to teach and declared that she had never introduced her political views into her school work. Yet despite the support of Labour councillors, the London County Council dismissed her.[56]

The causes of Margaret Clarke and John Towers were causes célèbres for the teachers on the left in the Union. In both cases their prosecution and dismissal were connected to their active support of the working class — in the General Strike. For Clarke, Union support was not as readily forthcoming as for Towers. Their cases illustrate the way in which the movement of some teachers to the left, particularly the Teachers' Labour League, placed them in a perilous position in the late 1920s as the earlier mass movement of teachers (the 'forward' industrial policy) had shrunk with the counter-reaction of the employers, and the later divisions in the Labour movement itself. The broad alliance for educational progress in the Union appears to recede in the 1920s, leaving a left rump exhorting the remainder of the Union to take actions on educational cuts which it was unwilling to do. At the same time, a move against Communists, particularly Communist teachers, by the Labour Party reduced the support available to these teachers when they were prosecuted by employers or Conservative Party activists.

Margaret Clarke was a Birmingham secondary school teacher who was prosecuted and fined under the Emergency Powers Act for typing material used in the local Strike Bulletin, the *Birmingham Worker*. She was then suspended by the chairman of the Technical Schools Committee and on July 5th 1926, received a letter from the Board of Education requesting the return of her teaching certificate. The issues at stake were the same as in earlier cases of teacher victimization; it was an infringement of their political liberties as citizens expressed outside the school, and it was another example of victimization of socialist teachers (not those from any other political group). The latter was forcefully illustrated by the fact that her replacement at the school was a prominent worker for the Conservative Party and a member of the Executive of the Birmingham Fascisti. The NUT encouraged Miss Clarke to apologize to regain her post and teacher's licence. The form of the apology was one in which Clarke was, in effect, apologizing for her political opinions and actions. It was most unlikely that Clarke would accept this form of apology; she was closely involved with the Teachers' Labour League, as a delegate to the Education Workers' International in Vienna that August, and in January 1927, was elected to its National Executive. After assurances from the Union, Miss Clarke did eventually apologize, got her certificate back and in April 1928, was given a post in an elementary school by Birmingham Education Committee. However between November 1927 and April 1928, she did not receive sustentation from the Union, which had received several appeals from her local Association and from many other local Associations in the country, helped by a special committee on her case organized by the Teachers' Labour League. The Union Executive even ignored the Tenure Committee recommendation that sustentation be granted. So, the Clarke case was a symbol for the socialist teachers of the backward policies of the Union Executive and in turn, must have been seen by Mander and the Executive as a personal fight to control elements in the Union who, in their opinion, were bringing it into disrepute. It was not what Clarke initially did that was the problem for the Executive but her stand and the support it gained within the Union. Again, for Clarke, and other socialist teachers, the issue was one of Union support for an action which was legitimate and involved a double punishment — a fine and the loss of employment.

John Towers was headmaster of Hedley Hill School in Durham and had volunteered to take charge of a canteen supplying food to the children of locked-out miners in 1926. Two children, whose father had returned to work, continued to eat in the canteen and Towers caned them for their disobedience. He was fined for assaulting them as the use of corporal punishment out of school was inadmissible. His teaching certificate was also withdrawn. After accepting a union-drafted apology, Towers was eventually reinstated though as an assistant teacher, with the Union paying the salary difference.[59]

These cases were only the most visible aspects of a process of controlling teachers by sacking key activists — a process made easier after 1926 by Labour and Communist divisions. The Board of Education might not have started prosecutions — as an indirect employer it could not — but it had a conscious policy of radical teacher surveillance and was in correspondence with 'grassroot' Tory organizations about individual cases or the general problem of the subversive teacher. The tone of the correspondence was one of dismay that some teachers were unpatriotic and of a rising feeling of impotence that the 'normal' channels of control, their school governors and local councillors, were sometimes unable to eliminate these teachers. At the Board there was, as expressed in Percy's notes and speeches, a further concern for the stability of the State when the Conservatives lost control over the younger generations to their Labour teachers. At the same time, it was Percy's policy, reflecting a Baldwinian political approach, that direct action was inadvisable on these teachers. Instead, some radicals were to be removed, if at all possible, their organization (the Teachers' Labour League) was to be attacked (especially after its break with the Labour Party) and the remainder of the teachers were to be praised in their professional commonsense. This latter appeal to their professionalism was significantly 'weaker' than Fisher's own appeals; the climate of uprising and militancy had gone and it was not now necessary to talk of a 'self governing profession' in the same way that the idea had been mooted in 1919. Instead, Percy generated a tactical control over the education system that was based on a lifting of further restrictions on teachers and their training and an appeal to their professionalism and love of teaching; divisions in education became a question of extremist socialist teachers, not of extremist Conservative school governors. Talk of autonomy did not mean ceasing to control from the centre but choosing instead to directly control, or indirectly control when the issue was important, and creating a general climate of opinion about what was and what was not reasonable in education and in teaching.

This policy of Percy's was created in counterpoint to the rising demands of the Teachers' Labour League, always well reported in *The Times*. In many respects the policy of the League on teachers' unity and a new curriculum had a wide currency amongst teachers although expressed in terms increasingly out of joint with them. The concern which Percy expressed publicly about school propaganda was directed at a school curriculum, influenced by pacifism and social issues which, while not directly socialist, was supported by socialist and other teachers — in itself, a difficult subject to control centrally and yet one which he described as expressing a 'revolutionary frame of mind' seen as a 'positive principle of education'. More than just the League, this creation of, for him, a divided education system on class lines, was to be seen in the Labour Party. In his memoirs, Percy mentions the 1926 resolution on Education passed at the Labour Party conference as an example of the revolutionary tendency in education.[60]

The resolution had six parts. It argued for a scheme of self-government in education, similar to workers' control of industry; a proletarian curriculum; civil rights for teachers, and for secondary expansion. It was overwhelmingly passed by the conference.[61] It is no wonder then that in his reply to Sir Charles Yate in January, 1927, he argued that making teachers servants of the State would make them available to a future Labour Government who could tell them what to teach; he argued for a 'reasonable independence', not subordination. It is this point which John White has tried to illustrate[62] in an essay which explores the possible motivation Percy had to remove curricula regulations from the 1926 code. One of his hypotheses was that it forestalled a Labour government operating with centralized powers, which is confirmed by his letter to Yates, and that this was unlikely to be repeated by Labour as it would be unpopular with teachers (to reassert central control), which the other elements in this study confirm. So, Percy managed to forestall a centralized socialist curriculum (or at least, the possibility of one) and to earn some respect for a Tory education policy with teachers, and, at the same time, retain a tactical or indirect control over schools by use of His Majesty's Inspectors (HMIs), education reports (like Hadow) and by secondary regulations.

This significant move on the 1926 Code seemed to solve many of the pressing problems with the socialist teachers and of a Conservative appeal to teachers, and left Percy free to continue his policy of isolating the Teachers' Labour League and their ideas of a socialist curriculum.[63]

Notes

1 Simon, 1974 *'Politics of Educational Reform 1920–1940'* p. 46/47 from 'Lord Riddell's Intimate Diary of the Peace Conference and After' 1933.
Schoolmaster, Nov. 3, 1922 Editorial. Following election of a Union official, Chuter Ede in by-election at Mitcham as a Labour Party MP and on an education platform, the editorial talks of the teachers' line of work spoiled, profiteers robbing schools and threatens Liberals and Conservatives with a Labour drift if present policies continued.
2 Simon, as above.
3 PRO ED/24 1753 and PRO/ED 24 1757 Public Records Office.
4 PRO ED/24 1753 Hansard, 22 May, 1922.
5 PRO ED/24 1757 HN, 06250
6 PRO ED/24 1753 28th May, 1926.
7 Percy, Eustace (1958) *'Some Memories'*, Eyre & Spottiswoode, London, pp. 121–123.
8 PRO ED/24 1753.
9 Percy op.cit. p. 95.
10 *Westminster Gazette*, 4 Oct. 1924.
11 *Morning Post*, Oct. 4, 1924.
12 PRO/ED/24 1757. Letter 17 Nov. 1923.
13 PRO ED/24 1757 Memo.
14 PRO ED/24 1757 Memo.
15 PRO ED/24 1757 Letter from Woods (Pres. Board of Educ.) to Cadogan.
16 PRO ED/24 1757 Memo 20th Nov. 1923.
17 All places of current Union dispute.
18 PRO ED/24 1757. Sheffield had tried to sack several headteachers on efficiency grounds, which a High Court case overruled. Percy, in his memoirs said that Labour won control of Sheffield in 1926 and the leader of the Council said he could guarantee to hold it for Labour on the educational issue alone, p. 96.
19 This view was consistent with a view he expressed two months earlier at Philip Stott College, to trainee teachers. He argued that the 'teacher should never be the servant of the State in this way, that he preaches and teaches what he thinks the Government would like to have him do' (Earl Baldwin 1938 Ed.) *On England*, Penguin pp. 154. It was not the 'victory of party' (p. 166) but a concern for truth and unfolding the child's personality which was the teachers' task. This latter comment, made in an essay 'Teachers and Taught', written in November 1924, is a by the way reply to the move of teachers to the left and a statement of educational principle and values which the Conservative teacher deputation required. Baldwin, it made clear, was on the side of educational progress (including pay) and for the teachers of the new democracy. Although this contrasts with his actions up to that date, it is a sign of Conservative awareness of the problem of the teacher and a justification of the way Percy was dealing with them.
20 Simon, (74), p. 74.
21 PRO ED/24 1757. Dec. 12–14 1923.
22 Simon, (74), p. 73.
23 *Daily Herald*, May 23, 1922.
24 *Yorkshire Post*, Feb. 13, 1925.
25 B. Edwards (74) *'Burston School Strike'* Lawrence & Wishart — referenced throughout to curriculum content and approach.

26 Lawson, W.R. op.cit.
27 1919, Headley Bros. London.
28 *Herald*, Jan. 27, 1917. The article mentions a Govan teacher dismissed for refusing to collect from his scholars for the War Savings Committee, and a Portsmouth teacher fired by her local Education Committee for having 'seditious literature' in her possession.
29 Starr, Mark (1929). '*Lies & Hate in Education*', Hogarth Press, London.
30 Morgan Jones, MP, a leading spokesman for the Labour party in the Twenties, was himself a conscientious objector, sent to prison, deprived of his teaching certificate and not reinstated.
31 Percy, p. 106.
32 Starr, p. 20.
33 Simon, (74), p. 73. Starr felt this Bill was mainly directed at Socialist Sunday Schools.
34 The *Schoolmaster*, Oct. 8, 1926.
35 The *Schoolmaster*, Dec. 26, 1924.
36 Reported in Starr, p. 20.
37 See Chapter 3.
38 *The Times*, 8 Dec. 1924 'Politics in Schools'.
39 Starr, p. 86.
40 *Daily Mail*, May 5, 1925.
41 *Daily Herald*, Dec. 10 and Dec. 22, 1924.
42 PRO ED/24 1761 Political Activities of Teachers 1926–1934.
43 PRO ED/24 1761. Letter from President of Board to W. Wellock MP — if the activities were 'prominent' then they may be inconsistent with being a teacher.
44 W.J. Brown, 'Civil Service Trade Unionism' in Cole, G.D.H. (Ed.) (1939) '*British Trade Unionism Today*', Victor Gollancz.
45 This claim to action by the Board on socialist teachers also applied to their work outside schools, for instance in Socialist Sunday Schools. If there was evidence that a teacher was 'teaching children out of school what he was not permitted to teach them in school' they would try to get him dismissed. PRO ED/24 1757. Corr. 23 Feb. 1934.
46 *Llanelly & County Guardian*, Nov. 3, 1921. Starr, op.cit. p. 88.
47 *Stratford Express*, June 4, 1923. Parent complained that children in a local school did not celebrate Empire Day because headteacher was a socialist. Inquiry held. *Newcastle Weekly Chornicle* June 2, 1923. Parent complains that teachers were absent from Empire Day celebrations. Mayor of Newcastle inquiry reveals only one or two teachers left to organize Empire Day.
48 *Kingsbridge Gazette* June 12, 1925. Also reported in *Western Weekly News*, June 13th 1925 and Starr, p. 90. NUT Pamphlet (1927) (No. 55). '*Accusation of Teaching of Communism and Atheism*' and *Schoolmaster*, 19th June, 1925.
49 *Kingsbridge Gazette*, June 12, 1925.
50 No issue was taken with her admission (echoing the advice of the *Workers Weekly*) that she had taught her children about child welfare and the physical deterioration of Devon schoolchildren.
51 Starr, p. 90. After the 1926 strike, the Ratepayers' Association asked the Education Committee to sack Spurrell because of a speech where she was reported to have said 'Thank God for the strike'. In November, 1926 another attempt was made because of her reference to 'The cant and hypocrisy of Armistic Day'. Anonymous letters were repeatedly sent to the Press as well.
52 *Blackburn Times*, May 29, 1926. 'Schoolteacher's wife distributes mischievous literature'.

53 *New Leader*, 23 July, 1926.
54 *Blackburn Times*, July 17, 1929.
55 Mahon, John (1976) '*Harry Pollitt — a biography*', Lawrence and Wishart, p. 121. She had been married to Pollitt for a year and been a Communist for about the same period. She met him in St. Malo with two friends of hers from the West Ham Socialist Sunday School; at that time she was in the Independent Labour Party.
56 Starr, p. 92.
 The Times, May 1/May 10, 1927.
57 Starr, p. 92.
58 *Educational Worker*, Vol. 1, No. 11 Sept 27. i.e. 'Those abnormal conditions have long since passed away and are not likely to occur . . . I will not knowingly take any steps in future which would expose me to proceedings of a similar kind'.
59 Starr, p. 93.
 Barker, p. 151.
60 Percy, '*Memories*' p. 103.
61 Labour Party Annual Report — 1926 Conference.
62 John White 'The End of the Compulsory Curriculum' in '*The Curriculum — The Doris Lee Lectures*', University of London, Institute of Education 1975.
63 Further discussion of the Teachers' Labour League can be found in Lawn, M.A. 'Deeply Tainted with Socialism: the activities of the Teachers' Labour League in England and Wales in the 1920s' in *The Australian and New Zealand History of Education Review*, Autumn 1985.

Chapter 9

Engendered Professionalism

The difficulty of trying to control the conditions and direction of work in elementary schools was always exacerbated by the fact that the employers saw two kinds of teacher available for employment in them. There was no difference in the labour power of these teachers nor necessarily in their qualification, the difference lay in their sex. The employer always paid a lower fixed sum or salary to the woman than the man. The employer was also capable of inventing new groups of 'teachers' who could be used in an emergency, a situation defined at the whim of the employer, such as Article '68ers or'guinea girls'. Only the certificated teachers were really organized and not until 1919 did the union change its policy and begin to admit the non-certificated. In 1919 the conference which endorsed a policy of radical self-government for teachers and a strong policy on action for better pay was also a conference described as being full of active women teachers. The very conference where the high point of union confidence coincided with a fuller participation by women teachers, the adoption of a syndicalist or industrial union policy and the start of an equal pay referendum (which was successfully accepted) also saw the formation of a separatist men teachers' association. In the twenty years since 1900, men had apparently begun to move from a position of outright dominance within a 'craft' union to establishing their own 'craft' union when industrial union policies, strongly supported by women teachers, were adopted.

In the main, the arguments drawn from socialist ideas were to be used against the men secessionists, but against women secessionists there was apparent silence. Women teachers seceded over the lack of enthusiasm in the Union for pushing on for equal pay, within the Burnham Committee and in LEAs.

Although women were the majority of teachers, as high as three-quarters or four-fifths of the elementary workforce by 1914, very few were organized in the Union in 1900. Of course, only certificated teachers were

139

eligible and a large number of women teachers were uncertificated or supplementary,[1] yet within the certificated only a third of women teachers eligible were Union members in 1895.[2] The presence of women in the Union began to be felt after 1904 and this was a reflection of the rise of the women's movement organized around votes for a proportion of women and equal pay. The two parts of the programme were of equal concern to women teachers and they were involved in organizations which concentrated on one or the other, the Equal Pay League or the Women Teachers' Franchise Union. For a number of women teachers, the source of their energy and organization among other women teachers came from their involvement in the Pankhurst's suffragette organization, the Women's Social and Political Union, founded in 1903.

Before we explore the rise of the women's movement among teachers we should mention one group that took a different course, preceding in some ways the actions of the Union militants in the Rhondda. A small National Union of Uncertificated Teachers (later, the National Union of Schoolteachers) had been formed in 1913 by a Miss Walsh, who organized it from Manchester. The National Union of Schoolteachers was extremely bitter at the attitudes towards the uncertificated and supplementary teachers prevailing in the NUT. The injustices placed upon these teachers, who were the victims of family poverty and unable to support themselves in training or had qualifications not recognized as full certificates fuelled the NUST. Its supporters saw themselves working in a sweated industry where other teachers got better renumeration, smaller classes, and pensions. The cry of 'equal pay for equal work' was welcomed by their allies in the Trades and Labour Councils and in the Trades Union Congress.[3] The arguments that Miss Walsh offered to the TUC were based on qualification and experience, not on divisions by sex; in other words, she argued for parity not because the NUST and its women members deserved equal pay because they were women but because they were doubly exploited by their employers.

There was a separate and growing movement among women teachers associated with the Women's Social and Political Union. The fight for equal pay was part of the fight for their political emancipation. It was not based on arguments of industrial exploitation or sweated labour but was part of their recognition as full citizens with economic, political and social rights. Within the NUT, they demanded their due — they were paid less for the same work as men. Initially they may have been influenced, like the early organizers of the Women's Social and Political Union, by the aims of the Independent Labour Party, which included women's suffrage as part of a full adult suffrage, but gradually, within and without the Union, the movement took on a political and tactical direction that was not linked to political parties or class arguments but based on sexual divisions in teaching.

Several of the early group that created the Women's Social and Political Union were Independent Labour Party teachers. For instance, two of the leading organizers of the Women's Social and Political Union between 1903 to 1910 were Teresa Billington[4] and Mary Gawthorpe,[5] both ex-elementary school teachers. (Although these two teachers were from working-class backgrounds, Beatrice Webb has argued that it was middle-class women newly entered into teaching who were the agents of the new women's movement in teaching.[6] Class arguments, as Sylvia Pankhurst argued, did not prevail long in the Women's Social and Political Union except in the sense she describes Christabel, as an 'incipient Tory'.) The first secretary of the National Federation of Women Teachers, Miss E. Froud (the NFWT was the successor to the Equal Pay League) was a member of the Women's Social and Political Union and had been selected for the post on the basis of her organizing ability in the Women's Social and Political Union.[7]

The Equal Pay League had been formed in 1904 by Mr J. Tate, who, in turn, had been converted by a London teacher, Miss E. Lane who had fought for equal benefits for male and female teachers from the Benevolent Fund. The League encouraged increased representation of women teachers at the Union Conferences and on the Union Executive, as well as equal pay. In 1904, it had 73 members, of which 5 were men; the latter dropped out when it became the National Federation of Women Teachers in 1906. One of the arguments for a separate organization was that women had to 'stand on their own feet' in a period when they were beginning to take their place as paid workers. A separate organization, it was felt, would help them 'to know what they wanted and how to get it through their own efforts'.[8] Within the NUT Conferences, resolutions for equal pay caused uproar[9] and in the London Teachers' Association (in 1907 and subsequent years) the attempt was stopped after 'whistles were blown, feet stamped, comic songs were sung by an organized opposition . . .'[10] A member of the NUT Executive, Allen Croft, speaking to a resolution on women's suffrage, was faced with a 'furious and sustained uproar'.[11] From 1908, the NFWT concentrated on trying to get the Union to declare itself in favour of women's suffrage and placed equal pay in abeyance. Getting a Conference resolution on the agenda was made extremely difficult by the tactics of local Associations, which included allowing delegates to vote regardless of the decisions of their Association. The Union Conference (1914) resolved that women's suffrage was outside the NUT's purview — this was an odd decision considering that teacher-sponsored MPs were sitting in Parliament. In accordance with its early principles, the NFWT tried to get women members of the Executive increased in number. To some extent this was a success, but they decided in 1916 not to persist due to two factors. The first, interestingly, was the 'apathy on the part of a very large number of NUT women'.[12] The other reason was the control of election machinery by men — they created fraudulent voter's lists or tampered with the voting papers, etc. Apart from the contacts with the Women's Social and Political Union and the cultural milieu which the NFWT shared with it, there are other clues to the NFWT membership. One area which had a strong influence on the organization in London and the national leadership of the NFWT was West Ham. The women teachers in West Ham had formed their own Association, within the NUT, in 1912, after the debate at the 1911 NUT Conference at Aberystwyth where Allen Croft was shouted down.[13] In the following year they joined the Federation. Other strong Associations which had been capable of influencing local authority negotiations on pay and producing an equal minimum for men and women teachers were Swansea, East Ham, Wood Green, Leyton and York.[14]

The National Federation of Women Teachers began to secede from the NUT, tired by continuous battles and of the 'apathy' of the women teachers. In 1915 it had rented offices, then employed a paid organizer and by 1917 was holding its own Conference at a different time of year to the NUT. After furious debate, its original object 'to recruit women teachers to join the NUT' was deleted and by 1921, it forbade its Central Council members to hold joint membership with the NUT. The Federation was against any kind of compromise over equal pay and opportunities with the men teachers in the NUT, and by compromise it meant any delay whatsoever. It was argued that unity was not possible between:

> those who believe that payment should depend on sex and those who believe that it should be based on the value of the work done (and those who think) ... that it is derogatory for a man to serve under a headmistress but not derogatory for a woman to serve under a headmaster.[15]

In a publication called 'Why I left the NUT', women Federation members wrote about their reasons, which were mainly a lack of belief in the Union's policy on equal pay and its attempt to achieve it, and a freedom to pursue pressure on local authorities without NUT interference.

The NUT in 1918 and 1919 was deeply altered by the influence of the women delegates to the annual Conferences and the severance policy of the Federation seemed in retrospect inopportune. Miss E.R. Conway, the NUT President in 1918, spoke on the problems of women teachers and chaired a debate on equal pay.[16] She made the point that equal pay should wait on schemes for State endowment of motherhood and taxation relief for children. A referendum was agreed on the principle of 'equal pay for men and women of the same professional status' by a margin of over 2:1. It is

Engendered Professionalism

possible that influential opponents of equal pay, like C.W. Crooks, felt that a compromise which was radical in theory but inactive in practice might keep the NUT from splitting; in fact it satisfied neither the conservative male teacher nor the feminist teacher, as both groups left. Again, in 1919, Goldstone in the *TES* remarked upon the number of women delegates at the Cheltenham Conference, and their activity[17], and perhaps pointed out the area of mistrust between the NFWT members and the Union Executive. He suggested that after the equal pay referendum, Union pay scales would have to be re-formulated but:

> The Executive is spared the difficult duty which some delegates would have thrust upon it, of not only propounding a new scale but also of presenting it to local education authorities in the form of an ultimatum.[18]

From the point of view of the National Federation of Women Teachers, the men and women of the NUT betrayed women teachers by not using their power to achieve equal pay and so allowed local authorities to employ women teachers cheaply. The irony is that although the men teachers of the secessionist NAS directly opposed equal pay, and perhaps many men in the NUT may not have directly supported it, it was the majority of teachers in the NUT, women teachers, who could not be drawn into active political support for equal pay. In the 1920s, the NUT was more directly concerned with protecting the Burnham agreement and the salary scales of its members. Without the direct pressure from within the union, as a single, strong, issue, equal pay took a backseat. The teachers of the NFWT were articulate and organized.[19] They were used to campaigning, through the activity of many of them in the suffragette movement. They were of a different class and generation from many other women in the NUT: they were the products of the new secondary schools, deliberately recruited after 1904 by employers keen to raise the social level of entry into teaching. They were independent at a time when the older, conservative, male argument about a family wage was rising again in the NUT with the economic difficulties of the 1920s. It was the *principle* they were fighting for and it built up their cohesion and identity as a group; even before 1921 they could argue that their organized pressure on some LEAs had gained them equal minima on the pay scales and sometimes equal increments — in Wood Green, Tottenham, East Ham, Leyton, Acton, Swansea and York.

'Equal pay' meant, to the NFWT, equal pay between men and women with the same qualifications, and not, as with the NUST, equal pay for equal work, regardless of qualifications. Equal pay they saw as related to qualification, and so a discussion about the value of the Swansea settlement where men and women college-trained certificated teachers were paid one sum, and non-collegiate teachers less, and uncertificated teachers half as much, was regarded as fairly satisfactory to the NFWT. For them, the Burnham Award was a retrograde step in the London areas mentioned because it increased the differentials between men and women and removed the equal minima. It was this, and not the fact that in urban areas it often reduced overall salary gains for teachers, that the Federation regarded as an 'outstanding evil'.[20]

The Burnham reaction was part of a number of defeats in which the gains made by women were being pushed back.[21] The Federation called a number of large demonstrations in London on the issue of equal pay in the early Twenties, and against the Geddes proposals (in 1921).

The main enemy of the Federation was the NUT. Evidence of its perfidy was culled from the *Schoolmaster* or Conference reports. It was not just a question of recruitment, though the NUT was a rival, but the fact that 'men teachers had vested interests in the maintenance of existing inequality of conditions',[22] and women teachers needed to rely upon themselves and organize.

It was not just equal pay that was the issue, there was also the question of a marriage bar from women.[23] This had been a problem since 1900; some LEAs had imposed marriage bars on women teachers but only on teachers new to work, not on teachers who were already married;[24] others banned all married women.[25] The movement developed with the shortage of pupil-teachers (from 1908) and before recruitment from secondary schools and colleges was really underway. The grounds for the bar were probably a form of economy; it was cheaper to employ a young teacher who was energetic if not experienced, than the older teacher. This would apply in areas that had salary scales; the pressure in the rural areas was not as acute as they did not generally have scales. Yet the bar could not have operated if the social climate of the period, influenced strongly by male assumptions of the nature of families and family support, did not unite some of the male teachers with the employers. Discrimination against the married woman teacher increased divisions among teachers. A marriage bar had also operated in the Civil Service for some time. Before 1896, it had been customary to resign on marriage, but after that date it was made a universal rule.[26] It was the Civil Service that was mentioned in discussions of a marriage ban. Beatrice Webb talked of an 'Association of London Married Women Teachers', formed in 1909 to defend their interests against serious attacks. The London School Board and the London County Council always employed and protected married teachers (due, probably, to the influence of the teachers' associations and shortage of staff) except for a period in the late 1920s and early 1930s but voluntary schools in London often tried to dismiss these teachers, and in one case, there was a large demonstration organized by the London Teachers' Association.[27]

The war changed this situation. The married women ex-teachers were treated as a reserve army of labour, drafted in to replace the conscripted men.[28] With the political reaction of 1921, local authorities again imposed bans and dismissed teachers who were about to be or were, married. Again this was generally an urban policy; rural areas had difficulties enough retaining staff on lower scales; bans were recorded in Nottingham, Lincoln, Leeds, Rotherham, Sheffield and Smethwick.[29] The official record of the work of Smethwick's education service, after describing the valour of its men teachers in the war, discussed its bar by means of a euphemism:

> ... mention should also be made of the readiness shown by former women teachers in Smethwick who had married and left the profession, in coming forward to fill the vacancies caused by the withdrawal of the men from civil duty. At one time during the war period, and for a year or two afterwards, the Local Authority had as many as eighty married women serving in the Elementary schools, and it was only by utilising their services that the Committee were able to carry on the schools. However with the gradual return to more normal conditions this number has been reduced, and the services of the married ladies have been dispensed with, so that there are now very few, indeed, occupying any posts under the Authority.[30]

Legal action was taken by the NUT to support any of its teachers faced with a marriage bar.[31] The East Ham branch brought an action against the Borough Council to restrain it from dismissing one of its teachers. The High Court gave judgement against the teacher and so all the married women teachers in East Ham were dismissed.[32] Sometimes married women teachers were allowed to continue if they had dependants or were widows, but rarely if their husbands were working.

In the Rhondda, the married women teachers had been threatened with dismissal in 1919, as had all those qualified for a pension. Local women teachers met representatives of the Labour women's organizations and co-operative guilds (and W.G. Cove) to form a permanent women's organization to enforce women's rights and participate in municipal elections.[33] In February 1920, they organized a deputation to the Council on the issue of a married women bar and dismissal of pensionable-age teachers. Marie Stopes, who had just written a book called *Penalising Marriage* led the deputation. She pointed out the waste of public money that would be involved in the teachers' dismissals (the cost of their training and experience); the stability that these teachers brought to schools filled with unmarried teachers;[34] and that they were enslaving women to their husbands. Without much reported discussion, except in favour of their continued employment, the Council voted eleven to eight for dismissal by August 1920. In 1922, some of these teachers, still working, appealed to the NUT Legal and Tenure Committee for help. The NUT solicitor told them not to continue legal action, although other lawyers were more favourable. The report in the *Daily Herald* added that 'the majority of local teachers are not in sympathy with the married women'.[35] A High Court injunction to stop the dismissals was rejected and the court decided that the local authority was within its rights.[36] High teacher unemployment and strong sexual divisions, reflecting continuing structural differences in the service over pay and conditions and a cultural milieu unfavourable to women's rights, served to aid the dismissals. As the London Teacher Association was to comment some years later:

> It has been the custom of LEAs to regard married women teachers as the means whereby they can solve staffing difficulties dismissing them when there is a surplus . . . and re-employing them when there is an insufficiency of supply.[37]

The other major issue for the NUWT was promotion. This was closely connected to the large school amalgamations that took place in the 1920s and the reservation for men teachers of many of the new headteacher posts created. Although infant departments were usually controlled by a woman headteacher, when they were amalgamated with junior elementary schools that took boys and girls, the post nearly always went to a man. The rule invariably was that if boys were present in single or mixed schools, headteachers were male. This was a reflection of the interests of the people controlling the Education Committees or voluntary schools. The NUT policy was that the 'best person' should be appointed, but the NUWT felt that, in practice, the NUT allowed the domination by men of these posts. The NUWT policy was that infants schools should have women headteachers and that there should be open competition between men and women for mixed school headships. In school amalgamations, the NUWT policy was that the better qualified teacher should be appointed. In practice it seems experienced or better qualified teachers might be passed over for the man teacher. In 1927 and 1928, deputations from the NUWT visited the Board of Education to complain of the continuing loss of headships for women.[38] The Union fought hard to retain separate infants schools and to oppose the amalgamation of boys and girls schools.[39] It has also been argued that the very way in which the NUWT worked went beyond a campaigning Union; that it was also a cultural and social support network to its members, in contrast to women's role in the NUT which was never to determine nor to alter the way of working in the union.[40]

The National Association of Schoolmasters (or the National Association of Men Teachers as it was called at first) was formed in response to the 1919 Equal Pay Referendum. Its first branches were formed in places where equal pay had started to appear (equal minima etc.) and the National Association of Men Teachers was established in West Ham, East Ham, Cardiff and Walthamstow, and other places in Merseyside and the North East. [41] It continued as a National Union of Teachers' pressure group until 1922 when the National Association of Schoolmasters was formed. Initially, it claimed no hostile intention to the National Federation of Women Teachers or the National Union of Teachers.[42]

The main strength of the NAS was initially centred upon Liverpool, where 97 per cent of men teachers were in the NAS by 1925. Other strong areas were Leeds, the North-East and London (where they recruited about half of the men teachers by 1924).

An issue which is referred to in the histories of the NAS as one of 'bad faith' was the referendum on equal pay, taken after the 1919 conference, when men were 'still absent in the forces'.[43] The accusation says something about the importance they felt their counsels would have, not the sheer numbers of them (as there was a 2 : 1 ratio in favour, at least, of equal pay). A history of a local NAS association, Hull and district, shows that it was fifty ex-servicemen who founded the association, and their list of rules said that it was their purpose to 'watch the interests of ex-servicemen teachers particularly with regard to matters which have been dealt with during their absence'.[44]

Only later did it refer to the interests of 'all men teachers' — about the time it seceded from the Hull NUT. By 1920 the NAS had about thirty-eight branches and over 3,000 members nationally.

An NAS recruiting pamphlet, published later, described the year 1919 like this:

> Ignoring the stark realities of war, its women preferred to stress their part in the classroom and 1919 produced a situation and an atmosphere of sentimentality of which they took full advantage. With men still embodied in the Army, the NUT adopted 'equal pay' as its salary basis. With men's posts filled by women who wanted to keep them, the NUT found itself unable to advocate 'Men Teachers for Boys'. Women comprising four-fifths of the membership, dictated the policy of the monopoly. After four years of war, men were stunned by such callous opportunism ... The men were muzzled.[45]

The anger and hostility which is expressed here must have been far stronger at the time. What generated it? A sense of betrayal that the Union had been 'captured' while they were fighting for their country was one reason. These teachers had left their Union with its salaries campaign stilled and in a period of unqualified patriotic support for the war; they returned to find it deeply altered by the events of the previous two years — politically radicalized, pushing for self-government, recruiting more widely and more influenced by its women members. Equal pay had not been a major issue in the Union when they left; in fact men teachers had tried to marginalize it at the annual conferences, and yet the Union had accepted it in their absence. They left to recreate the old NUT.

The enmity shown towards the women teachers seems to have been based on the breaking of what they felt were 'natural rules' in teaching. 'Men's posts' were senior posts, women had somehow got hold of them and refused to return them. Women teachers they described as:

> 'The worst group of profiteers that took advantage of the war to extort money'.[46]

The NAS argument was based on status and differentiated pay. They argued that the NUT had failed to gain teachers a standard of living 'commensurate with their perceived status in society'. This argument, old-fashioned by the prevailing standards of the NUT in 1919, was a reworking of the old NUT line on professional status for the few, as opposed to wage-working for the majority (the women).

Differentiated pay was necessary, they argued, for several reasons. Firstly, men were home and family providers, who needed more money than women teachers. In this guise they could also act as women's real champions, invoking a view of women as 'mothers' and 'homemakers' which would obviously deprecate going out to work (viz. women teachers), unless, of course, they were single, in which case they wouldn't need as much money anyway. This idea of the teachers' wives was explained thus:

> they would frequently have to undertake extraneous work in addition to, and almost always to the neglect of, their home life and domestic duties. The fact is often forgotten that 'motherhood is the noblest of all professions' and is of primary importance to the nation, and of worth above that of any other calling ... the men realise the truth of the fact that 'women's vital force can, and generally does, pour itself into motherhood'. They know too that the best women find in motherhood and prefer to find in it their

chief work, their most absorbing interest . . . what manner of bitterness is that in some women which makes them so blind to what is the most elementary justice to members of their own sex?[47]

So, men teachers were safeguarding 'real' women from the depredations of the selfish women in teaching. Secondly, they argued that low rates of pay in teaching would attract a poor quality man, giving boys a poorer quality of education. (As Littlewood has argued, this is an unusual example of workers arguing about their own inferiority to justify larger salaries for themselves, against people who were better qualified and more able.)

They argued that boys needed men teachers; they could be harmed by women who knocked the 'manliness' out of them and made them infantile or 'mother dependant'. 'Men Teachers for Boys' was a way of controlling their decline which would appeal to some employers in the local authorities and would reserve sections of the labour market for themselves against a cheaper labour force. It recruited help from well-known establishment figures and psychologists to justify its claim. So, in one pamphlet, it argued that, between 8 and 12 years, the boy passes into the 'first masculine phase' and that schools had the responsibility, now that fathers were away at work for most of the week, to meet 'the child's natural needs for male impact' and to surmount the 'mother-fixation' (aided by women teachers) which would 'cramp his development and leave him immature, effeminate, easy-going and afraid of the responsibilities of adult life'.[48] At other times its arguments were not so crude. It argued that men and women both had good qualities — they were different but not superior or inferior to each other. When the balance between them in schools was upset, trouble ensued; the balance was made up of men for boys, women for girls. With this formula it was possible to work out that there was a severe shortage of men teachers (or the reverse, over-representation of women teachers)[49]. Similar arguments were expressed in the NUT. The Executive debated one resolution that asked for 'men teachers for boys' in the two years preceding transfer to the senior elementary school. It was rejected on the basis of Union policy, which Alderman Michael Conway expressed, that it was a question of ability not sex that should be the issue.[50]

Inconsistencies in the NAS arguments were analysed in the *Schoolmaster* in the early 1920s, which were, presumably, a reflection of the influence of NAS arguments on some male teachers. In particular, NAS arguments about women's salaries and against equal pay failed to attract the post-Rhondda militants. One, in a Presidential address in Liverpool, where there was some conflict with the NAS[51], argued that:

> he could not give assent to the proposition that a decrease in the salary of women teachers was the necessary concomitant of an

increase in the salary of men. On the contrary, the economic tendency which operated in other trades and professions affected the teaching profession also; and a fall in the remuneration of any one section in the group of workers was the prelude to a fall in the remuneration of all... He failed to see that an increased differentiation between men's and women's salaries would in fact operate the other way and would tend to drive men out.[52]

Of course, the NAS did not accept this argument. It was true, they said, that in industry 'equal pay for equal work' was advocated but only because it could never be secured; women could not produce the same work as men.[53] So, the NAS continued, women before and after the war were better off than men, they did not do the same work as the men and they did not need the men's wage which was a family wage. The fact that women were rarely better off than men did not count; for the NAS, a man's wage should be a family wage and so women teachers paid less were actually on a better standard of living because they did not support a family.

Separating boys from girls, separating men from women teachers; no wonder the NAS invoked a passage from the Webb's *Industrial Democracy* which described the Union organization in the cotton industry: the different sections, such as overlookers or spinners, were organized in different sections and the whole joined in a federation. This the NAS proposed as the way in which teachers could organize — instead of sections divided according to occupation, now they would be divided according to sex. The NUT argued against this idea; any parallel between teachers and cotton workers was discounted, particularly as the two groups of elementary teachers, class teachers and headteachers, were both in the Union. Furthermore, the Union saw no differentiation between the work a woman or man teacher did — they worked under the same roof, with the same conditions. Goldstone, the NUT General Secretary in the early 1920s, wrote to Beatrice Webb with reference to the analogy used by the NAS. She replied that teachers were interchangeable in their work, unlike the overlookers and spinners, etc., and saw the NAS breakaway as wrong — particularly because they were trying:

> to protect one particular section of the members against another section in an occupation where the persons concerned are in fact largely interchangeable.[54]

The NUT's arguments were not, as once they might have been, that of a sectional craft union. The lessons of the last few years and the breakthrough of 1919 had altered it. A leaflet (No. 42) used the arguments of industrial unionism and of amalgamation — it too quoted from *Industrial Democracy*:

> It is one of the conditions of effective trade union action that a union should include all the workmen whose occupation or training is such as to enable them, at short notice, to fill the places held by its members,[55]

and later, talked of craft union strikes broken by 'female blacklegs'. It was probably W. W. Hill, who had argued for a guild socialist view of professional self-government at the 1920 and 1921 NUT Conferences, who wrote the Union pamphlet. In a *Schoolmaster* article of the same year he expressed very similar arguments, and this time referred to G. D. H. Cole, as well as the Webbs, to talk of industrial unionism.[56]

The teachers associated with people like Conway or Cove had little time for the NAS arguments and actions. They were seen as 'splitters' who were denigrating and damaging the NUT at a time when unity should have been paramount.

The NAS action in Southampton, during the strike, when the local branch secretary offered to take the men teachers back if higher increments were offered to them, was held against the NAS. Indeed Cove agreed that this action had revealed the true nature of the NAS to many men teachers and that many of them in Southampton rejoined the NUT.[57]

Although the challenge of the men's secession from the NUT obviously worried the Executive, they found it easy to muster arguments as to why this was a mistaken policy. They may not have been very successful but they did not find it difficult to raise arguments on unity, non-differentiation of pay, equal opportunity in promotion, etc. The economic argument on the futility of claiming a sectional advantage was offset by the cultural argument the NAS used, with parents and men teachers, about the superiority and natural leadership role of men. The changes in Union policy and ideas which took place in 1919 were too late for the women in the NFWT. Cultural and class differences were as much at work here as questions of tactics vis-à-vis the employer. The gap (filled by a resounding silence where a dialogue should have taken place between the two groups) continued in the 1920s. It was not just between the leaders of the NUT, who, regardless of their policies were as likely to be as paternalistic as the NAS, but with the NUT rank and file. Was this a question of lack of consciousness, of apathy or hostility, or even of class, between different groups of women teachers? Or was it a clash between a principle, already hard fought for in society, and tactics, defending what had been achieved in a period of reaction?

The very strength of the NUT in 1920 allowed secessions based on a single issue of 'equal pay now', regardless of the coming reaction, and on a right wing male-dominated elitist approach based on mythologies of patriarchy and craft unionism. Each of these secessions was probably incapable of being resolved within the NUT as each moved to the sound of a very different drum, yet each was to undermine the unity achieved by the NUT industrial or syndicalist ideas of the Big Union.[58]

Professionalism was not just affected by class or politics or state policy, it was also mediated through gender-based models. Copelman has argued that there was a consistency, pre-war, to the teachers' arguments on professionalism; that they were based on a male language of family support and lack of promotion opportunities:

> Men wanted to institute (professionalism) at the expense of the women teachers. This in turn also helps explain why women were not so active in professional politics as their numbers would warrant since they had less to gain.[59]

Separate pay awards and scales, combined with better if limited promotion opportunities for men were dressed up not only in a male language, but *the male language of the exclusionary craft union*, defining its skill as not only certificated but as *being male*.

If feminists in the NUWT intended to control the separate sphere of girls' education, it was to protect them from the dominant images of 'homemaker' and 'mother' and as a move towards equal opportunity. Equal pay was the first step towards equality: their professional view was based on a fair system of promotion giving access on the basis of qualification and ability to all posts rather than on sponsored, gender-based appointments. It acted as a pressure group, using campaigns and deputations, searching for other allies in the women's movement, to present a rational argument for change. They were also a support network for each other and shared a feminist ideology.[60]

The professionalism of the syndicalist self-government which had replaced the old male, sectional interest craft unionist side of professionalism, saw it secede and renew its arguments with gusto. At the same time, a new vigorous culture of feminism separated itself and formed a professionalism based on mutual support, a cohesive ideology and a clear, if single issue, programme.

Notes

1 The proportion of certificated females to males was over 2 : 1 and uncertificated 8 : 1.
2 Tropp, p. 157.
3 The NUST probably joined the TUC in 1919. It had six thousand members that year and 14 thousand by 1921. Allies speaking for NUST resolutions in the TUC were from

the Workers' Union (predecessor of the TGWU), dockers, cotton spinners and warehouse and general workers. TUC Annual Congress Reports 1919–1921.

4 Teresa Billington was a teacher and a member of the Manchester branch of the Independent Labour Party with the Pankhursts. She was a secretary of the Manchester Teachers' Equal Pay League in 1903, the second national organizer for the Independent Labour Party in 1906 and then the first paid national organizer for the Women's Social and Political Union. She was a socialist and an agnostic and had refused to teach religion in school; she was saved from dismissal by the intervention of Mrs Pankhurst, a member of Manchester Education Committee. She was a member of the small group of Independent Labour Party women who founded the Women's Social and Political Union in 1903.

5 Mary Gawthorpe was a vice-President of the Leeds Independent Labour Party and then a Women's Social and Political Union organizer. In 1909 she ran the Lancashire Regional office. Other teachers involved with the Women's Social and Political Union were Theodora Bonwick (NFWT member), Dorothy Evans, Edith How Martin, Annie Neligan and Edith New (a leading militant and the Newcastle organizer in 1909). An elder stateswoman of the Women's Social and Political Union was Elizabeth Wolstenholme Elmy who was a Manchester teacher and an early organizer of the Manchester Board schoolmistresses and women's suffrage champion.

In Rosen, A. (1974) *'Rise Up, Women: The Militant Campaign of the Women's Social and Political Union 1903–1914'*, RKP and Pankhurst, S. (1977) *'The Suffragette Movement'*, Virago, (1st Ed. 1931).

Winifred Holtby, the writer, was both a feminist and Independent Labour Party member in the late 1920s and wrote a column for the paper of the National Union of Women Teachers, as well as addressing their conferences. Brittain, Vera (1940), *'Testament of Friendship'*, Macmillan.

6 Webb, B. (1915), p. 8. Widdowson (1981) has argued that it was *lower* middle class women who entered teaching. This would tend to place them as products of the new secondary schools and college trained (as envisaged in the 1907 Pupil Teacher Memorandum).

7 Pierotti, A. M. (1963) *'The Story of the National Union of Women Teachers'*, NUWT, p. 6.
8 Pierotti, A. M. p. 3.
9 Partington, p. 10.
10 Phipps, E. (1928) *'A History of the NUWT'*, NUWT, p. 5.
11 Partington, p. 12.
12 Phipps, p. 14.
13 Phipps, p. 27. West Ham Women Teachers' Association. (The General Secretary, Honorary Treasurer and Chairwoman of the important Mutual Aid Fund were from West Ham. The West Ham Secretary was also on the Federation's Central Council).
14 Phipps, p. 85. West and East Ham were among the first NUT local associations that were troubled with the rise of a Men Teachers' Association. Indeed West Ham was taken over by it in 1919. Partington, p. 19.
15 Phipps, p. 34.
16 Partington, p. 19.
17 *Times Educational Supplement*, May 1, 1919. 'Not many years ago a large majority of the delegates were men. A steadily increasing proportion of women has been a noticeable feature of the attendance at recent conferences until at Cheltenham there appeared to be an almost equality of sexes ... [also] a marked change in outlook and debating power'.
18 *Times Educational Supplement*, May 1, 1919.

19 See Copelman, D. M. (1985) *Women in The Classroom Struggle 1870–1914* Princeton Univ. PhD.
   For further discussion on the effects of the equal pay debate in the NUT, see Oram, A. 'Sex Antagonism in the Teaching Profession: The Equal Pay Issue 1914–1929' in *Australia and New Zealand History of Education Review* Vol. 14 No. 2, 1985.
20 Phipps, p. 86.
21 Partington, p. 22/3. The Atkins Committee on Equal Pay, the 1919 Sex Discrimination Removal Act and the 1920 Hills Resolution were all rendered ineffective.
22 Phipps, p. 88.
23 See Oram, A. (1983) 'Serving two masters? The introduction of a marriage bar in teaching in the 1920s' in London Feminist History Group (eds) *The Sexual Dynamics of History*, Pluto Press.
24 Widdowson, p. 65.
25 The Stockport NUT unanimously decided to call for a ban on married women teachers. Campaigne H. (Nov. 1970) '*A Short History of the Stockport Association*', NUT 1871–1920.
26 Martindale, H. (1938) '*Women Servants of the State 1870–1938*', Allen & Unwin.
27 Webb, (1915) p. 8. Webb added that the 'precedents in State and municipal administration are against the employment of married women'.
   In 1909 in London, 40 per cent of headteachers and 23 per cent of class teachers were married women. Widdowson, p. 65.
28 i.e. in Bradford 'married women were encouraged to return to teaching from which they had been barred by reason of their married state', *Education in Bradford*, Bradford Executive Committee, 1970.
29 Partington, p. 28–9.
30 Smethwick Education Committee '*Fifty Years of Education in Smethwick 1873–1923*', p. 29.
31 Pierotti, p. 20.
32 Phipps, p. 44.
33 *Rhondda Leader*, Dec. 20, 1919.
34 Young teachers were often in a 'constant state of nervousness'. *Rhondda Leader*, Feb. 7, 1920.
35 *Daily Herald*, Sept. 28, 1922.
36 Partington, p. 31.
37 Partington, p. 33 quoting *Times Educational Supplement*, 9th Nov. 1929. Partington illustrates with numerous examples the serious attack on women teachers and women's rights in this period.
38 Phipps, pp. 74–78.
39 Pierotti, p. 28.
40 King, S. 'Feminists in teaching: The National Union of Women Teachers 1920–1940' in Lawn, M. A. and Grace, G. (1987) *Teachers: The Culture and Politics of Work*, Falmer Press.
41 Partington, p. 19.
42 *Times Educational Supplement*, May 22, 1919. 'Men, Women and Pay'.
43 Latta, G. (1969) 'The National Association of Schoolmasters' University of Warwick, M.A. diss. p. 9.
44 Ridealgh, W. (1975) 'The History of The Hull and District Schoolmasters' Association from 1919 to 1975', University of Hull, M.Ed diss. p. 24.
45 NAS '*A Reply and a Warning*', Pamphlet No. 45, 1940?

Engendered Professionalism

46 Littlewood, M. 'Makers of Men' in *Trouble and Strife*, No. 5, Spring 1985, p. 24.
47 NAS Pamphlet No. 49 *'Equal Pay in the Teaching Profession'*.
48 NAS *'The State and its Responsibility to the Boy'*, NAS Pamphlet No. 44, 1938?.
49 NAS *'Equal Pay in the Teaching Profession'*, NAS Pamphlet No. 49, 1946? It argued a gap of 16 thousand male teachers. The rise in juvenile delinquency was also related to this shortfall.
50 *The Schoolmaster*, April 11th, 1924. The Union also argued that the policy of the NAS would break up mixed schools and classes, create many small schools, and displace rural headmasters. NUT Leaflet 42 (1924) *'Group Home Rule'*.
51 Partington, p. 19. 'An NUT Mass Meeting supported equal pay by 585 votes to 382 in June 1919 after a bitter debate'.
52 *The Schoolmaster*, Jan. 2, 1925.
53 NAS Pamphlet No. 49 *'Equal Pay in the Teaching Profession'*.
54 NUT Pamphlet 42 *'Group Home Rule'*, 1924.
55 NUT Pamphlet 42 'Group Home Rule', 1924; 1920(ed.) p. 128, *Industrial Democracy*.
56 *Schoolmaster*, March 14, 1924.
57 *Daily Herald*, June 9, 1922.
58 These issues needed to be raised within this study even though primary sources are virtually non-existent and secondary sources extremely rare.
59 Copelman, D. op. cit. pp. 52/3.
60 King, S. op. cit. p. 55.

End Note

The first three decades of this century, pivoting particularly on 1919, were important for teachers as they developed an identity, a purpose and policy towards their role in elementary education, towards each other and to the state. The discussions, arguments and conflicts they had tell us a lot about them; their problems in work with low pay and tight controls, their changing political roles; their view of themselves as men and women in teaching. This period is also important in the development of a central state policy towards education, and, particularly, in the control of it. This shift, from local to central, and then to indirect rule, is paralleled by the development of a clear Labour programme for education and the Conservative struggle to produce a positive education policy.

Teachers were employed by a variety of people, from various religious groups, ratepayer parties, citizen coalitions or rarely, Labour associations. What united these people, with the exception of some Labour representatives, was their determination to manage without interference an education service which had to be cheap or efficient. Between 1900 and 1919, disputes and conflicts were local, centred around individuals known to each other or living near each other. The question of the management or the employing class being geographically remote didn't arise. Managers lived near, and came in and told the teacher what was and what was not required. Dismissal could result from disputing these demands. Management, whether in villages or cities, fought hard for the right to manage without interference from the teachers, the local education Committee or the Board of Education, depending on the type of school and area. Management meant deciding the local rate for the job, imposing duties and dismissing teachers. It rarely concerned itself with the content as opposed to the infrastructure of education in the sense of direct imposition on teachers. A teacher's duty was to obey management. There was no other duty. Central government rarely impinged on the teacher's work except through Inspectors and laws which may or may not have been observed locally. The Board of Education produced a number of Circulars and Reports after 1900 in which situational reviews or policy options were offered or recommended but grants-in-aid were not withdrawn nor was it the Board's decision (but the Treasury's) to reduce their overall value after 1911. Local authorities often seemed to feel that the Board was their opponent in a way that the teachers were not. At least the teachers were employees and could be controlled, yet the Board and its suggestions and hints of new requirements complicated their task of controlling the expansion of services and keeping rates down. As salaries were a large part of the budget and there was no specific grant attached to them, it was essential to reduce them or severely control them, and that meant ignoring the local teacher associations. All combinations of employees were a threat to the rate policy and so to the right to manage.

Not until 1917 is there a growing appearance of State policies for education, that is, a direct long-term view of the relationship of the State to its education service, in which options are reviewed, rejected or created for the management of schools and teachers, and the relationship between education and society expressed. Education took on a positive quality rather than the minimal, begrudged compulsory one it had had previously. This was under a wartime government that had taken a number of steps envisaging wider powers of intervention in industry to control a grave management crisis, help the war effort and to provide the foundation for ambitious reconstruction plans. Education was viewed in a similar way — it was becoming a danger to the State, at the same time as it had a new, vital role in the rebuilding of industry, accumulation of capital and creating social cohesion. For teachers, a Whitley Committee with joint, national employer-employee negotiations and an enhanced professionalism of duty and responsibility were on offer. Local management seems strangely uninvolved with this grand design. After taking the new salary grants, encouraged by national economy campaigns, it was not long before teachers were back in the old routine with local authorities. Refusing to recognize the union, importing blacklegs, refusing to negotiate — all were back. National policy, as defined by Percy, was bent on creating the social cohesion aspect of education by encouraging Conservative and ratepayer attacks on, and by the isolation of, left-wing teachers. Ideological definitions of teachers' work were emphasized — civic and patriotic duty and the possibility of oaths of allegiance — yet within a State policy which was operating an 'indirect rule' model.

The central State always removed itself from direct control of teachers; it rejected civil service status, Exchequer payment and Board of Education direct management. One of the reasons for this was the relative strength and unity of the teachers and a lively local management, intent on retaining independence, financing control and keeping teachers in their station. By subtle interference, private encouragement and exhortation, the Board of Education used a changed political climate in the 1920s to shape and order as much as possible a teaching force in ways that suited its purpose. Ideological domination was two-fold: the exclusion of radicals from teaching and a public campaign built on notions of the civic responsibility of teachers. Yet, earlier in the 1920s, during a crisis in public spending, financial cuts alone took precedence over ideological arguments. The State is not then an homogenous institution. At different levels of government service, central and municipal, different aims in management take precedence over other 'outside' aims. There is a tension between the local State and the central State. In periods of economic crisis or working-class unrest or unity, compromise or negotiation may be paramount or, where there is weakness, straight diktat precedes ideological argument. To talk of the State's 'determination' of teachers is to take on face-value what some elements of the State aspired to, rather than what they were able to achieve, and to ignore contradictions between competing groups in government. When teachers had a local or national unity, management was in disarray — united in local areas only by common policies on finance which broke down with strike action into different camps. Were teachers a social danger? Even within the short period contained in the case study, there is a sense of unease in Conservative observers at firstly, the growth of a major secular force in society which had ousted the Church, and secondly, the tentative alliance building up between the socialist societies and teachers in particular areas on education policy. It was not until the war that the 'social danger' thesis grew. Up to then it would have been centred on local authorities' right to manage their employees and the rise of teacher unionism which shaped or affected this right. In wartime, there was a growing clash between organized workers in key industries and the Government's right to govern and intervene in many new parts of the industrial world. Teachers were seen as a force which could, because of their class background, interests and audience, serve to continue the political and social unrest in schools to new generations. With the new 'human capital' argument in reconstruction plans, teachers became a central pivot in social rehabilitation and reorganization. Teachers emerged as the crux of the State's stability as defined by the employing class. They were also the main agent for a new social democracy and/or a strengthened independent working-class education as seen by Labour. The question of whether teachers were a social danger has to be artificially separated. From the view of the State a new importance for education as a generator of skills and a source of civic unity and patriotism was created by the industrial unrest and the need for a revival of economic power. The social danger was not just what teachers did, which was not comparable to actions on Clydeside or Sheffield by industrial workers, but, at that crucial moment, that any radicalization or working-class alliance could undermine the State's plans.

Radicalization in the pre-war period, when elementary education had merely to be cheap, was very different from radicalization in the war/post war period. Now it threatened the State. It was part of a general insurgence and it was central to plans to contain that insurgence. There was also unease about the emergent class of teachers. A previously unknown quality (seen as narrow or ill-educated), they were emerging as a force for radicalism. Teachers were at the head of revolutionary socialism abroad. Though these were individuals their actions were seen as symbolic by people like Lloyd George and Fisher. In the 1920s it was this potential for radicalism which was covertly observed by the action of the Special Branch; the social danger became an electoral danger. Although Conservatives saw themselves as the natural party of government and even as the guardians of the State, who needed to act to preserve teaching from socialist teachers as a patriotic duty, they were also preserving themselves. It was not just future generations but the electoral attraction of teachers to the Conservative Party that needed action. Baldwin was not too convinced about teachers and Labour, or the importance of education, but he supported Percy's plans to isolate the radicals and create a Conservative education policy. The social danger existed not so much as a concrete threat but as a potential weapon. A vision of professionalism as a duty, with attendant status and registration, was offered by the very agency of the State that was part of the teacher's main problem. The social danger had been, in part, created by the actions of the local and central State, and it became the duty of the Board to provide an ideal vision of responsibility seen within a new professionalism (Fisher) or a semi-autonomous body 'harnessed' within an 'indirect rule' (Percy). The causes of the creation of this teacher unrest were only partly resolved in the Burnham settlement but it was not initially guaranteed by the central government, and the problem of control over entry (and so over skill and unemployment) was not involved in any vision of responsibility. Duty was defined elsewhere — not by teachers!

Educational work meant that which was required by the employers, at a salary and in conditions decided by them. An arbitrary or penny-pinching approach to working-class education did not win teachers' consent. It had to be enforced through management demands. Resistance to these interventions is recorded in urban areas in the resolutions and demands of the well-organized teacher Associations and even in rural areas in continuous small-scale struggles involving extra fines, school attendance officers and encouraging a childrens' or village solidarity. In areas of teacher shortage, certificated teachers may have left, voting with their feet, but employers licensed others to fill their places. Work did not necessarily mean education

— it meant schooling, discipline and moral control. (The Bishop of Hereford wanted the children back in schools, not because they were missing their education but because they were developing out of moral control). Teacher resistance to compulsory extra duties did not mean that they resisted extra work. Clues exist to the formulation of other definitions of work than that of the employers.

Teachers were involved in the growth of the social welfare facilities created in certain towns and cities — providing soup or drinks in the classroom, working with health workers, and organizing after-school health clubs. Furthermore, teacher interest in new curricula involved them in more work, retraining themselves, making resources or breaking down classroom management into new class groups. Not all teachers — there was still the considerable difficulty of corporal punishment, though it began to decline after the war. A gap existed between the logic of the businessman and ratepayer demands for cheapness and the service or duty felt by the teachers for their children. This was strengthened by the teacher's identification with the children, with the poor or working-class, and the managers with the shopkeeper, squirearchy or local employer class. This service ethic or 'professional spirit' was not necessarily at odds with the central State, only with its unruly local agents. Indeed, in common with many Labour supporters, the intervention of the State was actively demanded; it was seen as an impartial referee that was not sufficiently involved in the guarantee of conditions and fair play. It was at odds with clear management actions that cut across educational and social welfare as defined by teachers (among others). Work could be redefined with some success by Fisher, given this demand, as notions of altruism, vocation and selflessness contained within his call for a profession and a new education service could only be tested over time by teachers. Yet there was a strong, residual antagonism to this redefinition among teachers who associated the central and local State together, who were influenced by current socialist ideas and actions (in 1917–1919) and who took ideas of professional service to a new degree of sophistication in alliance with a confident Labour Party. Professionalism for teachers contained a service ethic which was a response to having work defined by interchangeability of staff and financial criteria, and began to appeal to the public on the basis of educational quality when faced with 'blacklegging' or untrained staff. Teachers even set up their own schools in emergencies.

Professionalism was not opposed to unionism. The dividing line is unclear. Were the teachers approximating to 'trade union' or 'professional' approaches to work? The strongest professional argument that included support for the Teachers Registration Council, Conservative Party membership and the apolitical nature of the NUT, came from *within* the Union by people who also talked of dilution and a salary campaign. The argument for a strike fund, one union for all teachers, full-time organizers and strikes, within a materialist frame of reference, could also talk of professional self-government and join the TRC. There were differences. The same vocabulary disguised different approaches. Whether the NUT could be dissected and pronounced to be a Trade Union or not, even by close observers, is not important. In all practical ways, it was. If there was confusion about striking or whether petitions were more effective, it was no different from many other unions or parts of unions in this period. What was at stake, within this exchange, was whether the State could be trusted in its description of a new education system where teachers had more power, or whether this was a sham, a diversion from acting to take power. The arguments over the TRC or civil service status or Whitley Committees were all within this tension. A self-governing profession was the cry of the syndicalist left in the Union, not the old guard 'professional' elitists; a shared language hid deep divisions.

An undercurrent in the exchange over teachers and professionalism lay in the NUT's movement from being a craft to an industrial union. Craft attitudes which depended on qualification to protect skill were giving way to an industrial strategy, based on one union for certificated and uncertificated teachers, that protected skill by unity and organization. Control over the marketplace became essential for this strategy to succeed. It was not important to metamorphose into a state-licensed elite body within teaching, for that, it had been shown, could be easily undercut by dilution, cheap untrained labour and school closure. What was very important was to unite the teachers to control the supply of teachers. If they could not control the technical point of entry, the colleges or local authority employment points, then they would control the supply of teachers for jobs, raise the salary and protect educational quality. A self-governing profession was the specific application in education of the syndicalist guild socialism. This idea was strengthened by links with Labour and plans to democratize society. Though the people who held these ideas were probably few, in G.D.H. Cole's phrase, they were 'working with the grain' in teaching. The State could not be trusted. Power had to be taken to resolve that central contradiction for teachers: their relation with their employers. The point seen within the speeches of Cove and the contemporary observation of Thompson is that a strong union protected professionalism and was not in contradiction to it. It was an active defence of altruism, perhaps, but more likely, of service and quality and the power to shape the education system.

The Labour movement could mean several things to teachers. After the socialist revival of the late 1890s, and the decline of payment by results, a natural alliance between radical teachers and working-class socialists in the Independent Labour Party or the large general unions, like Will Thorne's

Gasworkers, was created on the basis of the centrality of education in the changes to come. Education was an obsession with those socialists — as a matter of improving the lot of the workers' children, physically and mentally, and as a way to study and improve yourself and your class. The vague appeals to working-class organizations, made by the NUT in 1909, on class size was made specific by the Labour Party referendum of 1917. In the meantime, teachers were joining together in Associations which then joined local Trades and Labour Councils (political and industrial bodies), working with the Independent Labour Party in Yorkshire and Lancashire, Labour councillors in West Ham, the miners in South Wales and agricultural workers in East Anglia. Ideas which were rooted in libertarian, collectivist or industrial versions of socialism affected the arguments and actions of teachers. Not only individuals, bright working-class students to whom teaching was the only avenue of further education, but groups of like-minded activists in Bradford, the Rhondda or Merthyr and London. The wider Labour movement had no single dominant strand of socialism and neither did the teachers. At different periods, advances made in West Ham or Bradford or South Wales by the local working class were affected by different socialist ideas and organizations and by the fast-moving social and political scene. Municipal socialism, collectivism and syndicalism, extended services and an independent working-class education were all part of the move forward. Local teachers benefited from these advances and were part of them, then or later, but their effect was much wider — West Ham teachers (with G.D. Bell in the area), Michael Conway from Bradford and W.G. Cove from the Rhondda all altered the way teachers saw themselves and their capabilities. The Union was revitalized by these people who debated up and down the country and on the Executive — teachers were not isolated, education was part of a wider problem of public services, industrial and political power could be taken. The Labour movement wanted the teachers to help in a new democratic society. The message differed sometimes — that teachers should join the organized party of Labour which could protect them, or that they had a strength of their own if they did but recognize their place in the construction of surplus value. There was a further factor in the influential writings of Wells, the Webbs, Tawney, Cole and Neill. In their different ways, they established a value for teaching which the teachers felt had not been widely recognized before. It was detailed and consistent and placed them firmly in the middle of the reconstruction of society. Whether they were advisors or socialist missionaries or autonomous workers was shaded but the import wasn't — socialism and the Labour Party were the natural, and eager, allies of the teachers. A new State could be created with teachers in a central role.

Of course, socialist ideas did not just bring the promise of Utopia. They could bring self-recognition. Teachers were not just the natural allies of a labour movement eager for power and education. They now had the opportunity to see themselves as workers. In common with other white-collar workers, although well-organized before the clerks and local government employees, teachers had been separated from the manual working class yet open to the same influences at work. The proletarianization of the white-collar worker by dilution, grading and mechanization was similar to the changing work conditions experienced by workers; so were the employers' tactics of making slight concessions encouraging a 'superiority' and creating a reserve Labour force. The production of a new analysis of the white-collar or black-coated proletariat was two way. In teaching it came from the Marxists involved with the Plebs League or the Social Democratic Federation (and later the British Socialist Party and Communist Party). In turn, it came back from the left in the Unions or socialist groups. Each tried to convince its membership — the teachers or the Labour movement. The division between the teachers and the manual working class was generally wide, but for Marxists and other socialists, in pockets throughout the country, it was closed. Teachers being a part of a working class was a position fully argued in the affiliation to Labour referendum. It brought with it an identification and a reasoning based on the production of value. For some socialist teachers, notably in the Teachers' Labour League or postwar pacifist organizations, it also brought a direct assault on an ideological hegemony based on patriotism; being defined in the main by Conservatives, sometimes with the assent of Labour politicians, as teachers being apolitical, supporters of Empire Day and the Navy League, anti-strikes, supporters of religious education, etc. In other words, it meant whatever the Conservatives chose it to mean — naturally defined in this way, it opposed many socialist ideals and practices. One way or another, these teachers tried to create a critical or a socialist practice in schools; by resisting patriotic ceremony, cultivating critical outlook in their students, supporting internationalism in the curriculum, etc. Many Labour teachers did not do this. Teachers were divided.

As the Labour Movement split and fragmented in the 1920s and the Labour Party was created in a particular way, excluding Utopian and materialist socialists and their policies, so the left-wing teachers split. They took different paths — as advisors, voters and Labour Party politicians on the one hand, and on the other, as activists, revolutionaries and so on. These splits occurred in a period of industrial decline and reaction, with union membership in a dive. Arguments for self-government, as workers, lost ground and survival, defence of gains, took precedence. Judging by the criticism of the Labour League (representative of only one strand of a Labour minority in the Union), the Union lost its way almost as an act of will. Given that fighting was extremely difficult for the Union and occupied its members, officials and organizers in many local authorities, the gains of an earlier period seem to be put aside. The League kept reminding its readers of working-class unity, of alliances and tactics that teachers had formed, and of accumulated ways of fighting that it had experienced. Perhaps like white-collar unions in the post-1920 decline or like some craft unions, the NUT was not able to build upon its new-found ideas and notions. Teachers were divided. As militancy submerged, old ideas were dusted off in the Executive about the danger of a Labour Party alliance. The uneven organization of the Union in rural and urban areas led to divisions over what was attainable, what was a gain. The vigilance against local employers, resumed again in the 1920s, seemed a poor second at times to the sexual divisions that were creating conflict between teachers.

Groups of men and women teachers, influential in a wider way amongst their colleagues, developed or re-developed ideologies of separatism, distancing themselves from the NUT. Returning ex-servicemen, left out of the social and political changes of the later war years, felt that the union had betrayed them by adopting equal pay resolutions. They argued for a separate section of men teachers, protecting themselves by adopting restrictive labour market policies, such as 'men teachers for boys' and opposing equal pay. Women teachers, increasingly strengthened by their growing place in teaching and the influence of a women's movement built around the extension of the franchise, were disappointed, not by the resolutions of the NUT, but the lack of real progress in achieving equal pay: without equal pay men and women teachers could not be equals at work. The NUT lost members — some men teachers in a few areas and some women teachers (though the NUWT had recruited among secondary teachers as well). The secessionist organizations developed their own identity and their own versions of professionalism.

Several of the major features of the present education system were formed in the 1920s. One of the most consistent has been the idea of autonomy, associated with 'indirect rule', and the 'partnership' of teachers, local and central government. Teachers moved from the position of self-government to the acceptance of consultation and counselling. It is fitting that in a period when power is being re-taken by the central state and the teachers are poised on the brink of a new 'servitude' that the teachers and employers should be reminded of a past when this was clearly rejected.

Index

Abertillery strike 8
Ablett, Noah 49
Acts of Parliament
 Agricultural Children's (1873) 5
 Education
  1870 4, 7
  1902 8, 42
  1918 66, 99
  Coalition Government's 73
  Emergency Powers (1926) 131, 132
  Schoolteachers' Superannuation (1918) 64, 98, 99–100
  Trade Union (1927) 128
Adams, Mr H.C. 104–10, 112
Advertiser, The 102
Agricultural Workers' Union 38, 39
Amalgamated Society of Engineers 13
Ammon, C.G. 99, 117
Arnett, John 37, 108
'Article '68ers' 139
Askwith, Lady 124
Assistant Teachers, National Federation of 24

Baldwin, Stanley 119, 120, 121–2, 123, 160
Bell, G.D. 77, 85, 86, 163
Benchley (headteacher) 122
Best, Duncan 27, 31
Billington, Teresa 141
Birmingham Education Committee 132
Birmingham Post 44
Birmingham Worker 132

Blackburn Grammar School 131
Blackburn Times 131
black-coated proletariat 63
Board schools 4, 6, 12
Boyd Carpenter, Major 129
Bradford Teachers' Association 83
Bradford Trades Council 83
brain-worker 60, 63, 78
Bramsdon 22, 23
British Schools 5
British Socialist party 39, 164
British Womens' Patriotic League 124
Brown, Norah 131
Burnham, Lord 97, 126
Burnham Committee 55, 64, 89, 95, 97, 100, 101, 139, 143, 144
 Agreement 100, 102–9, 112–3, 121, 122, 143–4, 160
Burston, Vicar of 38
Burston strike 37, 38–40, 111, 125
Byford, Councillor 28

Cadogan, Edward 123
Central Labour College 49–50
certification 1, 99–100, 101, 139, 140, 143
 NUT and 3, 4, 6–7, 13, 15, 70, 140
Chamberlain, Austen 64, 120
Chamberlain, Neville 120, 121, 126
Church of England Schools 4, 5, 127
Civil Liberties, National Council for 125
Clarke, Margaret 131–3
class, social, and teacher recruitment 10–12

167

Index

Code of Regulations (1904)   9–10, 30, 151
  (1926)   134
Cole, G.D.H.   73, 78–9, 88, 162, 163
  Chaos and Order in Industry   88
  Guild Socialism Restated   79
  World of Labour, The   88
Communism   129, 131–2
  Communist, The   129
Communist Party   164
Conservative party   9, 73, 117, 118, 120–3, 125–6, 132, 160
  Conference (1926)   127
  education policy   120
Conservative Teachers' Group   128
Conway, Alderman Michael   82–3, 86, 88, 163
Conway, Miss E.R.   113, 142, 151
Cook, A.J.   49, 53, 55
Cooperative Union   99
Copelman, D.M.   152
corporal punishment   12–13, 161
Cove, W.G.   49–57, 76, 77, 89, 97, 102, 110–11, 145, 151, 162, 163
  'Helps to the Study of Capital'   50–1
craft professionals   63
craft unionism   1, 3, 8, 13, 61, 95, 139, 150, 162
Croft, Allen   141, 142
Crook, C.W.   66, 69, 85, 86, 87, 120–1, 122, 142
curriculum   3, 6, 9–10, 80, 95, 111, 161

Daily News   26, 43–4, 128
Daily Chronicle   46
Daily Herald   62, 74, 82, 83, 98, 99, 100, 102, 111, 124, 129, 146
Daily Mail   124, 128
Daily Telegraph   97
Decies, Colonel   43, 45
Drift of Teachers towards the Labour Party   118
duties, teachers' extraneous   5, 6, 14

Eastern Counties Union   37, 39
Education, Board of   7, 8–9, 12, 13, 30,, 34, 54, 64, 68, 95, 105, 133, 157–8

Circulars
  573 on Pupil Teachers   11
  709   10
  and grants   99, 100, 103, 104
  and salary scales   70, 98, 113–14, 121
Education, Department of   3, 4, 13, 14
  see also Education, Board of
education policy, Conservative Party   120
Education Workers' International   132
Educational Institute of Scotland   43, 80
Educational News   29
Edwards, George   39, 108
elementary education   9–10, 11, 98, 139
elementary teachers   10–11, 14, 61, 75
Empire Day   125, 130, 164
Equal Pay League see Women Teachers, National Federation of (NWFT)
Equal Pay Referendum (1919)   141
Evans, Gwen Ray   32
Evening Chronicle   28

Fabians   3, 57, 73, 75
Fisher, H.A.L.   59–71, 73, 83, 87, 95, 97, 99, 101, 117, 120, 123, 160, 161
Froud, Miss E.   141

Gas Workers' Union   25, 163
Gawthorpe, Mary   141
Geddes, Sir Eric   98
Geddes Committee   98–101, 117, 144
Gee, Captain   127
General Strike (1926)   126, 131, 132
Godfrey, Mrs   108, 109
Goldstone   65, 69, 89, 143, 150
Goodwin (teacher)   53
Gower, Mrs   127
grants-in-aid   4, 9, 21, 34, 41, 44, 99, 111–12
Gray, Major Ernest   122
Grey (Member of Parliament)   13
Griffiths, Dan   129
Guild Socialism   57, 73, 77–9, 90, 162
'guinea girls'   62, 139

Haldane, Lord   70
Hampshire Advertiser   101
Hampshire Telegraph   23

Hapton, Reverend William   42
Hardie, Keir   34
Hargreaves (parent)   131
Hayday, Councillor   28
Head Teachers' Association   31
Herald, The   41, 125
Hereford, Bishop of   42, 45, 161
Herefordshire strike   8, 37, 41–6
Higdon, Anne   38–9
Higdon, Tom   37, 38–9, 108
Highland Road School   23
Hill, W.W.   79, 88, 89, 90, 151
Hilleary, Dr   29
HMIs *see* inspectors, school
Holton, Bob   77
Howard, William   81
Hutt, Councillor   30
Hyndman, H.M.   25

Imperial Fascisti, The   124
Independent Labour Party (ILP)   3, 9, 13, 34, 37, 74, 77, 81, 82, 83, 140, 141, 162–3
inspectors, school   4, 6, 7, 38, 80, 111, 126, 134
'intellectual workers'   60, 63

Jessel, Colonel   121, 122
Jones, Councillor   29
Joplin, John, Jr   108, 109, 111
Junior Imperial League   127

Kingsbridge Gazette   129, 130

Labour and the New Social Order   63, 74, 75
Labour Party   25, 60, 63, 111, 134, 162, 164
   alliance of teachers with   63, 73–87, 114, 117, 118, 120–5, 127–31, 161
   and Communists   132
   Conference (1917)   83
Ladies Imperial Club   124
Lane, Miss E.   141
Langdon-Davies, John   125
   Militarism in Education   125
Lawson, W.R.   11–12, 125
Leadbetter (teacher)   108

Liberal party   9
Littlewood   149
Lloyd George   59, 63, 98, 117, 123, 125, 160
London Board Schools   6
London County Council Education Commiteee   99
London Married Women Teachers, Assocation of   144
London Teachers' Association   141, 144, 146
Lowe, Robert   4
Lowestoft Education Committee   103–12, 121
Lowestoft Journal   103, 104, 108, 109
Lowestoft strike   103–13, 122
Lowestoft Teachers' Association   104
Lowestoft Trades and Labour Council   39, 107
Lugard, Lord   120

MacMillan, Margaret   9, 82
MacNamara, T.J.   5
Mainwaring, Miss   51, 52
Mainwaring, Will   49, 53, 54
Manchester and Salford Labour Party   39
Mander, Fred   107, 110, 132
Mann, Tom   22
Manfield, Councillor C.   28
Maskelyne   86
Masterman, C.F.G.   11
'Men Teachers for Boys'   147, 149, 165
Men Teachers, National Association of *see* Schoolmasters, National Association of
Merthyr Local Education Authority   62
Metropolitan Board Teachers' Association (MBTA)   6
Miners' Federation of Great Britain   49, 57, 77
Miners' Lodges   49, 50, 53
Moore, Mr H.   124
Morant   13
Morley, John   11
Morning Post   11, 12, 119, 124, 128
Morris, William   80
   News from Nowhere   80

Index

Morrison, Herbert 100
Municipal Alliance party 30
Murray, Gideon 118, 124

National Citizens' Union 124
  National Expenditure, Committee on 98–101, 117, 144
National Guilds' League 78, 79
National Union of Teachers (NUT) 1, 8, 11, 26, 32–3, 63, 67, 140
  and certification 3, 4, 6–7, 13, 15, 70, 140
  and equal pay 141–4, 151
  ideology 13–14
  membership 3, 4, 6–7, 57, 112, 113, 139
  and professional register of teachers 13–15, 16
  and salaries 40–6, 49, 52–7, 61, 106, 143
  and women teachers 61, 141–5, 147–50, 151
  Salaries Committee 62
  Tenure Commiteee 41, 132, 146
Navy League 125, 164
Neill, A.S. 73, 79–81, 163
  Dominie's Log, A 79, 81
New Age 77, 80, 81
New Dock School 129
New Education 10, 73
'New Social Order' 63
Nonconformist schools 4
Norfolk Education Committee 38, 39
Norwich Trades and Labour Council 39
Notley, Alderman 106

Oath of Allegiance 118–20, 124
Observer, The 44
Organ, Mr T.A. 24
overtime, compulsory 22–4

Pankhurst, Christabel 141
Pankhurst, Sylvia 141
Parochial schools 5
Pay *see* salaries
'payment by results' 8, 14, 16
Peel, Sir Mervyn 127
Penhale Road schools 23
Penny Bank supervision 6
pensions 13, 64, 65, 98, 99–100

Percy, Lord Eustace 118–20, 123, 124, 126, 128, 133, 158, 160
Plebs 50–1, 129
Plebs league 49, 50, 51, 57, 77, 129, 164
Pollitt, Harry 131
Pollitt, Marjorie 131
Portsmouth and District Teachers' Association 22
Portsmouth School Board 21–2, 33
Portsmouth strike 21–5, 33
Powell 88, 90
Primrose League 131
professionalism 1, 10–11, 13, 15–16, 57, 61, 63, 66, 73, 124, 152, 162
  and unionism 110–11, 113, 161
promotion 146
Provisional Minimum Scale 97, 102, 113
pupil/teacher ratio 10, 21, 41, 98
pupil-teachers 4, 7, 10, 14, 22, 28, 41

qualifications *see* certification

Railwaymen, National Union of 39
rates, local 21, 25, 44, 52, 105
Ray, Gwen 50, 51
Rees, Noah 49
Regulations, Code of (1904) 9–10, 30, 151
  (1926) 134
Rhondda Class Teachers Association 51, 52, 53
Rhondda Leader 52–6
Rhondda Socialist 51
Rhondda strike 1, 49, 51–7, 76–7
Riddell, Lord 117
Rouse, W.H.D. 11
rural teachers 1, 4, 5–6, 37–46, 65–6, 97
Ruskin College, Oxford 49

Sainsbury (President of NUT) 122
salaries 1, 3, 4, 22, 31, 33, 40, 41–2, 95, 97, 98–101, 157
  scales 7–8, 26–7, 49, 52–7, 63–6, 97, 101–3, 113
    Provisional Minimum Scale 97, 102, 113
  women's 1, 7, 139, 141–4, 147–9, 151, 165
  see also Burnham Agreement

170

Salary Campaign 52
Samuel 120
School Boards 4, 80
School Inspectors *see* Inspectors, school
school meals service 9, 82–3
school medical services 9
Schoolmaster, The 5, 23, 24, 28, 31, 32, 40, 41, 42, 46, 73, 85, 89, 90, 111, 112, 127, 144, 149
Schoolmasters, National Association of (NAS) 102, 143, 146–51
Schoolteachers, National Union of (NUST) 140, 143
Shaw, George Bernard 80
Shepherd (Member of Parliament) 128
Simon, Brian 123, 124
Smaller Classes and Better Teaching Staff 10
Snowdon, Philip 117, 131
Social Democratic Federation (SDF) 3, 9, 13, 25, 164
Socialist Review 81
Somerset Womens' Unionist Association, The 124
South Wales Minders Federation, Unofficial Reform Committee of the 49
South West Ham Free Church Council 29
Spurrell, Miss 129–30
Standing Joint Committee *see* Burnham Committee
Stanton, C.B. 125
Starr, Mark 50, 126, 127
Steer 88
Stopes, Marie 145
  Penalising Marriage 145
Strange (teacher) 37
Stratford Express 28, 31
strikes and disputes 13, 62
  Abertillery 8
  Burston 37, 38–40, 111, 125
  General (1926) 126, 131, 132
  Herefordshire 8, 37, 41–6
  Lowestoft 103–13, 122
  Portsmouth 21–5, 33
  Rhondda 1, 49, 51–7, 76–7
  West Ham 8, 16–17, 25–34, 41
Sunday School 5

supplementary teachers 4, 6, 7, 69
syndicalism 77

Tasker, Mr 84
Tate, Mr J. 141
Tawney, R.H. 60, 73, 163
Taylor, T. 86
Teacher's Certificate 7
  see also certification
Teachers' Labour League 77, 85, 86, 119, 123, 128, 131, 133, 134
Teachers and the Oath of Allegiance 118
Teachers' Registration Council 66, 68–9, 70, 76, 84, 85, 87, 89, 161–2
tenure 5–6
Thomas, D.W. 50
Thompson 162
Thorne, Will 25, 26, 34, 162
Times, The 49, 60, 65, 69, 70, 87, 127, 128, 134
Times Educational Supplement, The (TES) 61, 63, 65, 66, 67, 68, 69, 70, 83, 87, 143
Towers, John 131–2, 133
Trades and Labour Councils 9, 26, 49, 51, 74, 107, 140, 163
Trades Union Congress 140
Trevelyan, Charles 128, 130
Tribune 27
Tropp 7, 97

Uncertificated Teachers, National Union of 140

Vaughan Morgan, Colonel 118, 119
Voluntary Schools 4–5

Walsh, Miss 140
Webb, Beatrice 15, 16, 73, 82, 141, 144, 150, 163
Webb, Sydney 73, 75, 79, 163
  Industrial Democracy 150–1
  Teachers in Politics, The 75–6, 79
Welfare Centres 111
welfare services, school 3, 8, 9
Wells, H.G. 73, 80, 163
  New Worlds for Old 75
Wesleyan schools 5
West Ham Council 25–8, 33, 34

171

Index

West Ham strike   8, 16–17, 25–34, 41
West Ham Trades Council   34
Westminster Gazette   120
White, John   134
Whitley Committee 87–90, 122, 158, 162
Williams, Celfyn   53
Williams, Francis   74
women teachers   61, 95, 139–52, 165
  and boy pupils   147, 149
  married   28, 33, 99, 122, 144–6
  pay   1, 139, 141–4, 147–9, 151, 165
  promotion   146
Women Teachers' Franchise Union   140
Women Teachers, National Federation of (NWFT)   61, 140, 141–4, 151
Women Teachers, National Union of (NUWT)   99, 146–7, 152, 165

Women's Social and Political Union   140–1, 142
Wood   123
Workers' Bulletin   131
Workers Dreadnought   54
Workers' Educational Association   99
Workers' Weekly   124
Working Men's Clubs, Institute of   99
World War I   37, 63, 66, 77, 82, 126, 144, 145, 165

Yate, Colonel Sir Charles   119, 120, 134
York Education Committee   8
Yorkshire Post   44
Yoxall, Sir James   13, 14, 26, 29, 42, 54, 98, 121